Sport Politics

An Introduction

Jonathan Grix

First published 2016 by
PALGRAVE

Palgrave in the UK is an imprint of Macmillan Publishers Limited,
registered in England, company number 785998, of 4 Crinan Street,
London, N1 9XW.

Palgrave Macmillan in the US is a division of St Martin's Press LLC,
175 Fifth Avenue, New York, NY 10010.

Palgrave is a global imprint of the above companies and is represented
throughout the world.

Palgrave® and Macmillan® are registered trademarks in the United States,
the United Kingdom, Europe and other countries.

ISBN 978–0–230–29546–9 hardback
ISBN 978–0–230–29547–6 paperback

This book is printed on paper suitable for recycling and made from fully
managed and sustained forest sources. Logging, pulping and manufacturing
processes are expected to conform to the environmental regulations of the
country of origin.

A catalogue record for this book is available from the British Library.

A catalog record for this book is available from the Library of Congress.

Printed in China

Sport Politics

To,

Matthew — thanks
for being a great
training partner!

bst, Jon

Xmas, 2015

To Stuart – another inspirational big brother

Contents

List of Figures, Tables and Boxes

Figures

Tables

Boxes

Preface

The writing of a book always comes with its own backstory and this volume is no different. A long time in the making – at least five years from its original conception to completion – the nature of what follows has changed over time. If it was first thought of as another, dense research monograph, the project gradually developed into a collection of my ideas on and around the theme of politics and sport, which is the title of a module I teach. This text is, in part, based on this module. I say 'in part', because the practice I follow is one of research-led teaching, so that there is always an iterative relationship between the two: fresh ideas are brought to the classroom and discussed; such discussions over time lead to alterations in the original ideas that end up in print. Thus, the students I have taught on this topic over the last decade need to be thanked, for without them, without the debates and insights that they have contributed, this text would have been a lot duller.

Interestingly, in a higher education climate that strongly favours pure research, a text that synthesizes debates and discussions is not valued highly by academe. Ironically, such texts are probably of more importance to student learners on their way to becoming critical thinkers, than narrow slices of research.

I would like to thank my small team at the University of Birmingham for their help – directly and indirectly – in shaping this volume. Ceri Wynne and Paul Brannagan kindly read over parts of the manuscript; Paul also offered invaluable help with the bibliography. While this assistance came at a price – usually coffees – it was gratefully received. Mark Griffiths offered sage advice on the topic of 'social capital' and Ian Boardley (without knowing it) is to blame for my inclusion of a chapter on doping due to his leading work in this area. Thanks too to Mike Dennis (from the University of Wolverhampton) for his help with the chapter on doping.

My brother Stuart – or 'big Stu' – is the second of six sons and this book is dedicated to him. Stu has a number of characteristics that are admirable, including being consistently reliable, possessing a great sense of humour and thoroughly enjoying his food. He also likes sport and wonders, still, when I am going to get a 'real' job.

Last, but by no means least, thanks to Andrea, Louis, Hannah and little Alfie for their continuing support.

JONATHAN GRIX, SEPTEMBER 2015

Chapter 1

Of 'Politics' and 'Sport'

Sport has the power to change the world. It has the power to inspire, it has the power to unite people in a way that little else does... Sport can create hope, where once there was only despair. It is more powerful than governments in breaking down racial barriers. It laughs in the face of all types of discrimination.

(Nelson Mandela, Monaco, 2000)

The purpose of this volume is to introduce the reader to sport politics. It was not all too long ago that this phrase would have been considered contradictory, as 'sport' was widely believed to be something quite separate from 'politics'. Avery Brundage, a former president of the International Olympic Committee (IOC), famously stated over 50 years ago that sport had little to do with politics and the former has no place in the dealings of the latter. He went on to suggest that 'sport... like music and the other fine arts, transcends politics... We are concerned with sports, not politics and business' (IOC, 1968: 10). Unfortunately, this view does not hold in the light of a history of boycotts (for example, the 1980 Moscow and 1984 Los Angeles Olympics), murder (the 1972 Munich Olympics), and sports events mirroring political struggles (for example, Hungary versus the USSR in Water Polo, 1956). In what follows, it will become clear that sport has been *always* inextricably bound up with politics, from the Ancient Greeks and Romans to the choice of Qatar as host for the 2022 Fédération Internationale de Football Association (FIFA) World Cup. Indicative of the intertwining nature of sport and politics are perennial debates about the rights and wrongs of Formula 1 taking place despite popular protests; discussions on the moral issues surrounding the World Anti-Doping Agency's (WADA) overruling of the British Olympic Association's (BOA) by-law that prevented British drug cheats from ever competing at the Olympics; and endless conferences, workshops and media coverage on whether sports mega-events (SMEs), such as the Olympic Games, really deliver value for (public) money. Simply put, sport politics is the

1

area of study where politics and sport meet. This may be government intervention into sport (for example, through school sports policy), it may be through the support of potential Olympic champions or the hosting of the FIFA World Cup; alternatively, it may be about people's rights to access sport and sports facilities. A more far-reaching discussion of sport and politics follows in Chapter 2, but for now a ground-clearing exercise of the term 'sport politics' is offered.

If the concept cluster 'sport politics' is relatively clear and understandable, the two key elements making up the phrase are less so and they have spawned cottage industries of their own within the world of academia. An understanding of the relationship between 'sport' and 'politics' that takes the latter simply to mean the formal institutions through which governments govern would rule out the wide variety of settings in which 'sport politics' has taken and takes place. For example, the act of defiance undertaken by Tommie Smith and John Carlos on the medal rostrum at the 1968 Mexico Olympics – the well-known and often cited 'Black Power salute' – falls squarely under the rubric of 'sport politics'; in this case the use of sport, and the sport spectacle (the Olympic Games), as a vehicle to express a particular political message. The murder of 11 Israelis and one German police officer at the Munich Olympics in 1972, the use of elite sport success by the East German regime and the marginalization of sportswomen and 'alternative' sport by the mainstream media and commercial sponsors are all examples of differing degrees of the politics of, or the political use of, sport. The appointment of a specific individual to head a sports funding agency, for example, can be a political decision, especially when decisions are made, or at least heavily influenced, by the incumbent government.

Sport (terms in bold are explained in the Glossary) offers both an individual and a collective experience, something recognized by modern states that invest heavily in elite sport in order to engender a so-called 'feel-good' factor among citizens which is said to exist around the collective experience of sporting events (DCMS, 2002). Riordan (1999: 49–50) rightly points to the nation-building potential of sport when he suggests that:

> It [sport] extends and unites wider sections of the population than probably any other social activity. It is easily understood and enjoyed, cutting across social, economic, educational, ethnic, religious and language barriers. It permits some emotional release (reasonably) safely, it can be relatively cheap and it is easily adapted to support educational, health and social-welfare objectives.

Riordan's quote also touches on a number of the reasons why sport is so popular throughout the world; some commentators even consider that the devotion to sport – especially from the side of fans – has become similar to, and even become a replacement for, religion (see Coakley, 2007). People are 'worshipped' (sports stars/religious idols), events take place in specific arenas (mega-stadiums/churches and cathedrals), and stars and clubs command a 'following' from devoted fans (in the way that some religions do). It is certainly true that many fans of football clubs in Europe act as if they were following a religion, moulding their lives around weekend games and offering unconditional support to their teams. The cross-cutting nature of sport – touching on issues of gender, local, regional and national identity, ideology, ethnicity, economics, socio-economic status, and a variety of policy domains (health, education and so on) – ensures that it cannot remain apolitical. Thus, the argument in what follows will be for a broader definition of 'politics' rather than simply one that focuses on governments and their institutions of power.

What is 'politics'?

One of the most memorable definitions of what **politics** is comes from Lasswell in 1936. He stated that the essence of politics was 'who gets what, when and how'. Such a definition is clearly concerned with 'resources' and their distribution; however, 'politics' or the 'political' use of something like sport is much broader. Within the academic discipline of politics and political science there is contestation around whether the study of politics ought to restrict itself to the analysis of the formal operation of politics, its institutions and the sphere of government, or be driven by a definition of politics which 'sees it (the "political") as a social process that can be observed in a variety of settings' (Stoker and Marsh, 2002: 9; see also Hay, 2002: 69; Leftwich, 2004). The latter understanding of politics highlights the power relations between individuals: be it state and subject, husband and wife, employer and employee and so on; wherever power lies, politics is said to be present. This is the meaning of 'politics' (Box 1.1) used in the present volume and it goes far beyond simply the institutions or ideologies of government.

Whichever definition of politics is used in the study of politics, most commentators agree that scholars are bound by their 'concern with the analysis of the origins, forms, distribution and control of power' (Leftwich, 2004: 2). From this concern derive other central concepts

Box 1.1   What is 'politics'?

In general, there are two ways of understanding the term. First, it refers to the formal institutions of government (parliament, government departments, ministers, the president or prime minister and so on) and the ideologies that underpin different political stances. Second, a much broader understanding of the 'political' includes everything to do with power, power relations, the distribution and origin of power. So, wherever there are power relations in society, 'politics' is said to exist. A good example is the funding for Olympic sports in many states. Increasingly, National Sports Organizations (NSOs) are set 'targets' by governments or by bodies or committees close to government. If targets are not met, funding is reduced. There is nothing apolitical about this asymmetrical relationship (see Chapter 8 for more on the governance of sport).

such as authority, **legitimacy**, **government** and **governance** (see Houlihan, 2008), all of which will recur in the chapters that follow.

What is 'sport'?

The concept of 'sport' is no less difficult to pin down and needs to be discussed. The initial problem arises from the fact that commentators often use 'sport', 'exercise' and 'physical activity' interchangeably. Another problem is that different nations use these terms to mean different things; indeed, Nicholson et al. (2011) in their comparative study of participation in sport even went as far as to say:

> ...in each of the nations [case studies in their book] a different interpretation of sport and participation has been applied, not necessarily by the authors [of the chapters], but invariably by a government statistical agency, peak sport agency or market research organisation. In some nations sport is interpreted as a competitive, formal and rule-bound activity, whereas in others it is interpreted as physical activity...

Despite this, and many other objections that could be made to an attempt to define 'sport', one way of distinguishing between 'sport', 'exercise' and 'physical activity' is to see them as sitting on a continuum (Figure 1.1), whereby 'sport', broadly speaking, is the most organized and competitive form of activity and 'physical activity' is the

Figure 1.1 *A 'continuum' of sport, exercise and physical activity*

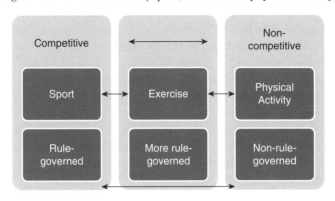

least. The World Health Organization, for example, defines 'physical activity' as 'any bodily movement produced by skeletal muscles that requires energy expenditure' (WHO, 2014). On the face of it, this could include any movement, including getting up to buy a drink at the bar. In general, however, physical activity is usually linked to health and citizens are encouraged to be physically active. They tend to do this by undertaking 'exercise', the next concept on the continuum. Exercise is 'physical activity that is planned, structured, and repetitive for the purpose of conditioning any part of the body' (*Medical Dictionary*, 2014). The key here is the phrase 'planned, structured and repetitive'. Any bodily movement that brings the heartbeat to a level higher than it would have been, had the person been resting, is physical activity: a swim, bike ride through the park and so on. These do not have to follow pre-planned schedules, whereas 'exercise' normally does. A good example here would be the burgeoning army-led exercise groups you see in local parks at the crack of dawn. These are pre-planned, follow a precise schedule and are designed to get or keep people fit. They are not designed to lead to a competition and they are not there for people simply to turn up and do their own set of exercises.

That leaves 'sport'. Clearly, training for a sporting event involves exercise and physical activity. However, 'sport' can generally be seen as physical activity that is governed by hard-and-fast rules, that is, set codes of behaviour and rules that have to be adhered to. A key difference is that, in general, 'sport' is competitive or contains at least an element of competition, whereas 'exercise' and 'physical activity' do not. Sport is rule-bound activities in which there are winners and losers, which is one reason why states of all political hues have been and remain fascinated with elite sport, as it pits social and political system against system (in the **Cold War** era, for example). Sport too is inextricably bound up with records, exact measurement and precision, or 'quantification', as the sports historian, Allen Guttmann, terms it. Guttmann, in his classic *From Ritual to Record*, outlines the development of modern sports from their historical beginnings as pastimes and rituals to the professionalized and specialized sport we know today. He also wrote in depth on the differences between 'play', 'games', 'contests' and 'sport' and noted the difficulty in disentangling them (Guttmann, 1978). A well-known definition of 'play' is that by Huizinga (1955), which covers a lot of activities on the continuum suggested above; he states that play is

> ...a free activity standing quite consciously outside "ordinary" life as being "not serious", but at the same time absorbing the player intensely and utterly. It is an activity connected with no material interest, and no profit can be gained by it. It proceeds within its own proper boundaries of time and space according to fixed rules and in an orderly manner.

For Simon Barnes sport '... creates archetypal situations of triumph and tragedy, and it does so bloodlessly, for at bottom, *all is play. Nobody dies...*' (2007: 84; author's emphasis). Lincoln Allison makes the valid point of perhaps not seeking a definitive definition of 'sport' but rather to grasp it – as he cites Wittgenstein doing with the term 'games' – as several things that share complex 'family resemblances' with one another (1986: 4).

Another attempt to distinguish 'sport' from other activities is the claim that athletes who partake in them ought to be able to exhibit high levels of cardiovascular fitness, succumb to tailored and disciplined training or show a high level of dexterity. Thus, debates on whether such activities as darts constitute a sport abound; yes, one needs a high level of skill to compete, but must an 'athlete' be at their physical peak to play it? The same type of argument could be made with any number of 'sports' or would-be 'sports'.

The outcome of sports competitions should be – as a rule – unpredictable; it is this very unpredictability of sport that makes it attractive to most (see also Cashmore, 2010: 3). Much cheating in sport is linked to overcoming this unpredictability, for example, match-fixing, doping and unsporting behaviour (see Chapters 4 and 9). When Erich Mielke, the Head of the notorious East German Secret

Police (the infamous Stasi), intervened to ensure his Berlin Dynamo team regularly won crucial football matches, fans on both sides were temporarily robbed of the beauty of sport: its unpredictability. And none of the fans were happy (Dennis and Grix, 2012), including those on the side of the victors.

Clearly the concept of 'sport' itself means several different things and has several ambiguities (see Allison, 1986: 3–8). For example, is kicking a ball around in the park with friends physical activity or sport? At which point does the one flow into the other? Soccer is a sport, but playing for fun may not be competitive. However, some would argue that playing soccer, even if it is for fun, using and following soccer rules (that is, no fouling, a specific number of people on each side, the use of a ball, goal posts, a 'pitch' and so on), constitutes playing a sport. The 100 metres Olympic final – the blue ribbon event – is considered a very serious elite sport. Few would disagree with this; however, some would suggest that darts and snooker should equally be included under the umbrella term of 'sport' along with such athletic events.

The etymology of the word 'sport' reveals its origins lie in the Old French *desporter*, which means 'to divert, please, amuse, play'. It would appear that from the fifteenth century a more recent definition emerged of a 'game involving physical exercise' (*Etymology Dictionary*, 2014). It is interesting to ponder whether these original meanings hold for what is considered 'sport' today in the twenty-first century. There is no doubt that there is a sense of continuity in the meaning of 'sport' (and especially sport spectacle) as a diversion from everyday life from the Ancient times up until today. Whether it be the Roman events known as 'bread and circuses' (*panem et circenses*) or a modern-day SME (see Box 1.2), sport spectacles have been and continue to be used to distract (or divert) the public's attention away from wars, poor governance, bad news and economic woes and towards the 'feel-good' factor that is said to accompany such events. In his classic study of sport in Greece and Rome, the historian Harris begins by offering this insight:

> By derivation the word 'sport' covers every diversion by which a man [sic] disports or amuses himself in his leisure time; it is essentially the antithesis of work (Harris, 1972: 13).

Further definitional problems surround the *level* of sport being discussed. It is usual to talk in terms of grassroots sport, community sport and performance (elite) sport. Often these three 'spheres' of sport – they are not as clear cut and separate as the labels make out – are

---

Box 1.2   Sports 'spectacles' as diversions

Large-scale sports events have long been used to divert and distract public attention away from immediate concerns through putting on a good show. The phrase 'bread and circuses' refers to the situation in which a ruling authority provides relatively cheap food and entertainment to the masses in return for acquiescence. Modern-day SMEs, however, are anything but cheap. States spend large sums of money investing in such events as the FIFA Football World Cup or the Olympic Games. The range of reasons why this is the case are discussed in detail in Chapter 7. However, 'diversion' and 'entertainment' of the public are still central to these events. Whereas Karl Marx suggested religion is the 'opium of the masses', some suggest that sport now plays this role. That is, sport provides a conduit through which people vent their frustrations and thus return home happier with their lot (see Chapter 3).

---

placed together to emphasize their interconnectedness. As will become clear, the health of grassroots sport is often looked upon as inextricably linked to the success of a nation in elite sport (Figure 1.2).

Although Figure 1.2 and the discourse that goes with it – the bigger the grassroots, the better the performance sport – appears logical and commonsensical, this notion is revisited in Chapter 7 and problematized in relation to elite sport development. In reality the distinctions made between levels of sport in Figure 1.2 are far from clear. It is easy to distinguish between elite sport as practised by top-class athletes and

Figure 1.2   *A simplified view of different 'levels' of sport*

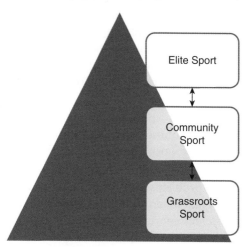

(usually) sponsored by commercial business or national governments on the one hand and 'grassroots' and 'community sport' on the other. Disentangling the latter two, however, is more difficult. Grassroots sport tends to refer to amateur sports participation played for fun, not involving any payment and with participants not necessarily striving to become better at the event in which they are taking part. As with all definitions, there will be, of course, exceptions. All Olympic athletes have to start somewhere, for example a taste of football in the park or dabbling with athletics at school; grassroots sport is where every future champion begins her or his career. The term 'community sport' overlaps with grassroots sport, but can be taken to mean more organized sports through local authorities, private and public sports facilities, private and community clubs, sports centres and so on. In many advanced capitalist states this 'policy space' is well known for being crowded with an array of organizations providing sport often competing against one another for scarce resources (see Harris, 2013).

In an interview with the author on another topic, a respondent offered an understanding of sport that went beyond a semantic definition when she said:

> To play sport you don't need to know the language (i.e. the technical terms associated with the game) – it's a bit like an instrument; you can play anyway, it is socially inclusive, it doesn't matter how old you are, you can play at a recreational level, with your family, you can play with others, even those with disabilities, the rules are universal (everyone understands the rules), in general it is something where it is attractive to join a club as it is not just sport but social, it goes beyond social class. When I played handball the goalkeeper was a butcher, others had been to university, but half had never seen the inside of a university; we never cared about this, we wanted to play. It crosses cultures, religions, class; in addition, it is something that is enjoyable, healthy and for me I love to feel I have done something, you get a real buzz and people can find the level where they experience a bit of this (Interview, June 2011).

As the reader will be aware of by now, the attempt to define sport and the wide variety of settings in which it is played, the types of sport involved and levels at which it is played, is fraught with difficulties. Definitions themselves come loaded with specific views of the world: a government definition of sport or physical activity cannot be without ideological baggage; the IOC sets out and defines which sport is deemed to be suitable to be admitted to, and counted among, the canon of 'Olympic sports'. The latter are ever changing and developing with golf being the latest (re-)inclusion in the Olympic programme for Rio 2016. How these decisions are made and why – and who they will benefit – are all political questions that need to be asked and answered. Further, as touched on above, who is it that decides whether snooker, darts or Frisbee are sports, pastimes or leisure pursuits?

It is worth noting at this juncture the rapid growth of what can be termed 'alternative sports'. These are sports seen to be outside the mainstream or 'canon' of traditional sports and, in some cases, the participants and fans are attracted to them for this very reason. The X-Games ('X' stands for 'extreme'), for example, have continued to grow in terms of participants and audiences: live and television. This is an annual gathering of extreme sports enthusiasts who compete for medals, but also prize money, by undertaking daring jumps and stunts in a range of disciplines. Snowboarding, skateboarding and motocross are at the centre of the action. Interestingly, the participants of X-Games come from a milieu that is anti-capitalist. For example, Terje Håkonsen, a top snowboarder stated in 1998 that

> snowboarding is about fresh tracks and carving powder and being yourself and not being judged by others; *it's not about nationalism and politics and big money.* (cited in Reuters, 2014; author's emphasis).

The irony is that X-Games is sponsored by and mediated through the US global sports broadcaster Entertainment and Sports Programming Network (ESPN). Nonetheless, it seeks to avoid the 'medal-table' mentality of the Olympics and the nationalism associated with team sports, for example, soccer. However, in the year of this quote, snowboarding became an Olympic sport and hence part of the nationalism and politics which this brings.

Other types of sport on the fringes of the accepted 'canon' are extreme sports like deep water diving, ultra distance running, paragliding and parkour (or 'freerunning'). These examples of sports outside the mainstream are all attempts to move away from the rationalization and exact quantification of modern sports and back to the spontaneity and the introduction of elements of 'play' that characterized early sports.

Finally, according to Hill (2011: 49), the attempt to define 'sport' and fix its meaning across time and space is of 'limited value', as sport is adapting and changing all the time. This is of particular importance when discussing sports history, as what is thought of now as sport is very different and rooted in a different social, economic and political context than even 50 years ago.

Approaches to the study of sport politics

The intention in this section is not to outline each and every academic approach to the study of sport politics. It is fair to say that the most developed 'approaches' to sport more broadly in the social sciences stem from sociology (see Coakley, 2007, for a good overview of sociological approaches). Approaches from political science, international relations (termed IR in the field) and policy studies have been used to study sport and the most relevant are discussed in more detail and applied to specific cases in this volume. For example:

- Chapter 6 introduces the concept of 'social capital' (which actually derives from sociology but was made well known by a political scientist, Robert Putnam).
- Chapter 7 discusses 'policy as discourse' when examining the rationale for state investment in elite sport.
- Chapter 8 introduces the theory of 'governance' and 'governmentality' and its relevance for understanding how sport policy is delivered.
- Finally, Chapter 10 introduces the concept of 'soft power' as a conceptual lens through which to understand states' investment in, and fascination with, SMEs.

Before outlining briefly the broad approach taken in this book it is worth noting that the process of the 'politicization' of sport over the last 30 years has not taken place in a vacuum. In part it is linked with, and is a reaction to, other processes that are taking place. For example, sport has changed rapidly with 'globalization' (see Box 1.3) and has become much more of a commodity. The latter process of 'commercialization' of sport is, as will be discussed in Chapter 5, bound up with the role of the global media. Thus, the politicization of sport that is central to this book must be understood against the backdrop of globalization and the commodification of sport.

The broad approach adopted by the author in this volume is a 'critical' social science to the study of all social phenomena (that is a stance that is not just sports-specific, but applies to, for example, the study of how to come to grips with the role of the masses in the collapse of the Berlin Wall; see Grix, 2000). Sugden and Tomlinson rightly

Box 1.3   What is 'globalization'?

There is very little consensus on what this term means. Some argue: 'What is the difference between now and the 1900s? We had global trade, many states had a global empire; there was world travel and so on'. However, the world has experienced an unprecedented increase in global travel, business interactions, in particular the spread of global capital; a homogenizing of culture (especially in the West), of which sport is a part. Economic globalization has seen the spread of capitalism and the spread of global production processes (for example, sports clothes made in India and so on), capital, labour and commodities. Political and ideological globalization have seen the abolishing of Keynesian policies, the dismantling of the public sector, the deregulation of economies, and the spread of the governance system of 'new managerialism', in particular among advanced capitalist states. All of these processes have far-reaching consequences that impact on states, regions and citizens in an ever increasing interconnected world. New technologies – the internet, social media, Wi-Fi and so on – have greatly contributed to shrinking the globe. Major sporting action, for example, is now witnessed by millions of people across the world in real time.

suggest that a good researcher ought to have 'a healthy disrespect for disciplinary boundaries, an adventurous cross-cultural curiosity and a commitment to critical social scientific scholarship not beholden to patrons, agencies or sponsors' (2012: xiii). Beyond this, however, a critical approach should not equate to polemic and should not slip into cynicism. For those interested, the approach taken is described in much more detail elsewhere (Grix, 2010a, 2010b). Suffice to say here that in terms of meta-theoretical position, the present work can be placed between the epistemological approach of positivists – whose chief aim is to find law-like patterns in the messy social world under study – and that of interpretivists who greatly emphasize the role of agents over structures in their accounts of how the world works (see Box 1.4 for an explanation of 'epistemology'). The approach adopted in this volume is termed 'hard interpretivism' and its origin stems from the belief that the sharp 'either/or' distinction between research paradigms in general (that is, between 'positivism' and 'interpretivism'), and the division between the epistemological positions of 'foundationalism' and 'anti-foundationalism' in research in particular, need to be problematized (see Grix, 2010b). In practice this leads to a position that gives equal weight to both structures and agents and their subjectivities in any explanation or study. Just as one academic discipline – for example, economics – is too narrow to capture the ever-changing

---

Box 1.4   What is 'epistemology'?

Formally, **epistemology** (see Glossary) is one of the core branches of philosophy concerned with the theory of knowledge, especially in regard to its methods, validation and 'the possible ways of gaining knowledge of social reality, whatever it is understood to be. In short, claims about how what is assumed to exist can be known' (Blaikie, 2000: 8). Derived from the Greek words *episteme* (knowledge) and *logos* (reason), epistemology focuses on the knowledge-gathering process and is concerned with developing new models or theories that are better than competing models and theories. Knowledge, and the ways of discovering it, is not static, but forever changing. When reflecting on theories, and on concepts in general, we need to reflect on the assumptions on which they are based and from where they originate. Two contrasting epistemological positions are those contained within the research paradigms: 'positivism' and 'interpretivism'. These terms can be traced back to, and are illuminated by reference to, specific traditions in the philosophy of human sciences.

---

complexities of the social world, so too are rigid textbook dichotomies between 'positivists' and 'interpretivists'. As discussed elsewhere by the author, it is often the work carried out 'on the border' between these research paradigms that is the most interesting and resembles that of the 'real-world' context.

The reader may be forgiven for thinking 'let us skip all this stuff and get on with the book'. The problem is that every assertion, concept, debate, argument and point of view underlies a specific view of the world. And it is this latter that shapes the points researchers make, the questions they ask and the issues on which they focus. Much of the trouble with academic discussion is that proponents of different approaches fail to take into account others' approaches or make clear their own approaches.

On a level down from the meta-theoretical (what has been discussed above), there are specific theories and concepts. All forms of conceptualization link back, of course, to the starting point at the meta-theoretical level. Take 'sport politics' for example. This is a concept cluster rooted in the belief that sport and politics are inseparable. It is impossible to discuss any form of sport – especially now that it has risen so high on political agendas around the world – without relating to the political context in which it takes place. Other commentators may have a different view of the world to the present author: neither is 'right' or 'wrong', just different. This volume rests on a broad understanding of 'politics' as a social process that can be observed in a variety of settings. This then will influence the choice of topics to include and, importantly, the questions asked about them. This is important as research ought to be 'question-led' (as opposed to 'method-led'), driven by a desire to find out, get to the bottom of and understand what is going on and why.

Other concepts used in this volume may not originate from a similar world view as the author's, yet encouraging cross-fertilization among disciplines and epistemologies is to be welcomed, as long as one remains clear about their origins and how they were originally used. The concept of 'soft power' will suffice to explain. In this book 'soft power' is used as a lens to understand the motives behind states' – in particular 'emerging' states – desire to host SMEs. Joseph Nye coined this term in 1990 and he is what is termed a 'positivist' in his academic approach. Now, working from a different perspective, in this book the term is employed to explain how states set about 'constructing' their image abroad through the use of sport (see Chapter 10). There is nothing inherently 'positivist' in the term 'soft power'; it is the manner in which it is used in research.

A final, yet crucial, point here is that there is a misguided belief that scholars need half a dozen theories and concepts to explain something; there is a need for some form of conceptualization (and 'sports studies' is often too descriptive), but it should be kept as simple as possible because the purpose is to seek to explain and understand, not baffle and confuse.

The structure of the text

In Chapter 2 the case is made for 'sport politics' as a burgeoning area of research. This is done by introducing a wide range of studies that come under this umbrella, also touching on the key themes that will shape the rest of this volume. Chapter 3, for example, offers a historical and contemporary discussion of sport, national identity and the state. The chapter shows that sport has been used for political means for many years and is inextricably bound up with national identity. The case of Germany is put forward to highlight the manipulation of sport for non-sporting objectives. Germany's role in sports history and in shaping the politics of SMEs is perhaps underplayed. Germany had not one, but two dictatorships, both of which made specific use of sport in promoting their ideology, seeking legitimacy for their state and attempting to promote a cohesive national identity. The second part of Chapter 3 discusses how national representative sports at the elite level have effectively become bound up with particular national identities. In Chapter 4 we turn to the story of the political economy of sport, that is, how sport has turned from an amateur pastime to a multibillion dollar enterprise within a relatively short period of approximately 50 years. Part of this chapter considers the journey of the Olympic Games, from being brought back to life in modern times (1896) as a celebration and gathering of the world's youth, to becoming one of the most commercialized sporting enterprises in the world. Chapter 5 looks at the role of the media in the development of sport. The mediatization of sport has run parallel with a process of commercialization and has had a profound effect on shaping modern sport. The media have acted as the conduit that has satisfied the high demand for sporting action by linking consumers with sport through 'live' television, internet, social media and traditional newspapers.

A discussion of 'social capital' (in Chapter 6) – difficult enough on its own – when coupled with 'sport' offers a wide range of opinions on the efficacy of sport and its ability to effect social change. Social capital as a concept presents several problems. Like many concepts in the social sciences, social capital has been used, abused and banded about often with little attempt to define it. As will become clear, it has come to mean the 'glue' that holds social relations together; 'sport' is often looked upon as a key ingredient in producing social capital, thus discussions that include both 'sport' and 'social capital' are usually upbeat and positive. The hope is that sport can change people's lives; a notion discussed in Chapter 6. Chapter 7 shifts to the politics of performance sport and it introduces the core discourse and philosophy underlying governments' willingness to invest in elite sport. This is carried out by putting forward the notion of a 'virtuous cycle' of sport in which elite success for a nation is believed to lead to a whole raft of benefits, including a fitter and healthier populace. A discussion of the governance of sport follows in Chapter 8. The burgeoning literature around 'governance' in political science and public administration is useful to help explain how sport is now governed (at least in the vast majority of advanced capitalist states). The second part of this chapter looks to the international governance of sport and focuses, in particular, on the organizations in charge of the two largest global sports competitions: FIFA and the IOC. These organizations are remarkable for the amount of political power they wield and for the lack of transparency and accountability they exhibit.

Chapter 9 focuses on drugs in sport, offering a brief overview of the development of doping and the struggle to combat it. The chapter discusses how many of the themes discussed in this volume – the commercialization and professionalization of sport – have contributed to an increase in doping in sport that shows little sign of disappearing. The logical step on from this is a discussion of the pros and cons of banning drugs; surprisingly, perhaps, a good number of commentators favour doing away with the attempt to prevent doping.

SMEs – of which the FIFA World Cup and the Olympics are the most sought after and most viewed – are increasingly being used by states as part of their 'soft power' strategies. That is, states seek to enhance their international image and profile by hosting expensive sports 'megas'. Chapter 10 looks at how standard diplomatic practices have been accompanied by 'soft power' strategies and state 'branding'.

A final summary chapter offers some thoughts on the future of sport politics: What are likely to be the key themes in sport politics in the future?

The discussion now turns to the wide variety of studies that could be included under the umbrella of 'sport politics' and how this burgeoning area of study sits with, and crosses over, other academic disciplines and sub-disciplines.

Questions

- Do you believe that sport and politics should be kept separate? Think of a good example where this would be possible.
- How would you distinguish between 'sport', 'exercise' and 'physical activity'?
- How would you explain the two broad meanings of 'politics' in this chapter?

Further Reading

- Allison, L. (ed) (1986) *The Politics of Sport*. Manchester: Manchester University Press.
- Guttmann, A. (1978) *From Ritual to Record. The Nature of Modern Sports*. New York: Columbia University Press.
- Houlihan, B. and Green, M. (eds) (2008) *Comparative Elite Sport Development: Systems, Structures and Public Policy*. Amsterdam: Butterworth-Heinemann.

Chapter 2

The Study of Sport Politics

Those who think sport has nothing to do with politics are living in a dream world.

(Lord Carrington, 1980, UK Foreign Secretary in Margaret Thatcher's Government)

This chapter serves as an overview of sport politics. The increasing political salience of sport globally has given rise to a growth in interest among academics, commentators and the general public in this area. New journals and groups of scholars attest to this: the *International Journal of Sport Policy and Politics* was launched in 2009, for example, three years after the creation of a 'sport and politics' specialist group of the Political Studies Association in the UK, which has grown from around five members to an annual conference with around 80 delegates. This chapter also functions as a brief survey of some of the mainstream literature that could be included under the rubric of 'sport politics'. As will become clear, this is not intended as an exhaustive review of all literature related to sport and politics; rather it should be understood as indicative of the area of study to be outlined.

For those who believe that sport and politics do not mix and should be kept separate at all costs, the last 30 years or so must have been a troubling time. The world has witnessed in this period the increasing politicization of sport on several levels. Sport is no longer a frivolous pastime – if it ever were just that – it is a key resource used by governments throughout the world for a wide variety of reasons, most of them little to do with sport. The story of why and how sport came to be political is central to this book. Rather than offer a blow-by-blow chronological account of the incremental shift from a time when sport is barely mentioned by governments and remained unrepresented in key government departments to the politicized debates around sport today, the following unfolds through a treatment of specific themes. The topics discussed are rarely, if at all, as distinct as presented in this volume: when discussing sport and the state in history

17

in Chapter 3, the subject matter also touches on sport and national identity, sport and international prestige and so on. However, despite the slight overlap in some of the chapters that follow, separating out discrete areas for discussion allows for a more probing investigation than otherwise may have been the case. As will become clear, politics has impinged on areas as diverse as school sport, **SMEs** (see 'sports mega-events' in the Glossary), doping, diplomacy and health.

It would appear that sport, in its transformation from a little used to a ubiquitous, and useful, resource, has taken on the quality of a panacea for all ills (Box 2.1). A cynic's view of sport's (new) healing qualities may consist of the following remedies: Having trouble with disaffected youth? Introduce them to sport. Want to bring countries together which have been torn apart by ethnic conflict, religious differences or war? Sport can help. Want to fix broken communities lacking the glue of social capital? You need some sport. Does your state have a particularly troublesome history? Then a sporting mega-event could help improve your negative image abroad. A more balanced view would accept that sport does have the power to effect social change, but ill-thought out, short-term interventions rarely get at long-term systemic problems, the roots of which may lie in deep-seated economic disparities, class and educational differences or age-old ethnic conflicts.

Box 2.1   Sport: a panacea for all ills?

There are no end of things 'sport' is thought to be able to do: for some, sports practice builds character, discipline and teamwork among participants; sport can be used to break down barriers between divided societies (for example Israel and Palestine), between states with poor relations (for example China and the USA); sport can help young offenders to find purpose in life; sport – along with physical activity and exercise – can go some way to halting the obesity crises plaguing many states; sport can – through a sports spectacle – change a nation's poor image in the world. British Prime Minister Tony Blair eulogized over sport as 'a pro-education policy, a pro-health policy, an anti-crime and anti-drugs policy' (Jefferys, 2012: 235). From these few examples it is easy to see why 'sport' has become politicized. However, Coalter (2007: 35) warns that causal claims made on behalf of sport are simplistic. He states

> ...in most cases it is misleading to argue that *sport* reduces crime, or leads to improved educational performance. Rather the contention is that sports may in certain circumstances lead to the development of certain dispositions which may, in certain circumstances, lead to a reduction of anti-social behaviour or improved educational performance among certain individuals.

Since the rapid increase in the political salience of sport, grass-roots sport, including school and community sport, and elite performance sport, have risen sharply up the political agenda. As Houlihan and Green point out, sport now appear to offer governments an 'extremely malleable resource to achieve...a wide variety of domestic and international goals' (2008: 3; see also Allison, 1986: 12, who suggests that sport 'creates politically usable resources'). Given the 'claim inflation' associated with elite and grassroots sport touched on earlier, one would expect a wealth of data evidencing sport's potential. Sadly, this is not the case and, apart from a section of literature in health studies, the evidence-base for sport's ability to effect change is very limited indeed (see Coalter, 2007). The reasons for this, discussed in later chapters, are not unique to sport's policy: it is extremely difficult to disentangle and unpick the influence of any type of policy intervention given the number of variables in any one scenario. For example, in evaluating a programme to get thousands of people, who had previously not been active, running within a year, we would need to consider whether any increase in the number of people running was actually attributable to the programme or would these people have started running anyway? Similar questions, as will become clear, arise when discussing 'legacies' from SMEs: Is any rise in participation in, say, athletics or cycling, due to the successful (they are all invariably 'successful') Olympic Games? Or was there a year-on-year increase prior to the event or any other factors that impacted on participation levels (for example, many people may switch to cycling in times of austerity and rising fuel prices)?

Government interest in the area of sport policy has led to growing funding for all levels of sport. For example, elite sport funding has greatly increased in the majority of advanced capitalist states and a growing number of 'emerging' states (sometimes termed the 'BRICS' states: Brazil, Russia, India, China and South Africa) have either recently or now seek to host SMEs. Such states are attempting to use sporting success and event hosting to bolster their 'image' and international 'prestige'. Interestingly, government investment often follows poor national performances, usually in the Olympics. This has been the case for the Canadian, French, Australian and UK governments in recent years (see also Taylor, 1986: 42). It was not always this way though, for up until the 1980s it was difficult to find a state willing to stage the Olympics. In recent years there has been a definite shift from advanced capitalist states staging SMEs (for example, Australia, New Zealand, Germany, Canada, the USA and so on) to a wide variety of states vying to stage an Olympic or even a Commonwealth Games or the FIFA World Cup (including 'small' states like Qatar). Tracing the increase in interest and investment in elite sport is one thing, but the question as to why this is the case remains unanswered. Governments worldwide justify high investment in elite sport on several grounds. The British Government's investment in 2012 was based on the idea that, among other things, the success of Great Britain (GB) athletes produces among British citizens watching a so-called 'feel-good' factor and the likelihood that they, the citizens, will be inspired to participate in sport. This participation in sport will make for a healthy citizenry. The net result of this increased participation will be a 'pool' of healthy people from which the elite stars of the future can be developed. The process whereby elite performances are said to inspire ordinary citizens to partake in sport and thus provide further potential for champions is what has been termed a 'virtuous cycle' of sport and is discussed in more detail in Chapter 7 in relation to the growing tendency of states to invest in elite sport (and to stage SMEs) to increase their international prestige (Grix and Carmichael, 2012). Each of the assumptions that underlie this virtuous cycle of sport is open to debate. As will be discussed, there is no clear-cut evidence that elite sport performance impacts on sport and physical activity participation among those who watch it. This is all a far cry from the UK Sports Council's concerns of too much government involvement in elite sport in 1982:

> ...some countries invest vast public funds in specialist facilities, training programmes and financial and status rewards for elite athletes, in order to win prestige and trade internationally. It is neither tradition nor policy to treat top level sport in this way in Britain. (Sports Council, 1982: 40).

Look closely at the build up to the London 2012 Olympics, and the above is a very good description of what Britain actually did. The British invested heavily in elite sport to ensure success; and the majority of the gold medallists from the Games received honours from the state.

Analysing the incremental importance placed on sport by governments and looking at why this is the case is of interest to this volume; however, sport politics does not begin and end there.

The study of sport and politics or 'sport politics'

It is not the intention in what follows to present a review of the vast literature dealing with various aspects of politics and sport or the politics of sport across the academic disciplines (see Houlihan, 2002c for a good early attempt at an overview). Rather, this chapter acts as a ground-clearing exercise and an attempt to simply map out the contours of the array of themes and literature available. The label for the academic study of sport, 'sports studies', is a very broad and generic term that includes a wide range of academic work from sports scientists dealing with how the biomechanics of a sprinter can be tweaked to improve performance, to reports by social scientists for sports funding councils on the governance procedures of the sport they fund. If 'sports studies' is understood as an umbrella term covering all scholarship dealing with sport, then at the next layer down – in terms of the social sciences – there are the established sub-disciplines of sports development, sports history, sport sociology (usually 'sociology of sport'), sports management, sport business and economics, and sport psychology. Each of these areas comes replete with its own conference circuits, journals, terminology and networks. Emerging areas of study include 'sport politics' (which includes 'sport policy') and the sub-discipline of 'sport pedagogy' (Box 2.2).

A great deal of work undertaken within the 'established' sub-disciplines above could be labelled 'political': sports development scholars analyse, among others, government initiatives and investment in community sport/interventions using sport to bring about social change; sports historians, aside from producing regular sports histories, look at the political use of sport made by states in the past; sociologists offer, among others, the more established 'approaches' to understanding the meaning of sport and its role in society; sports management scholars look at issues around sports event planning,

---

Box 2.2   Sports studies (umbrella term)

Sub-areas of study:
- Sports development
- Sports history
- Sport sociology
- Sports management and business
- Sport economics
- Sport psychology
- Sport pedagogy

Emerging cross-cutting area of study, touching on all of the above:
- Sport politics (including sport policy)

and 'leveraging' sports megas for benefits (see in particular, Chalip, 2006), while sport psychologists seek to understand such diverse themes as the motivation behind taking performance-enhancing drugs (see Boardley and Grix, 2013) and 'choking' in elite sport when under pressure. 'Sport politics' clearly cross-cuts *all* of these sub-disciplines. Interestingly, it is worth noting the lack of academic research that has been conducted by the very people one would assume would be at the forefront of sport politics analyses: political scientists and IR scholars. There are, of course, several exceptions, most notably Lincoln Allison on sport politics, Barrie Houlihan on sport policy and politics and Wyn Grant (also with Niemann and Garcia) on the political economy of football and the Europeanization of football (2007, 2011). Nevertheless, there is not a political science 'literature' as such with which to engage critically; only very recently an emerging IR literature around sport (see below) has been discernible. Much of the (good) political work that does exist has been penned by scholars working within the sub-disciplines above, for example, sports historians (although, as Hill, 2003, points out, not much historical work has been undertaken on the formal aspects of politics). Allen Guttmann surveys the work concerning politics and sport undertaken by historians and picks out several major themes from the vast, and diverse, extant literature. Of his themes, the most relevant for the current discussion include those scholars who have studied sport under fascism, sport under **communism** and those who have focused their attention on the politics of the Olympics (Guttmann, 2003). These themes clearly overlap and the Olympics has become a political site used by a variety of political regimes to promote their particular brand of ideology and an event which drives, steers and dominates sport policy-making and policy cycles. This makes the lack of analysis of sport by political scientists and IR scholars even more surprising; sport as a political resource has been used and manipulated for thousands of years since the Ancient Greeks and Romans (see Chapter 3 for more on states and sport): either externally in inter-state relations, or internally, among other things, as part of an attempt to create a sense of nationhood among citizens. As Roger Levermore rightly points out, elite sport usually represents a 'nation' in international competition and the national team is often equated with that nation; given that much of the understanding of IR is focused on the unit of analysis of the state, it is clear to see the potential of analysing and understanding elite sport. This also impacts on the manner in which sport is presented in the media with national 'stereotyping' and sport going hand in hand (see Chapter 5).

Box 2.3   What is 'sport politics'?

Sport politics is shorthand for an area of study that deals with the politics *of* sport and politics *in* sport.

- The politics *of* sport: as discussed, sport and politics are impossible to separate. A game of football or an athletics event may not be political in and of itself, but the manner in which sport is used by governments, by individuals and groups for ends that are not sporting renders them such. This includes the context in which sport is played; as soon as sport is funded, political questions arise. Who funds them? Why? What does sport give in return?
- Politics *in* sport: examples of this would be sports organizations acting like political units, for example, both FIFA and the IOC have taken it upon themselves to 'recognize' would-be states that had not been recognized by the international community or the United Nations. Political questions arise around the status of such powerful organizations: Who are they accountable to? (See Chapter 8.)

Despite these and myriad other examples of the political instrumentalization of sport (Box 2.3), the intermingling of sport, politics and sporting events, IR as an academic discipline and sport still suffer from a 'case of mutual neglect' (Taylor, 1986).

Polley (2012: 2) celebrates the move away from the early literature on this area with its narrow focus on 'IR and diplomacy' by such scholars as Espy (1979) and Hoberman (1984). The immediate 'post-Espy literature' (Polley, 2012: 2) saw Hill (1992) at least branching out to include international sports organizations and Houlihan (1994) offering some theoretical insights, albeit still from the discipline of IR. While Polley is correct in welcoming a broadening of sport politics topics beyond IR, the unforeseen consequence has been a dearth of studies on the international dimension of sport.

However, what has happened recently is the development of a nascent literature within IR that is taking as its focus the political use of SMEs by states (see, for example, Darby, 2002; Black and Van Der Westhuizen, 2004; Black, 2007, 2008, 2014; Cha, 2009; Finlay and Xin, 2010; Cornelissen, 2011, 2014). Black's work has been crucial in drawing attention to the use of what he terms 'second-order' SMEs by states: that is, it is not just the Olympics and FIFA World Cup that can be hosted for political gains, but lower-level events, such as the Pan American Games (PAG), can be central to a state's ambitions to host a major event. Brazil is a case in point, hosting the PAG in 2007 as a precursor to the Rio Olympics. Scarlett Cornelissen, in her numerous studies on South Africa's political use of sport, has contextualized the 2010 FIFA World Cup as part of an attempt to promote a pan-African identity by putting the continent on the map (Cornelissen, 2004, 2008, 2011, 2014).

Interestingly, the majority of scholars in the works spawned by the London 2012 Olympics, for example, and those involved in the wider field of 'Olympic studies' more broadly, are, nonetheless, not IR specialists or even political scientists, but sociologists, historians or communications experts (see, for example, Bairner and Molnar, 2010; Horne and Whannel, 2012; Miah and Garcia, 2012; Sugden and Tomlinson, 2012). All of these – apart from Miah and Garcia – offer at least some critical debate on the staging of the Olympics in general and the key actors involved more specifically. While the tone of much 'Olympic studies' literature can be anodyne, self-congratulatory and even full of pathos, drawing attention to the moral, physical and psychological aspects of (especially) Olympic sports, the critical literature tends to focus on opportunity costs (what the resources used in hosting could have been spent on instead), the key actors involved in ensuring their interests are served through hosting the event (politicians, sponsors, construction firms and so on) and the environmental damage wrought by the logistics of the world's largest sporting event (see in particular the work of Lenskyj, 2000).

Despite the (general) paucity of IR studies on sport, it is obvious that the Olympic medal table – and to a lesser extent the Commonwealth Games – is still used actively by states as a barometer of their standing in the (sporting) world (Hilvoorde et al., 2010). This was clearly the case in the Cold War, but now, in the twenty-first century, it continues to be of great importance to all regime types, whether capitalist, communist or otherwise. It is equally clear that simply being a host of a SME – or the 'second-order' or 'third-order' events (Black, 2014) – is seen as a signal of growing state strength, especially among so-called 'emerging' states (see Grix, 2014b for an overview of SMEs studies).

Holding a mega-event like the Olympics in the twenty-first century is very much a political decision, with the sporting aspect a distant second. Calculations by the host city/nation are based on the perceived international prestige and credibility that can be gained (for example, the 'consumer-communist' Games in Beijing, 2008), and/or the amount of urban regeneration and 'legacy' that can be leveraged from the event. Yet, despite the increasing instrumentalization of sport for political means in the last 30 years – and the interesting questions that arise about policy-making and delivery, governance, power and resource allocation – that is, very much the core focus of much of political science: only a handful of political scientists have turned their attention to this area of study. One of the reasons appears to be that the academic study of sport suffers from many of the same legitimacy problems as those disciplines with the suffix 'studies'. Academics working within 'area studies', 'gender studies', 'German studies' and so on can find themselves defending the methodological rigour of their research against attacks from scholars who work in traditional disciplines. The same applies to the student of sport: often seen as simply following a hobby, it is not recognized, by some, as a serious area of study. This appears to be particularly the case in the UK and the USA, where, in the main, the analysis and dissemination of research on politics and sport is not, generally, carried out in mainstream political science journals, but those specializing in sport (for exceptions see Allison, 1998; Chalip, 2004, 2006; Grant, 2007; Houlihan and Green, 2009; Goodwin and Grix, 2011; Grix and Phillpots, 2011). One early US example that countered this trend is an article penned by Andrew Strenk in 1978. In his article he manages to tersely outline the political nature of sport. This summary, written over 30 years ago at the height of the Cold War, rings true today:

> ...the tremendous investments being made by some countries in sports centers, facilities, training and talent development programs, medical and drug research and competitions have generated extreme pressure for success. Enormous human and natural resources are being directed towards producing and supporting star athletes and teams...The idea of unpolitical sports is, and always has been, a myth. Modern sports are, indeed, a 'war without weapons'. (1978: 140)

The phrase quoted by Strenk is, of course, a play on the famous words written by George Orwell, who, in the short essay 'The Sporting Spirit' wrote:

> Serious sport has nothing to do with fair play. It is bound up with hatred, jealousy, boastfulness, disregard of all rules and sadistic pleasure in witnessing violence: in other words it is *war minus the shooting*. (1945; author's emphasis)

Despite Orwell's prescient writings on the inherent political nature of sport as early as 1945, very few political scientists have turned their sustained attention to it. Lincoln Allison is one. His three edited volumes dealing with a wide variety of topics touching on sport and politics (1986, 1993, 2005) are indicative of the rapid politicization of sport. His initial book was titled *The Politics of Sport* (1986); just seven years later the follow up was named *The Changing Politics of Sport* (see also Polley, 1998: 13). The wide range of topics analysed by Allison and his colleagues – the majority of whom are *not* political scientists – reveal the extent to which politics permeates sport. From the obvious 'state and sport', the 'politics of the Olympics' and 'national identity and sport' through to 'sport and ideology', 'sport and law' and 'elite sport policy'. Despite Allison's pioneering efforts and subsequent work, the study of sport by political scientists in the UK has been conspicuous by its absence. In the USA, where there are thousands of political scientists and the country has one of the most successful elite sport systems in the world, the story is the same. The lack of studies seeking to understand the success of the US system is striking. This is partly because the USA does not compare easily with other leading elite sport systems globally. Whereas Australia, New Zealand, Germany, the Netherlands and even Norway exhibit strong similarities in the components that make up their sports systems (state-led funding systems, training, coaching, sports science, nutrition and so on), the USA can be understood as unique, with its uncoordinated grassroots system and college-based sports development programmes. Leading academics who have written on sport and politics in the USA come from disciplines other than political science: for example, a panoramic sociological study by Coakley (2009, 10th edition), political sociological studies by Markovits who is also a German studies expert (see below for an example of his work) and sport policy and marketing by Laurence Chalip. The latter has made several inroads in sport politics, in particular by introducing the management concept of 'leveraging' to the study of sport and sports events and developing a model that can aid governments/event organizers to pre-plan for and 'leverage' the legacies they wish to gain through sports programmes and major events (2006, 2014).

The breadth of sport politics

The gap in the study of the politics of sport left by political scientists has been filled, to a certain extent, by a wide range of diverse authors, concentrating on a variety of topics, many involving an analysis of politics and working within the more 'established' sub-disciplines mentioned earlier. This has been carried out in panoramic fashion by several historians (see Mangan, 1981; Polley, 1999; Hill, 2002; Guttmann, 2003). Guttmann, in particular, has made a major contribution to sports studies through, among other things, his study of the professionalization and specialization of sport and his masterly study of the history of the Olympics (2002). Several sociologists have had a similar impact in wide-ranging work, for example, the classic 'civilizing' process thesis of Elias (1939), which, when applied to the development of modern sports, places their development firmly among the development of societies from unruly rabbles who played 'mob' football to civilized citizens partaking in mutually agreed and rule-bound sport. Dunning (1999) has brought this work to a more recent audience and has dealt with several criticisms of this grand theory.

Leading sport sociologists, such as Richard Giulianotti, have tackled head on complex topics around fan culture and football, the securitization of SMEs and globalization with aplomb (2002, 2005b). Giulianotti's *Sport: A Critical Sociology* (2005b, 2015) remains a modern classic and is required reading for those wishing to understand how sociology can shed light on the study of sport and how the study of sport can reflect back on mainstream sociology. Giulianotti's colleagues from the same discipline have had a major impact on researching SMEs and their effects (Roche, 1993, 1994; Horne and Manzenreiter, 2006; Tomlinson and Young, 2006; Horne, 2007). In particular, Horne and Manzenreiter hit a nerve with their Special Issue of *Sociological Review* (2006) which looked at various aspects of the politics of SMEs. In many ways this Special Issue (also published as an edited volume, 2006) went some way to contributing to the 'mainstreaming' of the study of sport in the discipline of sociology.

Noteworthy studies from key sociologists on other important issues involving sport include detailed work on sport and nationalism (Jarvie, 1993; Jarvie and Reid, 1999; see also Houlihan, 1997b) and a now burgeoning area of research on the use of sport in attempts to overcome problems in divided and/or under-'developed' societies (Sugden and Bairner, 1986, 1993, 1999; Sugden, 2010). The latter is what is generally termed 'sports-for-development' and most advanced capitalist states have programmes designed to help the very poor in less developed countries via sport. There is a long-running debate as to whether such programmes achieve what they set out to do, especially given the deep-seated underlying problems behind the poverty in the first place. Fred Coalter, a sport policy expert, is one of the most outspoken in questioning the supposed healing power of sport. He is rightly fond of quoting Weiss' well-known critique of policy, which runs:

> We mount limited-focus programs to cope with broad-gauge problems. We devote limited resources to long-standing and stubborn problems. Above all we concentrate attention on changing the attitudes and behaviour of target groups without concomitant attention to the institutional structures and social arrangements that tend to keep them 'target groups' (cited in Coalter, 2007: 87; Coalter, 2013: 2, 35).

What Coalter's work and Weiss' quote do is to remind us that short-term interventions are unlikely to solve long-term, deep cleavages in society.

There is a wealth of material in sports studies on and around youth sports and school sports and the politics involved in this area (Kirk, 1992; Armour and Jones, 1998; Penney and Evans, 1999). Several sports and education specialists (Evans et al., 1993; Talbot, 1995) have taken school and youth policy as their focus of analysis. Griffiths and Armour (2013), for example, unpick the notion of 'legacy' (of the Olympics) and how it applies to youth sports and the development of social capital. Much of the work on youth sports and school sports touches on talent identification (Bailey et al., 2010) or the role of physical education in developing children's motor skills and impacting their attitudes towards sport. Often the focus is on the sport teachers themselves, their training and their skill set, given that this formative stage of young people's encounter with sport is crucial.

Work on sport and crime or violence is clearly relevant to sport politics (Young, 1993, 2000; Dunning, 1999), as is the literature on sports development, which includes analyses and critiques on interventions in society seeking to effect social change (Hylton and Bramham, 2008; Kidd, 2008; Collins, 2010; Coalter, 2013; see Box 2.4).

The use of sport by states to improve their national image, increase their political legitimacy or impart their political ideology is discussed throughout the volume and has a long history (Hoberman, 1984; Riordan, 1991; Dennis and Grix, 2012; Grix, 2013a; Grix and Houlihan, 2013). Suffice to say at this juncture that this theme touches on such topics as national representative sports, SMEs and the political use of the Olympic medal table.

Jennifer Hargreaves has been at the forefront of studies looking at the politics of gender and sport (1994, 2000), an area now driven forward

Box 2.4   What is 'sports development'?

Over a decade ago Houlihan and White (2002) wrote an entire book with the express purpose of disentangling just what 'sports development' refers to. The kernel of the definitional problem was already apparent on the front cover of their book, when they posed the question of whether sports development refers to 'development of sport' or 'development through sport'. The authors also pointed out, quite rightly, that sports development is situated in a very crowded policy field, along 'with other more powerful interests (education, health, foreign policy, social services)' (cited in Collins, 2010: 3). One of the earliest books on this area of study (Hylton et al., 2001; Hylton and Bramham, 2008) points to the difficulties in defining 'sport' (see Chapter 1), let alone 'development' and the compound noun 'sports development'. Nonetheless, the authors offer an insight when they suggest that the concept ought to be

> used to describe processes, policies and practices that form an integral feature of the work involved in providing sporting opportunities (Hylton et al., 2001: 1; cited in Hylton and Bramham, 2008: 1).

in the UK by the Women's Sport and Fitness Foundation (WSFF). The WSFF has commissioned several studies that show the poor representation of women in the top tiers of sports organizations, on sports boards, in top coaching positions and even the chronic lack, or lop-sided nature of, media exposure of women's sport (see Chapter 5). This, of course, is a widespread problem. Women's sport in general receives far less media attention globally and attracts a fraction of the sponsorship that men's sport does. Equally, in societies where women's movements, behaviour and dress code are strictly governed by religious law, few women participate in sporting events and few are allowed to attend or watch a sporting event. The jailing of British-Iranian citizen, Ghoncheh Ghavami, in 2014 by Iran is a case in point. Miss Ghavami was 'guilty' of watching a men's volleyball match (BBC, 2014b). Her retention in jail led to a warning by the Fédération Internationale de Volleyball that Iran will no longer be able to host events if women are not allowed to attend.

Other growing areas that deal with political aspects of sport are sports tourism and management (Chalip, 2006; Weed, 2008), areas in which there has been a growth of journals in recent years. Weed's work has enabled a bridge to be built between sports studies and the study of tourism, a fruitful union given the implications of SMEs for state tourist strategies. Chalip's work (2004, 2006), as cited in subsequent chapters, has been instrumental in developing an understanding of state strategies in how to 'leverage' the most out of sports events. 'Sports management' is another growing area of sports study that builds on a literature that tackles the 'economics of sport' (Taylor and Gratton, 2002; Slack, 2004). In Chapter 4 the volume turns to the 'political economy' of sport and thus draws from both the literature on and around sports management and sports economics (for one of the earliest treatments of this area see Nauright and Schimmel's classic text on the political economy of sport in 2005).

How sport policy, as part of public policy, is delivered and how the 'sector' is governed constitutes another new area of sport politics research and will be dealt with in detail in Chapter 8 (Houlihan and Green, 2009; Grix, 2010d; Goodwin and Grix, 2011). This area of research clearly indicates that states' involvement in sport – in particular in advanced capitalist societies – has increased rapidly in recent years.

The politics of sport and ethnicity could warrant a chapter of their own, along with separate chapters for sport and class and sport and gender. Each of these topics can act as barriers to participation in their own way and often an individual will be faced with them all: a working-class woman or girl from an ethnic background would be less likely to be involved in regular sport or physical activity than a male, middle-class and White counterpart (in the USA, for example). Throughout the volume these themes return and are discussed in relation to the political economy of sport ('class' and 'ethnicity') and the media and sport ('gender'; see also Cashmore, 1982; Hylton, 2008).

A final example of sport politics is doping and sport, including the motives behind athletes doping (Houlihan, 2002b; Waddington and Smith, 2009; Boardley et al., 2014a, 2014b). The reasons behind the increase in doping in sport mirror the sector's growing commercial potential and professionalization (see the entry **commercialization** in the Glossary). 'Doping' can be understood as a part of the corruption of sport, alongside betting, gambling and match-fixing; all of these have in common the intention to alter the outcome of sporting contests. Given that the undecided outcome of most sporting contests is what makes it most interesting and worthwhile watching, 'fixing' results runs counter to what most fans of sport want.

Sport policy specialists (Houlihan, 1991, 1997b, 2002b, 2005; Green and Houlihan, 2005; Coalter, 2007; King, 2009; Grix, 2010; Grix and Carmichael, 2012) have drawn heavily on policy studies, public administration and political science to shed light on how the sport policy sector works. The study of sport policy falls clearly under the heading of 'sport politics', as 'policy' is really the outcome of 'politics' and cannot be understood as separate from it. Some of the best work to date within this rubric has been carried out by the 'doyen' of sport policy, Barrie Houlihan. Through his work on politics and policy, Houlihan has introduced the tools, theories and methods of political and policy studies, which, themselves, of course, are taken from a wide cross-section of social science disciplines, to the study of sport. Houlihan has, in particular, along with the late Mick Green, focused on the sport policy community, adopting and adapting tools from public policy and public administration research to the study of sport. This pioneering work has introduced sports scholars to the tools and concepts of political and policy studies, including advocacy coalition frameworks, policy networks, multiple streams analysis, comparative policy analysis, the government's 'modernization' process, governance, social capital and more (for example, Houlihan, 1991, 1997; Green and Houlihan, 2005; Houlihan and Green, 2008; Houlihan and Green, 2009). Barrie Houlihan's oeuvre, touched on earlier, is not restricted to issues around sport policy, but ranges from analyses of schools, community and elite sport, thought pieces on approaches to the study of sport policy, through IR and sport to doping policy to name but few (Houlihan and Green, 2006; Houlihan, 2008; Houlihan and Green, 2009). The extensive treatment that sport policy has received from scholars like Houlihan – and those who have emerged from his stable (King, 2009; Phillpots et al., 2011; Harris, 2013) – has meant that in this volume the main focus remains less on policy mechanisms and processes but more on the outcomes of such policy. The work produced by Houlihan and others played a very important role in contributing to the study of sport and sport policy becoming more systematic and rigorous and, as such, has added to the emergence of 'sport politics' as a focus of study. There is a need for detailed in-depth analyses of specific areas of sport, for example, doping in sport, the governance of sport, the role of sport in international affairs and identity building, comparative sports systems and so on.

A final strand of 'sport politics' literature is the non-academic literature led by former athletes, sports pundits and sports correspondents (Downes and Mackay, 1996; Barnes, 2006; Jennings, 2006; Smith, 2009; Rowbottom, 2013). There is a mixture of cutting-edge investigative journalism uncovering malpractice and corruption in FIFA and the IOC (in particular, Jennings, 2006), the professionalization of sport (e.g. athletics, Downes and Mackay, 1996), and broader, more philosophical ruminations on sport and their meaning by those who have participated in sport at a high level or have reported on sport, providing insider perspectives (Barnes, 2006; Smith, 2009).

Gilchrist and Holden (2011: 151), in their thoughtful chapter on the politics of sport, are correct when they suggest that 'sport politics' – as suggested in this volume – is emerging as a recognizable focus of scholars from a wide variety of disciplines. This nascent, yet growing, literature has vastly expanded the notions of the 'political' discussed earlier, moving into areas unthinkable – and uncomfortable – to 'traditional' advocates of academic disciplines. Gilchrist and Holden's recent volume is a case in point, with contributions on the 'politics of canoeing' alongside more traditional areas such as sports development (Gilchrist and Holden, 2011).

The vast majority of studies discussed above represent what could be termed 'traditional' studies in the sense that they draw insights, tools and theories from a (established academic) discipline and apply them to a sub-field, in this case sport politics and policy (see Figure 2.1; this is similar to the sub-discipline of sociology of sport, for example). Scholars could, and should, however, turn things around too and take a topic from 'sport' – and there is a long list that would interest those working in political studies – as the independent variable (or the thing that impacts on another variable) with or through which one would wish to contribute to an understanding or explanation of some phenomena in the field of political studies, sociology and so on (Figure 2.2). Then, irrespective of whether one likes sport or not, this ought to have a wider purchase and aid an understanding of the 'established' discipline.

A clear example is that of sport governance; the sport policy sector in advanced capitalist states does not function according to the logic of the (dominant) new 'governance' literature, which, briefly put, asserts that public policies are being devolved towards the end-user and the state is effectively being gradually 'hollowed out'. Far from it – as Chapter 8 shows – the political salience of sport-as-policy has led to far more state intervention than before. This puts in doubt the many assumptions regularly made about other public policy sectors by the mainstream literature in public administration and political science.

Figure 2.1 *'Traditional' studies of sport and politics*

Figure 2.2 *The subject of 'sport' as an independent variable to understand issues in politics*

Given the fact that sport is a cultural institution within society, which have such a wide reach and affect many people's lives in a variety of ways (from player to spectator, gambler to match-maker, politician to policy, fans to heroes and so on), it could be argued that a cross-disciplinary approach is needed to fully understand and capture sport roles in an increasingly complex society. Markovits and Rensmann's (2010) treatment of sport is exemplary of the type of cross-disciplinary approach worthy of pursuit. They see sport as a cosmopolitan endeavour that has the ability to integrate and cross cultural boundaries, a globally understood universal language; in any given country there is a 'sports space' in which sports cultures compete; the latter are discussed in terms of those which are 'dominant' (for example, the 'Big 4' in the USA are baseball, American football, basketball and hockey), each with their own specific 'language'. The notion of a sports 'language' is taken further and used throughout their work to denote a commonality between sport (rather like Latin is to many European languages), but a specificity to each sport (you cannot discuss American football using the terms of reference learnt in association football; see also Taylor, 1986: 35, on the understanding of sport as a universal language). Interestingly, this study builds on Maguire's work on global sports (1999) in which the author uses Elias' approach (discussed earlier) to modern sports development, but does so in reference to the vast literature on 'globalization'.

The state and its interest in, and involvement with, sport is clearly only one aspect of this cultural phenomenon. Non governmental and supranational actors involved in sport have also increasingly politicized sport through their governance. Take, for example, the development of the world governing body for football, FIFA. In the past 20 years this undemocratically elected governing body has made several questionable decisions, has been involved in several corruption scandals, and yet remains a non-transparent organization which yields a vast amount of influence over national sports organisations (NSOs) of football (see Chapter 8 for more on supranational governing bodies of sport). Choosing the hosts of the FIFA World Cup is also a powerful decision to control, given that this is the most popular sport globally.

The above represents just a snapshot of some of the scholars and themes included under the rubric of 'sport politics'. The intention is to get across the usefulness of the study of sport for an understanding of the social world. As a subject area, 'sport' is very difficult to research, analyse and understand from a single academic discipline; thus, where politics meets sport one finds a rich seam of work from a variety of core academic disciplines and sub-disciplines that can and should learn from one another. 'Sport politics' scholars ought to return to 'established' disciplines with what they have learnt from others to test, contest and push the boundaries of 'traditional' studies (see, for example, Goodwin and Grix, 2011).

The argument that sport is a political, trivial, a diversion from 'real' life – apart from the deliberate 'diversion' of the public's attention through SMEs – does not hold up in the twenty-first century. Sport from the school level, through the community to the elite level, has taken on a new importance. The rest of this volume is devoted to thinking about why this is the case, starting with the political use of sport by states in Chapter 3.

Questions

- Which aspects of sport do you think is not political?
- How can the study of sport help scholars understand politics?
- Why is sport seen as a 'cure-all' for many of society's ills?

Further Reading

- Gilchrist, P. and Holden, R. (eds) (2011) *The Politics of Sport: Community, Mobility, Identity*. London: Routledge.
- Giulianotti, R. (2005/2015) *Sport: A Critical Sociology*. Cambridge: Polity.
- Houlihan, B. (ed) (2009) *Sport and Society: A Student Introduction* (2nd edn). London: Sage.
- Markovits, A. S. and Rensmann, L. (2010) *Gaming the World: How Sports are Reshaping Global Politics and Culture*. Princeton and Oxford: Princeton University Press.

Chapter 3

Sport, the State and National Identity

Sport is not an end in itself, but the means to an end.
(Erich Honecker, 1948, General Secretary of the Socialist
Unity Party, East Germany, 1970–1989)

Sport and the state

Throughout history, states have used and manipulated sport for political purposes. At different times in history, different regime types have drawn on sport as a resource to either entertain the masses and direct attention away from affairs of the state or unpopular wars, or as a vehicle to whip up domestic national sentiment and gain much needed international prestige and legitimacy. Sporting events and past glories occupy the 'national narratives' that make up a nation's past. For Hall (1992: 293) such narratives are made up of 'a set of stories, images, landscapes, scenarios, historical events, national symbols and rituals which stand for or represent, the shared experiences, sorrows, and triumphs and disasters which give meaning to the nation'. Australians hark back fondly to the 1956 Olympics – the 'glory years of Australian Sport' (Booth and Tatz, 2000, cited in Magdalinski, 2000: 306) – when re-telling their own national narrative, which has now culminated in the resurgence of their standing as a 'sporting nation' with the successful hosting of, and performance at, the Sydney 2000 Olympics. In New Zealand the All Blacks rugby team doing the 'haka' is an image that makes up a central part of the 'Kiwi' identity (*New Zealand Herald*, 2014). The 'Big 4' professional sports of American Football, Baseball, Basketball and Hockey are woven into many American citizens' sense of their own national identity; key sporting events, such as the Super Bowl, act as pivotal and perennial moments within the US national narrative.

In ancient times, both the Greeks and Romans used sport for non-sporting objectives, but not, as will become clear, in the same way as is used today. The intention in this chapter is to introduce some of the ways in which states in the past have manipulated sport for a variety of non-sporting political purposes and to discuss how sport and national identity are bound up with one another. To this end, an example of Germany's role in sport politics is highlighted, as the points raised by this case study touch on many of the key reasons why states intervene in sport today. Over and above this, Germany has played an extraordinary and underplayed role in influencing developments in sport politics that continues today. The latter sections of the chapter turn to sport and national identity more explicitly, outlining – and problematizing – the idea of the representation by athletes of a 'nation' and how this feeds into the creation or maintenance of a national identity. Finally, a discussion of domestic sport politics and state intervention in **community sport** is introduced to underline the increasing importance of this area to governments.

A measure of the popularity of using sport for political ends is the range of types of states that have done so. This is not simply the preserve of closed-off dictatorships or advanced capitalist states. Autocratic states such as Qatar have invested heavily in sport to put their rich, but tiny, state on the map (see Brannagan and Giulianotti, 2014); the latest trend is for so-called 'emerging' states to invest heavily in elite sport and elite sport events to showcase their increasing economic and political power.

Sport is truly one of the most universal cultural practices known to humankind. Civilizations around the globe played versions of sport thousands of years ago, from the Chinese to the Greeks and Romans; the civilizations of the latter two, however, have received much more scholarly attention. While the Greeks paid particular attention to the aesthetics of the body and physical beauty, they also used sport to prepare their people for warfare and to pay homage to their gods. The ancient Olympic Games – first recorded from 776 BCE – were, of course, a festival in honour of Zeus (one of four such Panhellenic Games held throughout Greece; Miah and Garcia, 2012). While modern-day athletics has its roots in Greek ideas of sport and the Ancient Olympic Games, Roman practices still have echoes today, especially in their use of large-scale spectacles. The Romans were very utilitarian, ordered and pragmatic and clearly used the training of gladiators as a preparation for war (training, sport and physical activity as a way of preparing – usually men – for war is a recurring theme in history). However, it is the brutal spectacles put on by the Romans to occupy mass crowds in what could be broadly understood as early versions of 'sport' that resonate today. This practice was understood as a clear 'diversion' by the Roman state of a warfare-weary citizenry and is encapsulated in the phrase 'bread and circuses' (literally, offering the crowds food and entertainment). Critiques of modern SMEs sometimes point to the modern-day version of this policy of 'bread and circuses' by ruling elites, the intention of which is to divert attention away from the mundane, or politically corrupt, reality of everyday life through offering the public spectacular sporting performances (see the origins of the word 'sport' in Chapter 1; see also Harris, 1972). The first modern Olympics of 1896, according to Tomlinson and Young (2006: 1), was seen by Greece at the time as an opportunity to 'both assert its incipient modernity and to deflect domestic tensions'. Arguably, states today seek to host spectacular sports events to improve a poor national image, stimulate economic tourism and give their populations something positive to focus on (see Chapter 10). Aside from large events, regular sporting occasions could be seen to have the same effect. In the 1970s Ralph Miliband suggested that one of the ways the working class sought release from the capitalist 'relations of production' under which they worked was

> …undoubtedly sport, or rather spectator and commercialized sport, some forms of which have assumed a central place in working class life. For instance, vast numbers of people in the countries of advanced capitalism turn out on Saturdays and Sundays to watch soccer being played (1977; cited in Allison, 1986: 15).

Baviskar (2010) adds a modern twist to the notion of 'bread and circuses' when referring to SMEs. She sees them as 'special time' in which the pursuit of both 'bread [material objectives] *and* circuses [psychosocial and identity-forging objectives]' is made possible (cited in Black, 2014).

Box 3.1 below illustrates the breadth of types of states interested in using sport to showcase their nation externally and stir national sentiment and identity internally. There are usually two ways of achieving this: either through the hosting of expensive SMEs or by investing heavily in elite sport development. There is a trend for a rush to the former by 'emerging' states, whereas elite sport success only comes from long-term investment in a state's sports system. Whichever method is used, it is clear that national identity is bound up with elite sport and where citizens of a particular state show any aptitude for sport at the elite level, this is duly exploited (see below). Domestically,

---

Box 3.1   All kinds of states

Irrespective of regime type, sport attracts the attention of all kinds of states:

- Advanced capitalist states, which usually refers to 'developed' countries such as Australia, Canada, the USA, Norway, Belgium and so on.
- 'Emerging' states is a term reserved for upcoming countries in terms of their economic, but also political power, for example, the BRICS countries of Brazil, Russia, India, China and South Africa, which have all hosted recent SMEs.
- An autocracy, of which Qatar is the best example. In an autocracy the state is ruled by a royal family, and citizens have little say in who their leader is.
- Authoritarian/communist: China, Cuba and East Germany.

Hoberman (1984: 17) summed up the broad political appeal to states of 'sporting competition' by suggesting:

> All kinds of governments, representing every type of political ideology, have endorsed international sporting competition as a testing ground for the nation or for a political 'system'. German Nazis, Italian Fascists, Soviet and Cuban Communists, Chinese Maoists, western capitalist democrats, Latin American juntas – all have played this game and believed in it.

---

there is no doubt that states invest in elite sport to engender a sense of national pride among citizens and create a 'feel-good' factor (see below and Chapter 7 for more on this). That sport can become inextricably bound up with local, regional and national identity is indisputable; this takes on a heightened sense of importance when mixed with religion and/or class. Thus, football clubs take on quasi-religious features for certain groups of fans, for example, Celtic Football Club (mainly Roman Catholic) and Rangers Football Club (mainly Protestant) in Scotland (see Bairner, 2001, for an in-depth discussion of sport, nationalism and globalization).

Germany's contribution to sport politics

Germany has played a central role in the use of sport for political ends and a discussion of this state serves a wider purpose of highlighting many of the ways in which sport has been instrumentalized.

Four key examples illustrate Germany's impact on the development of sport and on the manipulation of sport for political purposes, all of which touch on sport and national identity:

- First, the so-called 'Hitler Olympics' of 1936, which was arguably the first SME and has had an influence on the hosting of subsequent SMEs.
- Second, the Munich Olympics, held in democratic West Germany in 1972, which saw the first political and calculated use of a major sporting event by terrorists and greatly influenced the manner in which subsequent SMEs are 'securitized' (Cornelissen, 2011; Houlihan and Giulianotti, 2012); the purpose of this event, in part, was to signal a new post-War German identity based on democratic ideals.
- Third, the manipulation of elite sport in East Germany for political gains, which resulted in arguably the most successful sports system ever known (the key characteristics of this system – minus the systematic doping – are to be found today in the most successful elite sport systems; see Chapter 7).
- Finally, Germany's hosting of the 2006 FIFA World Cup. The success of this and the impact it had on Germany's international image and sense of national identity, it could be argued, have influenced recent and future SME hosts from 'emerging' states. In what follows, the emphasis is on the unprecedented politicization of, and state intervention in, sport by East Germany (Germany's successful hosting of the 2006 FIFA World Cup is discussed in Chapter 10).

The 'Nazi Olympics' (or 'Hitler Olympics') is widely recognized as the first and most blatant use of sport for political purposes. Young (2010: 96) labels the event 'the pinnacle of Olympic spectacle', comparable to the 'Hollywood show' of Los Angeles in 1984 (also known as the most commercial Games up until that time) and Beijing's bombastic affair in 2008. The Berlin Olympics have been immortalized by Leni Riefenstahl's beautiful, and extremely controversial, documentary of the whole event, *Olympia* (Arthaus, 2006). Both Riefenstahl and Joseph Goebbels, Hitler's infamous Minister of Propaganda, worked hard to create the impression of a link between the philosophical and aesthetic Greek origins of the Olympic Games and the emerging Third Reich. Riefenstahl, the author of infamous propaganda films such as *Triumph of the Will* (1935), begins her epic documentary-style film of the Games by making a transition from ancient

Greece to modern Germany, the prologue capturing physically perfect athletes (a half-naked Riefenstahl herself among them) against a backdrop which includes shots of ancient Olympia. Riefenstahl's link with antiquity ties in with the symbolism of Olympism and the lofty ideals of world peace espoused by the Olympic movement. Goebbels oversaw the introduction of the torch relay (the idea for which is generally credited to the sports administrator Carl Diem), a practice that continues to this day (Hilton, 2008), which sees a torch lit in Athens and carried by a succession of runners to the country in which the Games are taking place. Miah and Garcia (2012) point out the difference between the original *political* motives for instigating the torch relay, which were to propagate the Nazi regime, and its use now, as an integral part of community engagement by the Olympic movement, in an attempt to whip up enthusiasm for the event rather than for the hosts themselves.

Adolf Hitler's sporting dictum, fleshed out in his prison-penned biography, *Mein Kampf* (*My Struggle*), was as follows: 'Not a day should go by in which a young person does not receive at least 1 hour of physical training in the morning and 1 hour in the afternoon, covering every type of sport and gymnastics' (Hitler, 1926: 410; author's own translation); this sentiment was echoed in Walter Ulbricht's (East German head of state, 1960–1973) rather more catchy slogan (in the original German, that is) of 'everyone, everywhere, should take part once a week in sport' (DDR-Wissen, 2013; author's own translation). Hitler, like Ulbricht, was fully aware of the political potential of sport. Although Hitler was not known as a sporty type (neither was Goebbels), he clearly recognized the enthusiasm that accompanied national success in sport such as football. He was also well versed – through his rhetorical skills – in inciting a type of 'psychic exaltation among spectators at his mass rallies akin to the 'feel-good' factor' accompanying major sports events. And sport fitted well with an ideology based on a cult of youth, strength, and genetic and racial endowments. Sport lends itself to the simplistic narratives on which dictatorships rest. The binary opposites available in the arena of sport assist in drawing comparisons: contestants meet 'one-to-one', they go 'head-to-head'; usually sport is 'black and white', with clear rules and a clear 'winner' or 'loser'; participants' performances are judged 'good' or 'bad', and so on. Modern sports, with their emphasis on 'measuring' or 'quantifying' performance, exact times, distances, as well as national, European and world records and, above all, medal tables, appear to fit well with the crass racial distinctions made by the

Nazis and the simplistic *Klassenkampf* (class war) mentality of the German Socialist Unity Party (SED; Dennis and Grix, 2012). Interestingly, Young, in his study of the 1936 Games, concludes that the extravagant show put on by the Nazis – including 10,000 dancers performing a play and a 3,000-strong choir (Senn, 1999) – resulted in little change in perceptions of the country abroad, despite intense propaganda efforts (Young, 2010). Yet in the twenty-first century, showcasing the host nation and attempting to improve a state's international image is what drives hosts of SMEs more than any other reason for hosting (Grix, 2013a).

The events that took place in Munich in 1972 are a reminder of the Janus-faced nature of SMEs, especially the Olympic Games. Schiller and Young (2010), in their excellent in-depth study, carefully trace and uncover the meticulous planning and considerable effort Germany put into preparations for the 1972 Games. A few days prior to the deaths of 11 Israeli Olympic team members and one West German policeman during a kidnap attempt by the Palestinian group Black September (five group members were also killed), a 16-year-old German had won the Olympic high jump. Had the event finished there, the 'joyous leap to victory might well have stood as a metaphor for West Germany's successful rehabilitation on the world stage through the Olympics' (Schiller and Young, 2010: 2). Part of this rehabilitation would have been a change in the stereotypical depiction of Germans as war-loving, belligerent and boring. Unfortunately, politics viciously interrupted sport, completely overshadowing the planned 'coming out' party for the Germans, who were hoping to use the event to signal their successful transformation from defeated aggressor to democratic economic powerhouse.

The brief description possible here does little to unravel the complexities of what the 1972 Games meant: the bitter German–German rivalry and the German Democratic Republic's (GDR) delight at being able to use its own insignia for the first time at an Olympics, or deeper debates about 'overcoming' or 'mastering' Germany's recent history and how this affected the institutional and psychological development of Germany, the Germans and their sense of national identity. But it reminds us of the risks involved in staging a major SME and the legacies of Munich. Munich can be read as the starting point for the 'securitization' of SMEs, which reached its apogee at the recent London 2012 Games (see Chapter 11, as this is identified as a 'future area of development' for sport politics). In London, measures taken to prevent a Munich-type security disaster included surrounding the Olympic park with an 11-mile (17,703 metres), £80 million, 5,000-volt electric fence; the UK even stationed anti-aircraft missiles on residential roofs close to the Olympic park (*Guardian*, 2012a).

East Germany and sport politics

The East German dictatorship, founded in 1949, the same year as the Federal Republic of Germany, lasted almost four times as long as the Third Reich (1933–1945) and went on to develop a sports system that impacts on elite sport development today. The GDR was initially a pariah state in terms of international political legitimacy. Its founders were well aware of the power and potential of sport as a political tool, and as early as 1948 Erich Honecker, then Head of the Free German Youth Movement (*Freie Deutsche Jugend*) in the Soviet Zone and a future leader of the SED and the East German state, declared that 'sport is not an end in itself, but the means to an end' (Holzweissig, 2005: 1), effectively anticipating the politically focused use of sport by the GDR just prior to its inception.

East Germany's political instrumentalization of sport for international recognition and legitimacy remains unparalleled. East Germany's success in elite sport has had far-reaching and unintended consequences; the sports model developed and refined in the GDR continues to shape modern-day elite sport in advanced capitalist states. There is a certain irony that East Germany collapsed, yet its sporting legacy continues to influence its erstwhile opponents. Mike Carlson, who wrote the obituary for the *Guardian* newspaper on the death in 2002 of Manfred Ewald, the architect of much of the GDR sports model, aptly observed that 'despite being disgraced, in the end he [Ewald] had won, because the entire sporting world followed down the path he had blazed' (Carlson, 2008; *Guardian*, 2002). The central tenets of this system not only live on in the twenty-first century, but it would appear that the most successful elite sport systems globally are beginning to converge on a GDR-influenced model (see Chapter 7 for more on this).

Success in elite sport was intended to promote the tiny state of about 17 million citizens and gain it desperately needed recognition, as it was constantly in the shadow of its richer and bigger neighbour, West Germany. Examples of sport as a central part of nation-building abound – take Australia and its rather more recent attempts to construct a sense of community around sporting success (Stewart et al.,

2005) – but none compare with the efforts of East Germany, with its serious legitimacy deficit and lack of a cohesive 'national' history or culture, to gain *de jure* international recognition. Andrew Strenk perhaps overstates the 'soft power' role of sport when he suggests, as early as 1978, that the usual measures of 'trade, commerce, diplomacy and negotiation were not available to the GDR for use in influencing the world beyond the borders of Eastern Europe', so it instead 'turned to sport as a medium of cultural diplomacy to obtain [its] foreign policy goals' (Strenk, 1978: 348–9). Nonetheless, in 1969 official East German documents demanded not only that elite sport should contribute more to an 'increase in the international authority and image of the GDR', but also that sporting success ought to indicate the 'growing strength of the GDR' (Dennis and Grix, 2012: 19); these are clear indications that elite sport success was intended to influence world opinion on East Germany.

This was achieved by making a swift and impressive impact on the world of elite sport, improving from seven summer Olympic medals in 1956 (as part of a 'unified' German team) to a staggering 102 at the state's last Olympics in Seoul in 1988 (Dennis and Grix, 2012; see also Beamish and Ritchie, 2006). The 1970s can be understood as the period in which the GDR finally began to gain the recognition it craved from the international community. After formal recognition of the East German Olympic Committee by the IOC in 1965, East Germany had to wait until the Munich Olympics, organized by its *Klassenfeind* (class enemy), West Germany, in 1972, before it was able to compete as an independent national team, complete with national flag, national anthem and national kit (Riordan, 1999). While the Munich Olympics in 1972 can be understood as the beginning of the securitization of the Games, it also signals a high point in the pursuit of politics through elite sport by the GDR. The GDR not only beat its West German neighbours at their home Games, but the GDR flag and national anthem became commonplace and were televised around the world to a global audience watching and listening to the event. It is quite clear that the GDR leadership perceived a positive correlation between the achievement of their sportsmen and women and the international standing of the state, with East German sports representatives being dubbed 'diplomats in tracksuits' (Holzweissig, 1981), because of their contribution to breaking the diplomatic deadlock and isolation of their country (Dennis, 1988). Interestingly, the timing of the Munich Games (1972) touched on earlier coincided with the GDR's 'purple patch' in which, for a short period of time, it looked as if the country would prosper, with some claiming that an East German 'national identity' was beginning to emerge (Grix and Cooke, 2002).

Political aims are not far from any state's investment in sport, be it for international prestige or attempting to increase mass participation in physical activity and sport. Apart from outdated references to 'class war', the architects of the East German sports system, at its zenith in 1987, could have been describing the situation in the twenty-first century with regard to states' involvement in elite sport development when they stated that

> Elite sport has developed into one of the most important political and ideological factors in the class war. More and more countries are increasing their social costs in order to be successful at representative, international sporting events, in particular, the Olympic Games. (Federal Archives of Germany, Berlin, 1987)

It would appear that little has changed. In fact, and as discussed in detail in Chapter 7, with the growing number of 'emerging' states now interested in using elite sport to promote their nations, the 'sporting arms race' (Collins and Green, 2007) looks set to continue.

Sport and national identity

It should be clear from the discussion above that both international and domestic concerns are central to governments' decisions to intervene in sport and sports development. The motive to set a nation apart from others through sports events or elite sport success is highlighted often throughout this volume. The focus on a domestic audience, however, is no less important. The 'bread and circuses' argument touched on in relation to Roman 'sports' is *directly* geared towards appeasing citizens. The generation of national pride in sporting achievement also carries with it the idea of 'binding' the country together around a 'national identity'. Sport and sporting images generally play a central role in any description of a national culture (see Houlihan, 1997: 119). In fact, most states use sport in this way: to try to add weight to a sense of 'we-ness' among a nation's citizens, or, as Benedict Anderson memorably termed, to create an 'imagined community' (1983). Michael Billig, in his work *Banal Nationalism*, goes some way to explain the role of sport (sporting success and major sports events) in the psyche of a nation. For Billig (1995) an everyday form of national-ism – distinct from extreme or peripheral nationalism which is usually seen as a political problem – is what keeps people together in their 'imagined communities'. Billig's notion of 'the unwaved flag' both encapsulates the banality of this form of nationalism and its everyday-ness. In the USA, for example, the national flag is ubiquitous outside government or public buildings, such that people barely notice them. These flags, together with statues of important people, monuments of art and culture, however, all reinforce a notion of national 'we-ness' as citizens go about their business. Sport, sports images and sporting occasions could be understood as part of the cultural aspect of our identity: in part it defines who we are. The Australians, in particular, have long had – and continue to have – a self-image of a sporting nation, despite the year-on-year increase in levels of obesity among their citizens (National Health Performance Authority, 2013). Stewart et al. (2005: 5) suggest, for example, that

> Sport has, more than any other cultural practice, the capacity to unite Australians, whatever their background. Sport's nation-building capacity has been a feature of Australia's development, and reached its zenith over the last 10 years in the wake of Olympic and Commonwealth Games successes.

Representative sport has long been equated with a 'national identity', with national sports teams being seen to embody specific national characteristics and traits. Thus, the German football team used to be characterized by their ordered, structured, effective, but ultimately dull, style of play (both the German style of play and their attractive-ness as a nation has improved immensely since staging the 2006 FIFA World Cup, although this was built on over 60 years of democratic governance and years of public diplomacy). Clearly, judging a nation by its national team is akin to judging a book by its cover: it can lead to several misconceptions, not least because a given 'nation' is usu-ally very diverse in terms of ethnic mix, socio-economic backgrounds and citizens' access to sport and sporting facilities. The term 'national identity' effectively lumps together a very diverse set of individuals with multiple identities, be they local, regional, religious, racial, class and even sexual.

Further, some nations effectively 'buy-in' athletes from other nations, promising them a good or even lucrative living in exchange for a change of national allegiance. The 2014 Asian Games is a very good case in point: no less that 14 of the 22 'individual running events were won by athletes of African origin who had switched nationality, either to Qatar, Bahrain or the United Emirates' (Butler, 2014). Clearly then, trying to extrapolate Qatar's national identity from their athletics squad – and their football team for that matter – would be misleading indeed. Several interesting questions arise out of a reflection on 'foreign' athletes switching nationalities to compete for their adopted countries. Are we – as David Owen (2014) suggests – moving towards 'diplomatic doping', whereby the lure of championship medals and victories has states lining up to effectively 'buy' ready-made athletes (that is, rather than produce home-grown talent)? If this trend continues, will it lead to a situation where winning teams are made up of 'all stars', an assemblage of different nationalities brought together for a variety of reasons, mostly economic in nature? What impact will the influx of African-born athletes have on aspiring athletes in Asia, for example?

An interesting example of switching nationality to compete for another country is that of Tiffany Porter, a US hurdler who has dual citizenship and came to Britain in 2010 in order to make the London Olympic team. In a press conference in 2012 – and after the Dutchborn GB coach, Charles van Commenee, had nominated her as GB team captain for the World Indoor Championships – a *Daily Mail* reporter challenged her to cite the first verse of the British National Anthem (*Guardian*, 2012). This incident fuelled the so-called 'Plastic Brits' debate, a discussion on whether it is fair that athletes can switch to British nationality and take the place of a home-grown talent. A final example of 'nation hoppers' is the 2014 European Cross Country Championships in Bulgaria. The medals for the senior men's race were shared among 'three transferees': all African born. Ali Kaya, the silver medallist, was formerly known as Stanley Kiprotich Mukche in Kenya, where he was born and still lives (*Athletics Weekly*, 2014a: 114). The 'controversial "all-African" podium' (ibid.: 20) led to a lot of disquiet among spectators and competitors alike and adds to the debate on 'national' squads (in this case, the Turkish cross-country team, represented by two recent recruits from Kenya and one from Ethiopia) being equated with the nation they represent.

To add to the problems of equating 'national' elite sport teams and athletes with a 'nation' is the fact that some sports are still very much linked to social class and wealth, and even who participates at the highest Olympic level is linked to the latter (see Box 3.2). The English national polo team, for example, is not likely

---

Box 3.2   Olympic sport: the poor supporting the rich?

Of the lottery-funded Olympic British medallists at the 2012 Games some 37 per cent went to fee-paying schools and around 60 per cent went to top universities (*Telegraph*, 2012a). This tells us several things about investment in elite athletes in this case. First, the role of universities in the development of sports talent is becoming increasingly important, especially given that a high percentage of a state's population passes through them. Second, in the UK case, over a third of Olympic medallists are likely to be from a more affluent background, given their choice of schooling. Such schools tend to offer better sporting facilities, better qualified sports teachers and give more time to sport in general. These athletes are funded by the lottery; ironically, perhaps, research shows that members of the lower socio-economic classes purchase the lottery tickets that fund potential elite sport stars.

to be representative of the diversity of people in England as a whole. Rugby league, which developed out of a break from Rugby union – in Britain, but later also in New Zealand and Australia – has long been working class in character (Hill, 2011: 60). In the USA, American football and baseball are considered working-class sport, whereas boxing is probably one of the only truly global working-class sport; it is not for nothing that communist Cuba is famed for its boxing prowess. Association football has traditionally been the sport of the working person, with whole communities in England supporting specific teams and allegiances being passed on through socialization and generations.

With the hyper-commercialism of football – see Chapter 4 – including extraordinary wages paid to professional footballers (up to £200,000 per week), hikes in ticket prices (rising at twice the cost of living in the UK) and merchandise, the 'working-class' fan now struggles to follow their beloved team. A season ticket for Arsenal in 2014 cost over £2,000 with match-day tickets costing a cool £97, which equates to approximately £400 per month, close to the national average mortgage repayment (*The Independent*, 2015). In Germany, by contrast, prices are kept low, with Borussia Dortmund, Bayer Leverkusen, Bayern Munich and Schalke charging less than £13 for a match-day ticket (BBC, 2014a).

Part of the problem of equating 'national' representatives with a 'nation' is that the latter is not easy to define in the first place. A variety of factors are used to define a nation throughout the world; for example, Germany and Italy use a common language, while Israel, Pakistan and Belgium use religion. The USA calls on ideology to define its commonality. All do, however, share the common characteristic of a defined geographical territory (Allison, 2000).

Nonetheless, certain sports have become associated with specific regions or countries: there is little doubt that rugby is inextricably bound up with the international and domestic identity of both New Zealand and Wales. Some sports, such as baseball and American football in the USA, remain linked to a specific nation and have not internationalized in the same manner as others (despite some signs of growing popularity in Europe; see Markovits and Rensmann, 2010, for an analysis of why this is). Others still have taken root after being introduced through colonialization. Szymanski, for example, explains that 'cricket thrives in the former empire: Australia, India, Pakistan, South Africa, Sri Lanka, New Zealand, and the Islands of the Caribbean that were under British rule play and watch the game enthusiastically' (2009: 17). Indeed, as Hill (2011: 60) points out, sport (cricket) played a major part in signalling changes in the balance of power in the Caribbean in the late 1950s, early 1960s. Sport, politics and nationality take on a more complex relationship when applied to a state or 'would-be' states recognized by the IOC or FIFA, but not by several other states in the international system. The Palestine national football association is a case in point. Recognized by FIFA in 1998, but not recognized as a fully-fledged state by the United Nations (or, incidentally, by the USA, Canada and so on), the Palestinians made headlines by winning the Asian Football Confederation Challenge Cup in May 2014 (CNN, 2015). Although not yet a *de jure* nation, the Palestine football team clearly represent Palestine and Palestinians who invest their hopes and dreams of their own state in 11 men on the pitch.

Whatever the sport and wherever it is played, it is clear – as in the example above – that it has the ability to elicit feelings of a tribal nature around mythical bonds of a 'nation'. This is sometimes even more so in nations who have 'adopted' sports from the outside or, like Palestine, struggle to have their own 'state'. This, then, can lead beyond 'banal' nationalism to a way of playing out international rivalries 'on the sporting field'. George Orwell described sport as '... war minus the shooting' (1945) and subsequent events appear to prove him partially correct, for example, the vicious Soviet Union–Hungary water polo match at the 1956 Olympics and the numerous England–Germany football grudge matches. In countries with overlapping sporting boundaries, for example, the UK, sport is often used as a 'marker' to distinguish home countries from one another. The UK's quirky situation has led to the strange case of joint GB teams for the Olympics, but separate teams for 'second-order' events (Black, 2008, 2014) such as the Commonwealth Games (England, Scotland, Wales and Northern Ireland compete). Barrie Houlihan (1997b: 121) captures the 'ambiguities of the territorial basis of the nation' when he states:

> The overlap between British and English identity is clearly evident in sport. While there is only an English soccer team at international level, track and field athletes will compete for England in the Commonwealth Games, but for Britain in the Olympics. In Ireland the tension between Irish, Northern Irish and UK identity is also reflected in the definition of 'national' teams. In soccer the Irish Republic and Northern Ireland have separate teams, but in hockey and rugby union the teams are drawn from all thirty-two counties.

Sport and sporting events are similar to 'royal weddings, civic parades [and] remembrance gatherings' (Giulianotti, 2005b: 6), in as much as they engender a 'feel-good' factor that could be understood as an essential part of community bonding: local and national. The public outpouring of emotion attending such events suggests they play a role beyond that of mere entertainment. This is despite the fact that it is necessarily an ephemeral phenomenon, vanishing gradually after the event (see Chapter 7 and Chapter 11).

Back to basics

Despite a lack of evidence for the ability of elite sport to provide sufficient 'trickle-down' effects to inspire community and school sport participation, governments continue to favour elite sport over its much poorer cousin, mass sport. This is despite the fact that there is sound evidence to show that low levels of obesity among citizens and relatively high levels of physical activity are *not* necessarily linked to elite sport prowess, but rather to the type of society in which one lives. The more equal a society is – that is the gap between rich and poor – the more probable citizens are to be physically active and less obese. Four Scandinavian countries fare consistently better than all other states in statistics for income inequality and obesity by scoring low in both

(Wilkinson and Pickett, 2010: 92): in the hallowed Summer Olympic medal table these states finished 60th (Finland), 37th (Sweden), 35th (Norway) and 29th (Denmark) respectively. Norway did, however, finish second in the Winter Olympic table. Nonetheless, the point is that if governments want to get more people physically active, they ought to work on creating more equal societies. The increasing investment in elite sport is a *political* decision to bolster a sense of national pride and national identity through elite sport performance, hosting SMEs, and climbing up the Olympic medal table. Interestingly, de Courbetin, the founder of the modern Olympics, was against the creation of the latter: a table pitting nations against one another. This sentiment lives on today in the Olympic Charter (IOC, 2014: 21):

> The Olympic Games are competitions between athletes in individual or team events and not between countries. They bring together the athletes selected by their respective NOCs (National Olympic Committees), whose entries have been accepted by the IOC. They compete under the technical direction of the IFs (International Federations) concerned.

Given that health and physical inactivity are likely to be one of the most important topics in the future (see Chapter 11), politicians around the world need to reassess their involvement in headline-grabbing sports spectacles and focus on interventions that actually get communities active.

Domestic sport politics

Most of this chapter has concerned itself with the broad-brush discussion of states' use of sport in the past and present, with the emphasis on elite sport and SMEs. This, of course, leaves out a core area of sport politics: that of community sport. This area of government involvement in sport is less glamourous and takes place in a very 'crowded policy space' with a high level of 'sectoral complexity' (Houlihan, 2006a). A main aim of community sport is to provide the facilities and opportunities for the wider public to participate in sport and physical activity, with a further aim to raise the levels of participation among domestic populations. It is easy to see why governments and other policy providers would be interested in raising levels of participation in physical activity and sport; usually in the belief that such activity contributes to the health of a nation. For individuals, the potential benefits of participation arc in terms of well-being. For governments there is a clear built-in incentive to attempt to ease the burden on health systems and to attempt to increase the productivity of their workforce (this is more essential for those states who have a – for the most part – nationalized National Health Service; DCMS/Strategy Unit, 2002; Sport and Recreation Alliance, 2015). Participation in physical activity and sport is, therefore, seen as crucial to the health of the nation, and government-set targets for frequency of sport are designed to achieve health gains among participants.

There also appears to be a belief – more so in states with advanced elite sport systems – that from a greater pool of healthy citizens it follows that more champions will emerge. The performances of this elite, in turn, will help boost national pride on the one hand, and encourage the 'masses' to be physically active on the other. In Chapter 7 this 'virtuous cycle' of sport is examined more closely and left wanting. Although the belief that elite sport success and SMEs lead to greater mass participation is oversimplified and lacking in empirical evidence, there is strong evidence of the intrinsic health benefits of physical activity and sport participation (Oughton and Tacon, 2006). A large literature provides evidence that a lack of participation in sport and physical activity impacts negatively on health by reinforcing the occurrence of obesity and several chronic conditions such as cardiovascular diseases and diabetes (Gratton and Tice, 1989; Vuori and Fentem, 1995; Gratton and Taylor, 2005; Coalter, 2007). Linked to this evidence, the European Commission (2007: 8) claims that the sports movement has a greater influence than any other social movement on participation in health-enhancing physical activity. Given the clear link between increased physical activity and health, it is relatively easy to understand why governments are now keen on intervening in domestic sport politics to varying degrees. Some states, for example, Brazil, have poured scarce resources into large-scale sports events that make an impact globally, yet their school and community sport systems remain woefully underdeveloped. This would appear to be a trend in so-called 'emerging' states; the emphasis is less on long-term, grassroots sport development, but more on quick, big bang effects of global sporting events.

In advanced capitalist states there has been a rapid increase in state intervention in sport in the last 30 or so years. Community and school sport, traditionally the preserve of the volunteer, are gradually being professionalized, regulated and – most recently – privatized.

Community sport in many countries is now characterized by a complex array of bodies, 'government' arm's length agencies, charities and sports organizations with, often, overlapping areas of competence. For example, up until the 1990s the UK Government involvement in community sport was minimal. Today, community sport policy is set by the government-funded Sport England, and the government's Department for Culture, Sport and Media. Community sport policy is cascaded via Sport England from the 'top-down' to government-installed 'County Sport Partnerships' (CSPs) designed to arrange and facilitate sport policy delivery among an array of 'partners' (see Chapter 8 for more on 'governance' and 'partnerships').

The fact that community sport has not had a coherent and strong 'voice' or lobby has led to several interlinked developments: first, this has allowed the state to fill the void; second, it has done so by creating several 'enforced' partnerships between CSPs and NSOs to deliver on the government agenda of increasing participation rates in sport and physical activity, along with several other partners, including local authorities, universities and business (see Grix and Phillpots, 2011; Harris, 2013).

Effectively, UK community sport policy runs from the Exchequer down to street-level bureaucrats and successive governments now intervene in elite, community and schools sport. There have been clear advancements in GB's elite sport performance – often at the expense of sports disciplines' long-term development – while community and school sports have been subject to 'initiativitus' and the energy-sapping, creativity-blunting mode of top-down governance prevalent in many advanced capitalist states (also termed 'governmentality'; see Chapter 8). Australia, New Zealand and Canada all have governance systems based on new public management that has led to a tension between devolved public policy delivery on the one hand and increasing state influence on policy (sport, for example) on the other.

Summary

The use of sport by states has a very long history. While thousands of years separate the examples of Greek and Roman sport politics and those of the modern era, many of the motives behind state involvement in sport remain the same. Be it for fitness (to prepare soldiers or trim obese citizens), to divert the masses from the politics of the day (arguably what the Olympics usually achieves, for example, 2004, 2008 and 2012), to showcase a nation, its national image and strengthen its sense of national domestic identity, sport has and is set to continue to play a key role in a state's self-perception.

Part of this chapter revealed how Germany has played an understated role in the development of sport politics. From showing the world how to host an SME, to developing the blueprint for modern elite sport systems, Germany has been influential. Less positively, Munich 1972 signals the start of the 'securitization' of major sporting events. This has developed so far as to take a lot of the fun out of events for spectators and pose questions of the restriction of basic human rights for others (see Chapter 11).

National identity is a complex, socially constructed category difficult to define; add sport to the mix and it becomes clear why a chapter can really only be a brief introduction to such a vast topic. For Palestinians their national football team playing represents far more than simply a sporting occasion; rather, their hopes of a *de jure* homeland – a given for most people – are bound up with the team. For other football fans it may be a case of following a local team that their grandparents supported decades previously. Debates on 'national' teams and 'national' athletes have shown that such squads and people often do not reflect the nation that they are said to be representing: Kenyans running in Turkish or Qatari colours and former US citizens rallying GB troops as athletics captain. Such nation 'hoppers' complicate the notion of a 'national' team followed by citizens of a 'nation'. As yet there is little research to suggest that the success of such nation 'hoppers' produces less 'national' pride in citizens of the countries for which they compete. States continue apace to invest in elite sport in the hope of national excellence and pride, but also in domestic sport politics, usually with the intention of increasing physical activity participation among the population.

Questions

- How is sport linked to national identity?
- How do states intervene in sport for internal domestic and external international purposes?
- What impact has Germany had on the development of sport politics and its study?

Further Reading

- Billig, M. (1995) *Banal Nationalism*. London: Sage.
- Dennis, M. and Grix, J. (2012) *Sport Under Communism: Behind the East German 'Miracle'*. Basingstoke: Palgrave.
- Houlihan, B. (1997) 'Sport, national identity and public policy', *Nations and Nationalism*, 3, 113–37.

Chapter 4

The Political Economy of Sport

When sport is viewed solely in economic terms or as the pursuit of victory at all costs, we run the risk of reducing athletes to mere products from which to profit.

(Pope Francis, 2013)

Sport is big business – very big business. FIFA claimed that half the people on the globe watched at least one minute of the 2010 World Cup. Imagine what a sponsor or someone wishing to advertise goods for sale would make of that figure. The last game of the National Football League (NFL) in the USA culminates in the annual Super Bowl. Viewing figures for that nation's favourite entertainment have risen from around 75 million in 1990 to a staggering 114 million record in 2015; a figure higher than that of church attendance once a week in the USA (*Economist*, 2015: 43). It is for this reason that a 30-second advert during the Super Bowl cost advertisers no less than US$4.5 million in 2015 (*Time*, 2015). The economic knock-on effect of such events as those above are equally staggering; for example, according to the *Economist* 'more than half a billion chickens will have given their lives so that their wings might be dipped in barbecue sauce' by the time the Super Bowl is finished (ibid.). The figures generated by English football's Premier League are equally astonishing. In 2015 it signed a £5.14 billion television deal with Sky and British Telecom – up 70 per cent on the £3 billion from the previous deal – causing uproar among commentators who point to the simultaneous rise in soccer stars' wages and the dwindling numbers and deterioration of grassroots soccer facilities. Will Hutton sums up the view of many when he suggests:

> ...England's top football league cannot avoid the charge that it is now the most unedifyingly plutocratic and unequal sports spectacle on the planet. American football may be richer, but takes infinitely

more care to spread its largesse more equally...The leading Premier League clubs are joining Russian oligarchs, oil sheiks and English dukes as totemic exemplars of extreme undeserved wealth (*Guardian*, 2015: 38).

If any more evidence was needed that sport is big business, then a glimpse at the average annual wage of athletes from various leagues around the world should suffice. Leading the pack is the National Basketball Association (NBA) which boasts an eye-watering US$4.5 million; this is closely followed by the Indian Premier League (cricket), which has seen a huge influx of money in recent years (US$4.2 million). The Bundesliga, which produces some of the most consistent national (German) soccer team performances year in and year out, has an average annual wage of US$2.2 million, sandwiched between the NFL (US$2.0) and the National Hockey League (US$2.4; Business Insider, 2014). According to Forbes' (2014) annual list of highest paid sportspeople, the boxer, Floyd Mayweather, tops the bill with a total income of US$105 million. The spread of sport in the top ten are soccer stars (two), basketball stars (two), golf (two), tennis (two), boxing (one) and US football (one).

The economic benefits and profit of connecting sports and their star players to the paying public through direct and often live media are also great. Yet the sports 'industry' more broadly is made up of several things, including turnstile receipts – that is, what people pay to watch sport live and face-to-face – and the growing sales of sports-related clothing and sports-related merchandise. There would seem little let up in the very high demand for consuming sport, even in times of recession. Of course, the more eager people are to consume something, the more likely they are to pay to see it and the more likely someone will charge them to do so. The story of the commercialization of sport goes hand in hand with that of the development of the media, as witnessed in Chapter 5. In fact, it is often difficult to relate, retell and make sense of the one without reference or recourse to the other. However, the focus in this chapter is on the political economy of sport, a term that needs a little explanation before proceeding. The intention is not to enter into terminological debates and claims and counter-claims of economists and political scientists in turn. Wyn Grant, who contributed to the growth of this area of research, stated the following over 30 years ago:

...In talking of a 'political economy', one is not advocating a hybridization of the two subjects which would inevitably mean that the economics strain would be dominant. Rather it is argued that both disciplines need to bring their own particular insights to bear on problems of common interest...By proceeding in this way not only is an understanding of the specific problem enhanced, but the two disciplines can be enriched by a better understanding of the theories, methodology and terminology of the other discipline. (Grant, 1982: 3)

In addition, politics and economics are closely entwined and any substantive economic decision will have political reverberations; equally, many political decisions – for example, hosting a SME – will be closely bound up with economic questions, calculations and hoped-for benefits. In what follows, the idea is simply to sketch some of the political economic factors that make up the sporting landscape today.

High demand, uncertain outcomes and sporting rivalries

One of the most profound changes in sport between the codification of their rules and regulations in the latter part of the nineteenth century and now is the shift towards professionalism, the commercialization of sport and their global reach. One could also add the politicization of sport and government interest in it. All of these processes have developed alongside each other. The development of what could be termed a sports 'industry' has grown exponentially in the last 30 years and the media, as part of sports services within this industry, have become increasingly important (Gratton and Taylor, 2005), especially in connecting sporting action with those seeking to consume it: travelling fans, armchair fans and followers (see Chapter 5). As intimated in Chapter 1, globalization has had a profound effect on all aspects of life. The world has experienced an unprecedented increase in global travel, business interactions, and in particular the spread of global capital; as well as a homogenizing of culture (especially in the West), of which sport is part, and an increasing spread of labour, commodities and capital. Economic globalization has seen the spread of capitalism and the political and ideological premises on which it rests. The commercialization and the professionalization of sport must be seen against this backdrop; equally, the pace and scope of sport's global development would not have been possible without the media, the subject of Chapter 5. Once governments realized that money, prestige and national pride could be by-products of sport, it was only a matter of time before sport became a political issue too.

Just as one could argue – and many do – that the proliferation of doping in sport is inextricably bound up with sport commercialization (see Chapter 9 for much more on this), other developments have accompanied sport's increase in economic power.

Offshoots of the astonishing economic reach of sport and sporting events touched on above (Super Bowl, Premier League and so on) include the growth of cheating in sport in general. This ranges from doping, fouling and sporting brinkmanship to the development of whole industries around gambling and match-fixing. The latter services have grown alongside and out of the sports industry (Morris, 2013; see Box 4.1).

Szymanski (2009) makes several pertinent points that aid the understanding of the political economy of sport. These are developed and embellished below:

1. First, once there is a high demand in the form of spectators for a product ('sport competitions') business will seek to exploit it.

Box 4.1   Sports gambling and match-fixing

The commercialization of sport has brought with it both sports gambling and match-fixing. The USA has taken a tough stance against sports gambling, whereas the UK is much more lax. Of course, legal gambling is just the tip of the iceberg, with illegal gambling making up the lion's share of transactions. Once money is to be made, the attention of criminal organizations is likely to not be far away. Match-fixing is closely associated with illegal gambling. It usually involves attempts at influencing the result or outcome of a sports event, with the purpose of making a profit. As discussed below, this touches on several of the core principles of sport and why spectators find sport fascinating: the uncertainty of outcome is why people pay to watch events.

In many countries gambling on the outcome of the Olympics is illegal. Liam Morgan believes that

> Not being able to place a wager on the Olympics is seen by many in the United States as a positive aspect of the gambling culture in the country as sport continues to be littered with allegations of match-fixing across several sports on the Olympic programme, including football, tennis and badminton (Morgan, 2015).

Furthermore, several Olympic medals are decided by judges who are easier to influence than, say, tampering with a piece of equipment.

2. Second, the uncertainty of the outcome of a sports event is what makes it fascinating to the fan and very good for business, as the desire to know this bolsters demand (see Szymanski, 2009: 128).
3. Third, 'rivalries' in sport – be they between contestants or teams – are central to sport's appeal and adds to the excitement.

High 'inelastic' demand

It is quite clear that sport does not operate like any other market and that 'brand loyalty', especially around team sports, takes on a whole new meaning. Some sports lend themselves more naturally to fanatical fandom and thus a situation in which fans are effectively 'locked-in' with no exit route (see Box 4.2).

As touched on briefly in Chapter 3, the very high wages for footballers in the UK Premier League (up to £200,000 per week), the upward hike in ticket prices (rising at twice the cost of living in the UK; BBC, 2014a) and extortionate prices for sports and team-related merchandise, could see a decline in support among those who can no longer afford to follow their team. As stated in Chapter 3, an Arsenal soccer

---

Box 4.2   Sport and inelastic demand

In Chapter 8 the discussion on governance of global sports touches on the international governing bodies FIFA and the IOC. The argument is that given the 'inelastic' demand for sport – that is, in general, demand does not fall when prices rise – these unaccountable organizations are in an enviable (economic) position. Take soccer fandom as an example: demand for watching soccer teams is inelastic, as fans are effectively 'locked-in' with no alternative. If a fan's team is part of his or her DNA, through socialization, generational bonding, proximity and local culture, they are not going to support the opposition if ticket prices and merchandise prices rise. The 'locked-in' nature of fandom makes sport extremely attractive to sponsors, whose aim it is to make a profit by selling goods. Equally, if sponsors and foreign owners of a fan's club change the stadium name and make ill-informed decisions about the fortunes of a club, all the fan can do is despair. Hirschman's 'exit' option (1970) works better for commodities than sport, for, as Wyn Grant suggests in relation to English soccer

> ...if one starts watching a non-league club, the standard of play and facilities will be inferior. Switching to another sport is an unlikely option (Grant, 2007: 75).

club season ticket in 2014 equates approximately to the UK national average mortgage repayment (*Independent*, 2015). In Germany, by contrast, prices are kept low, with Borussia Dortmund, Bayer Leverkusen, Bayern Munich and Schalke charging less than £13 for a match-day ticket (BBC, 2014a). It is interesting to point out the stark differences between Premier League wages and tickets and Bundesliga wages and tickets. How do the latter manage to produce better home-grown players, pay them less and keep prices down for loyal fans? Part of the answer is that the Bundesliga is not an unfettered market, the majority of clubs are part-owned by fans, are not allowed to be sold to non-national billionaires and the country has a long-term view of sports development, which does not separate the grassroots so starkly from a cash-rich super league.

There is another observation to be made beyond the fact that a high demand exists for sport from spectators: it is that 'sport' as such represents an abnormal market, one that manages to exhibit characteristics usually associated with both communist and advanced capitalist states at the same time. On the one hand, some sports operate the most liberal and free of all markets (for example, the *de facto* unfettered transfer market in English Premier League football). Equally, the political economy of the Olympics (including sponsors, branding and so on), as discussed below, could be understood as the epitome of an advanced neoliberal, economic project, given the demands of the IOC on the hosting states, including concessions to Olympic sponsors (see Box 4.3) to operate in a tax-free zone. Both the Premier League and the Olympics sit very well with standard neoclassical economics which advocate free market competition. On the other hand, the sports market – especially since the involvement of governments – has come to resemble that of the Soviet planned economy. Elite sport development programmes in the top sporting nations have become centrally governed (see Chapter 7) and are driven by certain governmental expectations and norms. This often operates alongside rhetoric demanding the freeing up and exposure of markets to more competition. The paradox is that the two trends play alongside each other: professional sports and the major stake-holders behind major sports events are, or act like, profit-seeking businesses (officially the IOC and FIFA are not-for-profit organizations), while a majority of Olympic sports in nations that head the top of the Olympic medal table are supported by state-led funding programmes akin to a command economy and populated by state-funded, full-time athletes.

> ## Box 4.3   Olympic sponsors
>
> The Olympic Partner (TOP) programme is the highest level of Olympic sponsorship available. According to the IOC, the benefits of 'worldwide' partners are manifold:
>
> > In addition to the financial support generated by sponsorship, each Olympic partner's products, technology and expertise are vital to the success of the Games. Partners also help promote the Games worldwide through their marketing campaigns and sponsorship activations, helping the Olympic Movement reach a wide global audience. Through this commitment, the Olympic partners provide the foundation for the staging of the Games and help more athletes from more countries participate on the world's biggest sporting stage (IOC, 2012).
>
> Two of the top Olympic sponsors are Coca-Cola and McDonald's, whose 'products, technology and expertise are vital to the success of the Games'. Indeed, the McDonald's at the 2012 Olympics broke its own world record for being the largest outlet ever.
> According to the *Financial Times* (2011) to become one of the 11 TOP-tier Olympic sponsors at London 2012, corporations paid an estimated US$100 million. The IOC relies on fewer sponsors than in the past, but they pay significantly more for the privilege.

The uncertainty of outcome

One of the reasons why match-fixing and cheating are frowned on by regular sports consumers is that it robs sport temporarily of one of their most exciting aspects: unpredictability. Last minute goals, tries or runs; crashes, falls, fouls and trips all add to the highly charged nature of consuming sport; that is, when they are seen to be part of play and not premeditated action. The highly charged emotional atmosphere, however, only lasts as long as the outcome of the event is unknown: once the runners cross the line, the baseball scores are in, the final whistle is blown and the chequered flag is reached, then, at this point in time, demand turns towards the next race, match, game and its outcome. A classic example of sports diplomacy helps clarify this point. The so-called case of 'ping-pong' diplomacy – that is, a table tennis match between China and the USA in 1971, which symbolized a 'thawing' of relations between the states – only really worked because everybody *knew* that the US team could not beat the Chinese at table tennis. Thus, the outcome was *predictable*, given the superiority of the Chinese athletes over those of the USA.

Rivalries in sport

Rivalries in sport are good for business; they are also good for selling newspapers, stimulating demand for other types of media, but also for generating interest in a sporting contest. Hence, the media are central to whipping up rivalries in sport, and history reveals a great number of much-hyped 'one-to-ones' on the sports field, in the ring or on the track.

Rivalries can be at the level of a state, that is, the USA versus USSR during the Cold War (one reason why the 'ping-pong' example is so poignant). The rivalry in the sports arena echoed real-life rivalries between ideologically opposing systems of governance (capitalism versus communism), in which 'individual freedom' as opposed to the 'collective' was the underpinning philosophy. National insignia – vests, tracksuits, flags, badges, colours and so on – lend themselves to the display of national identity through sport and it is partly for this reason that states put so much effort and resource into the opening ceremony of major Games. Rivalries more commonly take place at the level of teams: Szymanski opens his book with the story of the rivalry between the New York Yankees and Boston Red Sox baseball teams, that dates back to over 100 years ago (2009: vii–xiii). The German–English rivalry in soccer is legendary, although – as discussed in Chapter 10 – since the FIFA World Cup in 2006, the antagonism towards Germany from the notoriously intrusive and, at times, rude, English press, seems to have abated. Australia's rivalry with England in cricket has several historical, and colonial, undertones, something Australia has in common with New Zealand, another 'Commonwealth Realm', whose head of state is, of course, the English constitutional monarch (currently Queen Elizabeth II). The notion of a former 'colony' beating the 'homeland' plays into the rivalries that sport seem particularly apt at engendering.

Rivalries at an individual level also seek to build interest in, generate an audience, and often financial backing for, a specific event or contest. The famous 'Rumble in the Jungle' world heavyweight championship fight in 1974 between George Foreman and challenger, Muhammad Ali, is a case in point. Held at 4 a.m. in the jungle of Zaire (now the Congo) to accommodate foreign television audiences, this million dollar bout has become – along with the 'Thrilla in Manila' (between Ali and Joe Frazier in 1975) – one of the most iconic sporting moments in history. Other, less financially spectacular, rivalries include those on the athletics track between Sebastian Coe and Steve Ovett in the

UK (see Chapter 5 for the media's role in creating this rivalry) which appeared to split supporters along class lines.

State, team and individual rivalries in sport all serve to stoke the emotions of the watching fans; emotional fans are, in turn, prepared to pay to see such events either live or, increasingly, via a variety of media outlets (see Chapter 5). One unique example of the commercialization of sport which adds another dimension to the examples of professional sport given above is that of the Olympics, to which this chapter now turns.

The commercialization of the Olympics

Discussion about the Olympic Games is often couched in a well-intentioned but unrealistic and mythical discourse of an amateur, peaceful sporting event far from the maddening crowd of politics and economics. Pierre de Coubertin, commonly acknowledged as the founder of the modern Olympics, would be hard pressed to recognize what has become of the modern event. He had envisaged bringing the youth of the world together to inculcate young people with the values of internationalism through sporting endeavour. Such values contained in the Olympic Charter are well intentioned, admirable, life affirming and out of step with what the event has become. The Olympic motto, for example, 'expresses the aspirations of the Olympic Movement' (IOC, 2014: 23); yet, 'Faster, Higher, Stronger' (*Citius, Altius, Fortius*) cannot disguise the fact that the event is *the* most quintessentially political sporting event the world has ever known. This is evidenced in two clear forms: first, the Olympic Games represent an exemplar of *laissez faire* economics, the ideology of which allows for tax breaks for multinational sponsors, forbids the use of the Olympic symbols and name, and provides a boon to (usually transnational) business in each city it is hosted. Horne et al. state:

> Perversely, the prohibition of advertising in the Olympic arena gives the [Olympic] symbol the aura of being above commerce and hence greatly increases its commercial value. This gives a clue to the resolution of a paradox at the heart of sport. Sport is capable of generating substantial profits although the key institutions were not formed as commercial endeavours. Yet, increasingly, beneath the cloak of traditional amateurism, they are reshaping themselves according to the nature and opportunities of the market-place (2006: 278).

Second, the whole debate about which facilities to build, who will benefit from them, how much ought to be spent and so on, is at its heart; that is, a contestation around resources, which is the very essence of politics.

It is interesting to note, before proceeding, that there is a distinct lack of critical research on the politics of the Olympics (critical in the sense outlined in Chapter 1, that is, not *negative per se*, but questioning). The general thrust of much work on the Olympics, including the majority of reporting and press coverage, is positive, celebratory and uncritical. Those who ask difficult questions about the Games – for example, whether the vast resources states continue to allocate to building new stadia and urban 'regeneration' projects despite the lack of evidence for post-event 'legacies' would be better invested elsewhere – are often grouped along with anti-Olympic protesters and looked upon as pessimistic cynics or simply moaners seeking to spoil the fun (see Lenskyj, 2000; also Bairner and Molnar, 2010: 13–14; Perryman, 2013). Yet, clearly, the Olympics, more than any other sporting event, are turning into a business fair driven by a mixture of political and economic calculations. While the motives for hosting SMEs may differ slightly across different regime types, the Olympics themselves and the signalling effects of the opening and closing ceremonies have become overblown, extravagant and often unnecessary affairs. Beijing's opening ceremony, for example, is said to have cost around US$100 million (*Telegraph*, 2012b), money that could have been directed to those in need in China.

Allen Guttmann, in his masterful account of the history of the Olympics, points out that the very inception of the modern Olympic Games in Athens, 1896, was political (Guttmann, 2002). Little has changed since to refute this view; the world's greatest SME has been used and manipulated by states of all political hues as a means to further their own interests in a variety of different ways. The event itself has impacted on states, their sport policies, systems of sport and has been the driving force behind sports funding by governments seeking to finish higher up on the Olympic medal table for decades. The long-term impact of a focus on *specific* Olympic sports, for example, is bound to skew sports development in such states and it will have economic implications for other sports and physical activity initiatives. While there would appear to be no end to the topics that could be discussed in which politics are integral to the bidding for, staging of, protesting against, reporting on and even – on occasion – taking part in, the Olympics, the focus here is on part of the 'twin suns of prestige and profit' (Guttmann, 2002: 175) that such events are supposed to produce.

The Olympics are big business. The hard-hitting, straight-talking Helen Lenskyj talks of the 'Olympic industry' (Lenskyj, 2000) refusing to engage with the 'fluffy' IOC terms 'Olympic family' or 'Olympism'. Lenskyj criticizes the IOC for its claim to be 'the moral authority for world sport' and the 'supreme authority' over the staging of the Olympics (Lenskyj, 2010: 23). She points to the extraordinary examples of the IOC effectively conferring political recognition on states (for example, East Germany), despite having no diplomatic status to speak of (2010: 23). The 'Olympic industry' is evident in the 'neo-liberalization' of the Games in general (Horne and Whannel, 2012: 135–6). Sugden and Tomlinson go as far as to state that

> The most compelling and fundamental change is the way the Olympics have moved steadily and inexorably away from being an amateur, peoples', sporting festival towards a state-choreographed, commercially driven, internationally controlled, media mega-event (2012: 243).

It would appear difficult to reconcile the original underlying values of Olympism – that is, an emphasis on peace and the educational and moral value of taking part in sport (McFee, 2012: 37) – with the rampant commercialization of the Games. Both of the descriptions above were relevant for the most recent Olympics in London 2012.

While 'legacy' promises are made, founded on hope rather than any tangible evidence or clearly spelt out leveraging strategies, the 'corporate' side of the Games is a reality. The majority of arguments in favour of the commercialization of the Olympics also cite the 'legacies' that will accrue by virtue of staging the event. However, perhaps the call for the Games and its aftermath to 'inspire a generation' of youngsters, through elite sport, to take up physical activity and reduce the UK's increasing rates of obesity (figures indicate that some 31 per cent of boys and 28 per cent of girls between the ages of 2 and 15 are classified as 'obese' in the UK; NHS, 2011) should be questioned, if the event is sponsored by the transnational companies often linked with the obesity crises in the first place (Coca-Cola, McDonald's and so on; see Finlay, 2011: 379). The London Olympic Park had already broken records before the Games even began: the Australian-owned Westfield Stratford City Shopping Centre is the largest in Europe and the site boasted the largest McDonald's outlet in the world. As part of the IOC stipulations, the Olympic Park acted as a quasi-tax haven for the 'core sponsors' selling their merchandise, so that no tax was paid on transactions within the Park and no money went back into the public purse that paid for it, although after a large-scale online protest, some of the major sponsors opted to pay tax. For Horne the compliance by hosts to the IOC's increasingly long list of demands leads to the Olympics becoming

> ...'fat cat' projects and media spectacles benefiting mostly the corporations that sponsor the Games, property developers that receive public subsidies, and the IOC which secures millions of dollars from television corporations and global sponsors (2010: 28).

As argued in Chapter 11, there appears an inevitable slide towards the (hyper) commercialization of the Olympics that has little or nothing to do with the actual sport on show.

The impact of commercialization on sport

One of the perennial questions for students of sport is 'How has commercialization changed the nature of sport?' or, better still, 'Has commercialization ruined the very essence of sport? Give examples'. Before considering these questions, it ought to be pointed out that sport has always been commercial; betting and prize money in handicap running races in Australia, for example, have been around since the late nineteenth century. The Stawell Gift race is Australia's oldest (established in 1878) and most lucrative (Stawellgift.com). However, the difference lies in the sums of money pouring into sport. The consultancy company, PricewaterhouseCoopers, estimated that the North American sports industry revenue will top US$67.7 billion by 2017 (North America includes the USA and Canada; the 'industry' refers to sponsorship, media rights, gate receipts and merchandise; Bloomberg, 2013). This is a large part of the global sports market revenues estimated to be around US$145 billion in 2015 (Sport and Recreation, 2015). To put the North American figure in some perspective, such a sum is greater than most small states' gross domestic product (nominal GDP, that is, the market value of all goods and services from a nation in a given year), including the vast majority of African states. It is also greater than the 2013 GDP of over 120 states listed by the World Bank (World Bank, 2014).

A recent report suggested that sports sponsorship in Australia is worth some US$735 million per year (Sports Marketing, IMR, 2013). Coupled with the Super Bowl statistics and the English Premier League television deal outlined above, it is easy to see that the sports sector is witnessing an unprecedented era of prosperity. Before getting too carried away, it is wise to qualify this by stating that popular and rich sports appear to be getting more popular and richer; the Premier League, already the soccer league that generates the most money globally (and is only surpassed by the American NFL, Major League Baseball and NBA), has only just begun to tap into lucrative overseas markets. Top teams, such as Manchester United (£433.2 million revenue in 2014; Deloitte, 2015), have become 'brands' in their own right, attracting millions of fans in population-dense countries, such as China (around 1.4 billion inhabitants), India (around 1.25 billion) and other parts of Asia (See Rofe, 2014). A recent survey suggests that Manchester United have no less than 659 million fans worldwide (*Guardian*, 2013a). Given the extortionate price of a replica soccer shirt, if only half the fans bought one, it is easy to see why the global sports market revenue figure is so high. While it is indisputable that more money is being pumped into sport, it is not the case that all sports benefit equally. Less 'glamorous' or 'marketable' sports suffer from a chronic lack of funding, from a lack of media exposure and, as a consequence, a lack of sponsorship. Sports which are heavily reliant on government funding – including many Olympic sports – have their futures linked to their current performances (that is, if they do less well than expected, funding is cut). The fate of some sports, incidentally, depends very much on their place in their country's sporting culture. Take basketball, for example, a game played by the same rules with the same equipment on both sides of the Atlantic. However, in the USA, basketball is one of the 'Big 4' professional sports, enjoying a massive following, sponsorship and television coverage. The NBA is consistently ranked among the top three sports leagues globally in terms of the size of its revenue. In the UK, in stark contrast, basketball has suffered from a lack of funding and does not have the same iconic status among fans as in the USA. One of the GB men's basketball team sums up the situation when he was reported as saying:

> members of the squad were living off £15 a day, had to sleep in beds too short for them, and were forced to take early morning flights on budget airlines the day after late night matches in order to save money (BBC, 2014).

There is an interesting debate to be had about how sport – such as basketball – becomes embedded in a country's sports culture. In Chapter 2 the work of Markovits was flagged up, in which he sought to explain the dominance of certain sports (in this case the 'Big 4' in the USA) and how it is very difficult for other sports to penetrate long-existing markets (soccer in the case of the USA; basketball in the UK case).

The student's perennial question on the impact of commercialization on sport, however, remains unanswered. One clear effect of all the money pouring into sport can be read off the changing names of teams (the 'Qantas Wallabies'; FC Red Bull Salzburg) and the arenas in which they play (Commerce Bank Ballpark, New Jersey; Red Bull Ring, Spielberg and so on). Does this matter? Probably less to the younger generation who may have adapted more to the advanced capitalist principles that underlie all the states in which the world's most lucrative sports leagues take place (mostly the USA, UK, Canada and parts of Europe). It could be argued that the influx of money into sport has improved its quality, for example, providing clubs and organizations with the resources to buy the best talent available and offer the best support structures. A counter argument would be that money has tainted sport, ruined its very 'essence'. The shift from amateur pursuit to professional career has witnessed an unprecedented improvement in performance, but at the expense of the character building and social aspects of sport.

While it may be premature to announce the 'end of history', as Francis Fukuyama did when communism collapsed in the late 1980s, early 1990s, it is clear that the most dominant – and for the most part intellectually unchallenged – economic paradigm in the twenty-first century remains neoliberalism in its various guises. While some countries are more immune to such a paradigm (Germany and Japan, for example, espouse more long-term investment), it is clear that the market of sport is driven by the profit motive and changes will take place as a result (see Chapter 5 for the impact of the media on sport).

Summary

The above has and can only offer a brief introduction to what is a vast topic: the political economy of sport. As discussed, sport is a highly unusual 'market' which does not operate according to the usual rules of supply and demand. In a 'normal' market one would expect to see an 'exit' from a product at a certain point of rising prices. In sport – especially the popular team games – fans cannot exit and will put up with extortionate prices, poor management decisions and undemocratic international governing bodies. This 'inelastic' demand for sport, built as it is on the uncertain outcomes of games, races, matches and so on, is a sponsor's dream.

The Olympic Games was put forward as an example of the hyper-commercialization of sport in the modern era. This global event with the loftiest of ideals has become an exemplar of organizational profit making. Preparing the athletes for this event has become a state-sponsored, government-funded, glory-seeking enterprise. The impact of such Olympic-driven sport policy on the development of sports disciplines – and the commercialization of sport more generally – is likely to be profound.

Questions

- Has commercialization ruined the 'essence' of sport?
- Why has sport become so commercialized?
- What positive and negative impacts has the influx of money into sport had?
- 'The Olympics is more about profit than sport' – Do you agree?

Further Reading

- Grant, W. (2007) 'An analytical framework for a political economy of football', *British Politics*, 2(1), 69–90.
- Lenskyj, H. J. (2010) 'Olympic power, Olympic politics: behind the scenes', in A. Bairner and G. Molnar (eds) *The Politics of the Olympics: A Survey* (London and New York: Routledge).
- Szymanski, S. (2009) *The Comparative Economics of Sport*. Basingstoke: Palgrave Macmillan.

Chapter 5

Sport and the Media

The story of the commercialization of sport in Chapter 4 goes hand in hand with that of the development of the media: it is difficult to relate the one without the other. If the academic literature around the commercialization of sport has developed into a sub-discipline of its own, so too has that of sport and the media. This chapter can but briefly touch on some of the milestones in the development of the 'sport–media' relationship. In what follows, a brief discussion of the historical development of sport and the media will be outlined. The chapter then turns to the role the media plays in constructing a state's national 'narrative', formed as it is around critical junctures in history and momentous, and usually glorious, occasions, of which sporting events and feats are part.

The 'media' is, of course, a very broad umbrella term encapsulating a wide array of methods of communication, ranging from the 'traditional' newspapers, radio and television, through to the much more recent on-line and social media platforms. The effects the media have on those who consume them are varied too: the commonsensical view, that consumers tend to believe what they see, read and hear in the media, and do so in a uniform fashion, is a belief not substantiated by research. Early studies on the media did subscribe to such a 'hypodermic needle' or 'magic bullet' approach, but subsequent research has shown that the context in which recipients receive the media message and their own personal make-up, socialization, background, educational levels and so on, have an impact on how they perceive, process and make sense of the media messages coming their way (see Williams, 2003 for an overview on media effects). The importance of being aware of this becomes apparent when one considers the extent to which sport consumption is in reality a 'mediated' experience, whereby matches, tournaments and races are effectively 'packaged' for (often very specific) audiences (Box 5.1).

An example where the media clearly fail in their role as the 'fourth estate' (see box 5.1 below) is in the coverage of women's sport in all forms of media outlets. Such coverage, if believed, would

> ### Box 5.1 What is the role of the media in (a democratic) society?
>
> The textbook role of the media in society has been termed that of the 'fourth estate' of government (that is, in addition to the Legislative, Judiciary and Executive in a democracy), attempting to keep the Legislative, Judiciary and Executive in check. Ideally, the media act as watchdogs for society, ensuring good governance, and act as agenda setters for news, pointing to the most salient events and developments and informing citizens about them. This then puts citizens in the position to make informed and balanced choices on the basis of such information.
>
> Unfortunately, not all forms of media fulfil this ideal–typical role in society. The media have the power to shape people's opinions and by focusing on specific issues and ignoring others, they can distort what is really going on. Also, not all individuals have equal access to a variety of media outlets, thus making it difficult to come to an informed and balanced opinion.

seem to suggest that women are far less interested in sport and that barely any females undertake sport, despite the fact that globally the human sex ratio is more or less one-to-one (that is, women make up half the world's population). A dearth of media coverage also translates into far less possibilities for female role models to be in the spotlight, who may inspire girls and women to take up sport. In Australia, it is estimated that around 9 per cent of media coverage is given over to women's sport (Australian Sport Commission, 2013). According to the WSFF in the UK (2014) only 5 per cent of sport media coverage is devoted to women's sport. It is perhaps no surprise that fewer women than men participate in sport (31 and 41 per cent respectively in the UK; Sport England, 2015).

The development of sport media

Cashmore (2003: 277) rightly points to the crucial link in the early days of newspaper developments between the media selling stories about sport and about the heroic sportsmen and women who played them, and the 'useful consequence of raising public awareness, so enlarging the mass spectator market'. This is important for understanding the role of the media in sport today: in the very early years (late 1900s to early twentieth century) the beginning of a number of key trends were already visible. The role of the media in connecting people to sport sports results and star players (the heroes and villains) cannot be overstated. The economics of this process afforded by the media ought to be clear: the more people made aware of, and who are interested in, sports competitions and rivalries, the more likely they are to want to see the game, race or match. As stated in the previous chapter, the more eager people are to consume something, the more likely they are to pay to see it and the more likely someone will charge them to do so.

The emergence of 'modern sports' and in particular the codification of sport and the founding of NSOs (firstly in England) is accompanied by the development of sports-related magazines. For example, *Sporting Life* was launched in Britain in 1859; incidentally, this magazine was immortalized through the saying: 'a rub down with a Sporting Life', which appears to be dying out in the English language. It used to pertain to a person who would rather spend time reading about sport rather than actually playing it. A US sports magazine existed as early as 1831, entitled *The Spirit of the Times* (Cashmore, 2010: 360). By the late 1900s the 'modern era of mass circulation popular newspapers began [1896] with the launch of the *Daily Mail*. The first sports pages began to emerge' (Horne et al., 2006: 162). In Britain, the initial sports reports simply reflected what went on in the public schools up and down England and the 'Oxbridge-educated male Victorian bourgeoisie' (ibid.).

It is no coincidence that the commercial 'turn' in sport in the 1970s and 1980s is reported around the same time as the (mass) introduction of modern television, with live colour pictures. From the 1980s there were significant changes in how sport is provided and consumed. First, satellite and cable television began the process of fragmenting television audiences according to specific interests, which served to increase specialized advertising; this was exacerbated by the introduction of pay-per-view television; further change in the consumption of sport is being driven by digital technology through which consumers can choose specific camera angles and 'produce the "feel" of "having been there"' (Rowe, 2007: 205). There is a certain irony here that while the armchair experience becomes more 'real', levels of people who are overweight and obese continue to rise unabated in many parts of the world, not just the wealthy advanced capitalist states.

The key point above, however, is the deliberate fragmentation into specific consumer 'markets' that advances in media have enabled.

Advertisers can target more precise audiences with a greater likelihood of shifting stock; thus, while it may be consumer friendly to be able to just pay and watch golf, such specialization benefits commerce greatly.

Media have allowed the growth of sport and in particular mass sports events. The scale of media coverage and scope in reaching consumers globally is staggering. For example, the official FIFA viewing figures for their centrepiece, the World Cup (here 2010 in South Africa), offer an insight into the media's incredible global reach:

Top-line coverage and audience summary (comparison against the 2006 World Cup in Germany)

- Total broadcast hours: 71,867
- Total territories reached: 214
- Total in-home audience reach (20+ consecutive minutes): 2.2 billion (+3 per cent)
- Total in-home audience reach (1+ minute): 3.2 billion (+8 per cent)
- Average global in-home audience per live match: 188.4 million (+6 per cent)
- Highest global in-home average audience (2010 FIFA World Cup South Africa final): 530.9 million (+5 per cent)

2010 FIFA World Cup South Africa final match

- In-home audience reach (20+ consecutive minutes): 619.7 million (+5 per cent)

2010 FIFA World Cup South Africa final match

- In-home audience reach (1+ minute): 909.6 million (+4 per cent)

(FIFA, 2015).

FIFA's claim cited in the last chapter that almost half the globe watched at least one minute of the 2010 World Cup gives some indication of the potential power of the mutually beneficial sport–media partnership and the obvious attraction to sponsors wishing to advertise and ultimately sell their wares to those consuming the sport.

Media: the national 'narrative' and 'stereotypes'

The media play a crucial role in how nations construct their identity, in particular how they contribute to retrospective 'image' building by interweaving the nation's collective memory with significant national markers. A national 'narrative' is a way in which citizens can connect with their own national cultures and heritage and was touched on briefly in Chapter 3; 'narratives' are not owned by anyone in particular and they are ever-changing, just as an individual's identity is likely to shift and recalibrate over time. Sporting feats and sporting events are central 'anchors' to the process of relating a national 'narrative'. While the Magna Carta may be a more significant precursor to British democracy, England's victory in the 1966 soccer World Cup is a cornerstone of English identity. According to the English soccer fans' controversial ditty, when playing long-term rivals Germany, England has won 'Two World Wars and One World Cup'. This may sound trivial, but (victorious) wars and (victorious) sporting events work together to form part of a nation's national narrative. Such narratives are far less concerned with correct historical facts; leaving out humiliating defeats or unpleasant episodes in a nation's history is all part of the glossing over and construction of a glorious and proud national past. There are not many fans' ditties highlighting Britain's expansion of its empire, for example.

Through the telling and retelling of a nation's past, sporting events can take on an iconic status. Sport does appear to be one of the very few things that can (momentarily) unite a nation and the media play a major part in this by transmitting the sporting experience to viewers. The manner in which the media represent sport can clearly inform 'our sense of our own identities and our characteristic *stereotypical images* of other nations...' (Horne et al., 2006: 177, author's emphasis). The reference to 'stereotypes' is pertinent to this chapter, for the media play on stereotypes as a 'cognitive' shorthand to both get a message across quickly, but also to 'sell copy' (see Box 5.2).

The media tend to highlight, exaggerate and repeat stereotypical traits of nations in reporting. In a study of British media attitudes towards the Germans in 2006 (interestingly, before the FIFA World Cup), the author found no fewer than 10.3 per cent of a total of 1,315 newspaper articles discussing Germany made reference to the sporting rivalry between Germany and England (the largest category, 36 per cent, unsurprisingly perhaps, was 'war prone', that is, the use of

---

> ## Box 5.2   What is a 'stereotype'?
>
> Often understood as offensive, pejorative and misleading, stereotypes in fact tend to act as necessary cognitive shorthand to enable individuals to understand the complexities of their environment and categorize individuals into specific social groups (see Fowler, 2001: 17). Without these socially constructed cognitive short cuts, parcelling the world into understandable but necessarily oversimplified segments (for example, 'women', 'the Americans', 'the media', 'academics' and so on), the world would remain a complex mass of unordered information. The danger arises when one relies solely on stereotypical views of the world or on 'automatic' stereotyping, resulting in an opinion based on little or no empirical experience against which to check and recalibrate these stereotypes. Against such a backdrop contemporary films based on older works, such as Charlie and the Chocolate Factory, are still able to portray a German boy as plump and clad in traditional, southern German lederhosen. The boy's father is a butcher who makes German sausage, thereby making the child instantly recognizable as German and representative of stereotypical Germans, above all to British and American audiences.
>
> The representation of women in sport through the media is – if aired at all – often stereotypical. Much of the limited coverage of women's sport is dedicated to 'titillation and human interest rather than on performance and achievement', with discussions often focusing on female athletes' 'families, husbands or children rather than focusing on their sporting achievements...' (Kay and Jeanes, 2009: 145).

war-related vocabulary; Grix and Lacroix, 2006). A good example of the sporting stereotype is that of the following:

> Britain's clocks went forward at the weekend but football still runs to German time. Wondering why they always seem to be drawing 1–1 in the 87th minute and leading 2–1 in the 89th is a bit like asking why the Queen has more than one birthday. She just does. (*The Daily Telegraph*, 27 March 2001)

Interestingly, sport also has the power to alter stereotypes – as discussed in Chapter 10 – through elite sport success and the hosting of SMEs.

The 'mediatization' of the Olympics began in earnest in 1976 at the Montreal Games, when the 'number of journalists, photographers and technicians (approximately 10,000) exceeded the number of athletes (6,028) taking part in the event' (Bairner and Molnar, 2010: 203). The figures pertaining to the media coverage of the London 2012 Olympics make astonishing reading. All 204 IOC-recognized National Olympic Committees (NOCs) were present, which meant all would have their own contingent of media in tow. Some 10,568 athletes (5,892 male; 4,676 female) competed, dwarfed by 20,000 journalists (IOC London 2012 Factsheet). The headline media figures for the London 2012 Olympics are:

- London 2012 was the most watched television event in American history, according to the National Broadcasting Company (NBC), with more than 219 million viewers.
- There were 59.5 million YouTube views in 64 territories in Asia and Sub-Saharan Africa.
- Olympic broadcasters provided a record combined total of more than 100,000 hours of Games coverage.
- London 2012's social media sites, including Facebook, Twitter and Google+, attracted 4.7 million followers.
- The London Organising Committee of the Olympic and Paralympic Games reported that there were 150 million tweets about the Games, including 1.55 million 'support your team' tweets recorded for all 204 NOCs (all information from the IOC London 2012 Factsheet).

Such incredible figures as those cited above for London 2012 offer an indication of the scale and impact of the Olympic Games and are grist to the mill for the IOC when it comes to tempting future TOP-tier Olympic sponsors.

Of particular note here is the role of social media in the consumption of sport. Clearly the technological developments that have allowed the global reach of social media have impacted on many aspects of human communication, including watching, reading about and distributing sport. The popular social media platform Twitter has over 300 million monthly active users and Facebook has over 1 billion (Statistic Brain, 2015; Twitter, 2015), while sports-related blogs multiply daily. Twitter, in particular, is used heavily by coaches, athletes and media companies alike, allowing insights into sport and sports personalities, globally, instantaneously, and, of course, while people are mobile. Given the nature of Twitter – allowing only 140 characters to be 'tweeted' in a message – the depth of what can be communicated is severely limited; however, with 500 million tweets per day (Twitter, 2015) an awful lot of communicating is going on. According to Browning and Sanderson (2012), Twitter has had a profound impact on sports communication, including sports journalists, broadcasters and sports clubs, most of whom maintain a presence on the platform. For the latter, such a quick and global method of reaching fans can be extremely useful for communication, updates and news; for the fans, they feel they are much more closely aligned to both their favourite clubs and the stars of their teams.

Social media are clearly changing the face of sport consumption. No longer are punters tied to specific places, times and days on which they have to watch their favourite sport. Nowadays, sport can be consumed on the move from a range of mobile devices, live or on 'play-back'. Sport consumers do not need to attend matches or watch a television; it remains to be seen whether social media and the ability to individually tailor sport consumption will impact on stadium spectator numbers and the atmosphere that goes with it, and the 'social capital' (see Chapter 6) that comes with a shared sports experience (meeting up to watch a soccer game on television, for example).

One thing is for sure, sports stars can now engage and interact with supporters/followers/fans instantaneously and directly, without having to go via 'traditional' media, for example, through the increasing use of Twitter. There have already been several instances where athletes have 'tweeted' something considered offensive or defamatory and have subsequently been fined. Sports on-line, available to subscribers, is clearly on the increase and is set to offer sports organizations yet another lucrative income stream with which to fund their sport and pay the – often extortionate – wages of their athletes.

As with all new revolutionary methods of communication, there are some dangers. For example, irate fans have been known to send derogatory – and often racist or sexist – 'tweets' directly to sportspersons after a perceived poor performance; athletes themselves have been known to (over)react and respond inappropriately to a remark made about themselves or about their behaviour in the sporting arena, which often leads to fines and bans from governing bodies of sport. Another, perhaps less important, negative aspect of Twitter in terms of sport is the development of the would-be sports 'expert'. Usually the mark of an expert in anything is their ability to maintain a sustained, generally logical, reasoned and evidenced argument. Given the fact that one can barely say anything on Twitter (in 140 characters), expert advice is reduced to short, sharp, and at times catchy, soundbites. Often the wisdom – and work – on which such soundbites ought to rest is non-existent, rendering the 'expert' merely a sifter of other people's ideas. One academic, Neil Hall, has even developed a measure to gauge the discrepancy between the number of Twitter followers a scientist has against the number of citations for their scientific work. Hall describes his tool as the 'Kardashian index' (Hall, 2014).

The impact of media on sports development

Both the commercialization of sport – discussed in Chapter 4 – and the media have impacted on how sport is consumed and even on how it is played. Fitting sport around busy television schedules is not new, but it reveals why marathons may be staged at inappropriate times of the day (for the athletes) to satisfy consumer demand on the other side of the world or, more precisely, to 'fit television's programming needs' (Coakely, 2003: 418). The start times of sporting events have always been shifted about to please television audiences and sponsors alike – from the Muhammad Ali fight staged at 4 a.m. in the middle of the jungle, to rescheduling 'fixture calendars and tournaments...at very short notice' in football (Guilianotti, 2005a: 25). Kerry Packer's interventions in the traditional world of cricket are a key example of the power of money and media to change sport. Packer was instrumental in introducing: short cricket matches with limited overs (an 'over' is a set of six balls bowled from one end of the cricket pitch towards the wicket; traditional games can take up to 5 days); colourful clothing (instead of the standard 'whites'); and cricket under floodlights (see Cashmore, 2010: 374–5 for a full account). Such changes have also led to the introduction of thumping music and scantily clad cheerleaders, much to the annoyance of traditional cricket fans. What Packer did was to introduce a form of cricket – a sport with roots dating back to 1787 – made-for-television: short, sharp, nail-biting, rather than long, slow and often ending in a draw. As seen in the previous chapter, the Indian Cricket Premier League is one of the most lucrative in the world for the players and it was only launched in 2008.

NSOs have very little influence on how their sports disciplines are 'televised, reported or covered' (Maguire, 1999: 150); this is usually linked to the fact that a great deal of income is generated in this way, so that sport becomes dependent on their links with the media and sponsors. Maguire (1999: 151–2) adds that 'Sport has also become a commodity whose media value is determined by the size and composition of the audience it can deliver to potential advertisers and sponsors of media broadcasts'. The viewing consumer sees a spectacularization of a sporting event which is 'truncated...injected with pace' and which tends to omit the 'dull patches' (Hargreaves, 1994: 144). Or put another way:

Television does far more than simply relay the event. It selects, frames, juxtaposes, personalises, dramatises and narrates. In the process space and time are re-composed in order to enhance the entertainment value (Horne et al., 2004: 169).

Such a 'mediated' version of events may be political too; for example, coverage of the PAG in Rio in 2007 never strayed beyond the large wooden boarding that 'framed' the stadium, thereby blocking off the view of the neighbouring favela (Curi et al., 2011). If the media 'package' is what viewers consume, they also, together with sponsors, determine which sport gets air time, column inches and thus directly impacts on consumers' perception of the sporting world. This clearly has implications for sports development, for if certain sports are privileged over others, made more attractive to sponsors, then they would be in a better position to finance themselves and their grassroots. The most obvious example of this is the media coverage of men and women's sport; as stated above, the coverage of women's sport ranges from approximately 5 per cent of all coverage in the UK to approximately 9 per cent in Australia. A consequence of this is the paltry level of sponsorship of women's sport, which equates to just 0.5 per cent of the entire market (Women's Sport and Fitness Foundation, 2014; see Box 5.3 below), meaning that very little resource is going into developing women's sport from this avenue. Along with the negligible media coverage of women's sport 'an image of female sport is perpetuated as being trivial and unimportant' (Kew, 2003: 54),

---

Box 5.3   Sport and sponsorship

While women's sport languishes behind men's in terms of media coverage and sponsorship, sponsors for men's sport are difficult to miss. They are now to be seen on athletes' kit, the banners around the arenas in which athletes play, adverts in programmes, television and websites and even taking the name of the facilities that house the sports games and matches. Individuals, for example the footballer, David Beckham, earn extraordinary sums of money through personal endorsements of products (that is, putting an already well-known face to a product or service) and, increasingly, their own products (perfume, underwear and so on). The idea that just because a particular sportsperson recommends a product, the buying public ought to rush out and purchase it, sounds absurd. The fact that sponsors pour many resources into such products and sportspeople would suggest that it must lead to a profit.

this is perhaps not the best message to send out to 50 per cent of the world's population at a time when physical inactivity is on the rise along with levels of obesity.

It ought to be added that of the 5–10 per cent given over to women's sport in media coverage, much of it is focused on the sexualization of the subject through either their appearance or their sexual orientation (Carlisle Duncan and Messner, 2000: 182), or on non-sporting aspects relating to gender. Thus, pictures of female tennis players with long legs and short skirts and shots of beach volleyball matches played effectively in small bikinis are favoured among media outlets. Female athletes are often portrayed as passive and not active participants in sport; they are not discussed in terms of their sporting prowess, but rather for the fact that they are a 'mother' (for example, 'supermum' Jo Pavey won the European 10,000 metres; Athletics Weekly, 2014; see also Rowe, 2007: 147). Rarely are male sportsmen portrayed in this manner. Rowe (2007: 147–58) goes further in his analysis of the differences in media coverage of women's and men's sports by drawing on evidence suggesting that a significant portion of the former could be seen as (soft) pornographic.

Another impact the media have on the coverage of sport is through so-called 'sex-typing'; that is, the notion that some sports are more 'typically feminine'. For example, sports such as 'figure-skating, gymnastics, tennis, swimming, diving – [are] all sports thought to be consistent with conventional "femininity"' (Carlisle Duncan and Messner, 2000: 182) and contribute to this understanding of what women ought to be participating in. It is noticeable that all of the sports named require only the bare minimum of clothing and most are carried out in very tight-fitting outfits that would appeal to the 'male gaze'.

Noting that media coverage is skewed towards men's sport and certain men's sports disciplines is one thing, understanding why is another. Much of the answer lies in Chapter 4 and the political economy of sport; sponsors are attracted to the big audiences and big audiences can be generated by media coverage.

Women's sport today does not attract big audiences regularly and only has a fraction of the available sponsorship. Another part of the problem is that those in positions of power in the sports industry and sector are predominantly men. There are few high-profile female coaches, few high-profile female sports administrators and very few female senior sports correspondents. In such an overwhelmingly male-dominated sportscape it would seem that women's sport has an uphill struggle to obtain more media coverage.

Just as the main media coverage focuses on mainstream, male-dominated events, it also tends to ignore Paralympic events. In fact, the Paralympics had barely been covered by the media prior to the Sydney Olympics in 2000. Cashman and Darcy (2008) remark that

> Before 2000, few countries were able to watch the Paralympic opening ceremony in its entirety. The only country outside the USA to broadcast the entire 1996 [in Atlanta, author] opening ceremony was Germany.

In 2012 the US media giant NBC was criticized for providing only partial coverage of the Paralympics (4 × 60-minute highlights and a 90-minute round-up; and not covering the opening ceremony) despite the USA fielding the third largest team of 223 competitors; Channel 4 from the UK, however, covered some 150 hours of live events while Australia covered 100 hours (*The Telegraph*, 2012a).

While it is a little early to say what the effect of the UK's widespread coverage of the Paralympics had on attitudes towards people with disabilities in society, there is no doubt that partial and patchy coverage is unlikely to have much. A lesson can be learnt from women's sport: attitudes towards women's sport are changing, but very slowly; this is likely to be the case for Paralympians and disabled sportspersons too. The downfall of the Paralympic star, Oscar Pistorius, sentenced to five years in prison for shooting his girlfriend, could be seen as a blow to the Paralympic movement. The star's trial, played out in detail and at length in the world's media, put an end to the South African's growing popularity around the world. It is fair to say that Pistorius was a media favourite and one of the most courted Paralympic participants for his views on disability and sport. He is also one of the very few Paralympians to compete in the Olympics, making Olympic history by getting through to the 400 metres semi-finals at the London 2012 Olympics. Thus, Pistorius' downfall may in the future be seen as negative for the Paralympic movement, as his constant media presence kept the movement's cause firmly in the eye of the public.

Summary

The intention in this chapter was to introduce the reader to some of the most important topics around the role the media play in sport. The ideal–typical role of media in a democratic society was outlined, whereby the media act as part of a series of checks and balances on democratic rule. Contrary to the media's moral obligation as a 'fourth state' in democracy, most media outlets are profit-seeking institutions and are guided by the need to fulfil this principle. It should be clear that the story of the development of sport media is bound up with the commercialization of sport discussed in the previous chapter. It is fair to say that sport is a commodity that brings the media revenue; it is also clear that it is the media that ultimately links the consumers with the products of sport, thus sponsors are able to sell their wares via media exposure.

The developments in media technology have added to the already influential role that media played in the development of sport. Sport streamed via the internet and through numerous social media platforms is revolutionizing the way in which this cultural practice is consumed, covered, packaged and sold. The diverse tastes of the discerning sporting public are catered for by a multitude of different media outlets, channels and mediums, including red buttons, cable television, YouTube and Twitter. The multifaceted media consumption of sport provides extra income streams for broadcasters, advertisers, sports themselves and other manufacturers; it also impacts on the make-up and development of sport, leading to rule changes, shifting start times and locations to suit media coverage. The profit-oriented nature of media coverage has seen less 'profitable' areas of sport covered far less: women's sport and disabled sport, including the Paralympics.

Questions

- What should be the role of the media in a democratic society?
- How has the revolution in social media and the internet impacted on the consumption and coverage of sport?
- Does it matter that the media coverage of women's sport is so poor relative to that of men's sport? What are the likely long-term consequences?

Further Reading

- Cashmore, E. (2010) *Making Sense of Sports* (5th edn). London: Routledge.
- Rowe, D. (2007) *Sport, Culture and the Media* (2nd edn). Maidenhead: Oxford University Press.
- Williams, K. (2003) *Understanding Media Theory*. London: Hodder and Stoughton.

Chapter 6

A Politician's Dream: Sport and Social Capital

As discussed in Chapter 1, 'sport' is a contested term. Increasingly, governments around the world understand 'sport' as a resource to invest in and utilize in the pursuit of a host of non-sporting social aims and objectives. If 'sport' has become a hot topic of late, the concept of 'social capital' has had an equally impressive rise in prominence in the past 20 years. It too has become a contested term that brings with it a great deal of hope for the betterment of society. It seems, therefore, inevitable then that both concepts would be taken together to form a concept cluster that makes politicians salivate: 'sport and social capital'. Given the intuitive, self-explanatory and commonsensical understanding(s) associated with both concepts – that they are intrinsically 'good' for society – it is little wonder that literature on sport policy and development has sought to combine the two.

As outlined in Chapter 2 (and in Chapter 11), it is good practice to draw on established debates in core academic disciplines and apply them to the study of sport. Inevitably there is a time lag between their emergence in a main discipline and their use in a sub-discipline and this is evident in the literature on this topic. Raging debates around the usefulness of 'social capital' to understand developments in society hit fever pitch on the publication of Robert Putnam's book *Bowling Alone* (2000). Apart from a few early articles, sports scholars only really engaged with the concept from the mid-2000s on.

The intention in this chapter is to offer an understanding of what 'social capital' means and how it can apply to sport. Sport is seen by many as a resource that can make a real difference to citizens' lives, including as a site for the development of social capital. Whether volunteering for a local sports club or a major sports event, participating in team sports on a regular basis or sitting on a club committee, sports clubs and associations are seen as ideal vehicles for generating trust between members and inculcating citizens with characteristics that impact ultimately on their (positive) engagement

Box 6.1   Capital that is social

Generally speaking, the higher the stock of social capital in society, the more democratic that society is thought to be. In line with other types of capital, for example, physical and human capital, social capital can increase and decrease. Interestingly, though, social capital is said to increase with use, instead of decreasing as other forms of capital tend to, and it diminishes with disuse, the opposite in fact to monetary capital. Furthermore, unlike physical and human capital, social capital does not belong to individuals, but rather resides in groups and incorporates expectations of reciprocity. The question of whether one can accumulate or invest in social capital has, in particular, fuelled the interest of academics, journalists and policy-makers alike.

with wider society. In the UK alone, there are approximately 150,000 sports clubs, the vast majority of which are run by volunteers (Collins, 2008: 98; Box 6.1).

Such volunteers undertake work for free, which saves governments billions of pounds in the bargain (it is estimated that to pay for the work that approximately 2 million sport volunteers undertake in the UK would cost almost £3 billion; see Sport and Recreational Alliance, 2015).

The last two decades have seen an explosion of literature on or employing the concept of social capital in a wide range of academic disciplines, including politics, social policy, economics and sociology and, more recently, sports studies. This literature covers a wide range of topics, for example, crime rates, health, economic growth, political participation and sport volunteering. Common to all accounts is the consideration that higher levels of social capital in a given region impact positively on the object of study, ranging across the examples given above. Confusion, however, as to what social capital is, whether it can be measured, maintained, mobilized or created, remains (Box 6.2).

The elasticity of the concept has added greatly to the confusion of its meaning and to the wide variety of ways in which the term is employed. In what follows, an overview of the 'original' social capital debate is presented to students of sports studies. The focus is on three key areas relating to sport and social capital: first, the core concept of 'trust' which is central to all accounts of social capital, irrespective of academic discipline; second, the need to differentiate between the *types* of associations and clubs in which social capital is said to be

---

> ### Box 6.2   What is 'social capital'?
>
> Broadly speaking 'social capital' has come to refer to the by-product of
> trust between people, especially within secondary organizations and asso-
> ciations, in which compromise, debate and face-to-face relations incul-
> cate members with principles of democracy. Given the fact that there
> are so many sports associations across the world in which large numbers
> of volunteers work, it is clear why 'sport' is understood as a site where
> social capital could grow. The active involvement and interest in civic
> affairs by citizens is thought to generate a collective good that facilitates
> collaborative action for all. It is through networks of civic engagement
> that information flows and is accessed by others. It is the supposed link
> between the existence of social capital in a specific region and the positive
> effect this has on governmental and economic performance – and ulti-
> mately on democratic governance – that has caught the eye of researchers
> and policy-makers alike. Sports clubs, especially through the volunteer-
> ism associated with running them, would appear ideally suited as havens
> of social capital and its generation (see below).

generated, as clearly not all are alike; and third, this chapter finishes
with a brief discussion of social capital and participation in sport or
physical activity. The latter is often linked to the key 'legacies' that
SMEs are said to produce (see Chapters 7 and 10).

The 'original' social capital debate: James Coleman

In his 1988 article on social capital in the creation of human capital, the sociologist James Coleman goes some way in presenting social
capital as the relation between structures and individual agents within
certain social networks. Coleman maintains that 'Social capital is
defined by its function. It is not a single entity but a variety of entities,
with two elements in common: they all consist of some aspect of social
structures, and they facilitate certain actions of actors...' (Coleman,
1988: 16). Importantly, and an insight not picked up on by Putnam
and many of his followers, Coleman highlights the closed nature of
many social networks, a fact that aids knowledge about, and assists in
the maintenance of, social capital (Coleman, 1988: 23–6). 'Closure' of
social networks allows for the emergence of effective norms, because
members can impose sanctions on others in their network, requiring
them to act according to those agreed norms. In an open network,

where some members have no contact with others in the network, effective sanctioning is impossible. Implicitly, Coleman highlights the importance of access to social networks for the individual and his or her ability to tap into the benefits derived from belonging to a structure that produces social capital. Additionally, for Coleman, another aspect of social structure that represented social capital was information channels.

For example, if social scientists wish to keep up to date on research in fields related to their own, they 'can make use of everyday interactions with colleagues to do so, but only in a university in which most colleagues keep up-to-date' (Coleman, 1988: 22). Access to information is essential, as this forms the basis of a person's subsequent action (Box 6.3).

Two important factors emerge here: first, the added value of having access to a certain social network; and second, the type of context in which the network itself is embedded. A network of this type in a remote university not well known for research would obviously yield different results for the individual than an established institution at the heart of a thriving research community. It is not difficult to see how this could link to a sports club. For an athlete the benefits of

---

Box 6.3   Sport volunteers and social capital?

The place of sports clubs in the social capital debate stems from the fact that the vast majority are run by an army of volunteers. By definition these people are (for the most part) investing in their community out of goodwill and not for financial gain. Hylton and Bramwell correctly state that

> Sport and leisure organisations can sometimes include those excluded from the serious world of work, religion and politics. In other instances, people experiencing social isolation can tap into a vibrant network of friends by becoming involved in volunteering in sport (2008: 170).

Ironically, as governments have intervened more and more in sport, accompanied by growing investment, they have attempted to change the amateur volunteering culture of sports governing bodies and clubs to a more 'accountable' professional culture in which 'good governance' ensures a better return on their investment. The irony lies in the fact that such top-down governance can lead to volunteers being replaced by salaried posts in former volunteering positions. It could be argued that organizations are run more efficiently, but it may come at a cost to the social capital volunteering used to generate (see Chapter 8; also Nicholson et al., 2011: 167).

being around or near people at the cutting-edge of their field (coaches, physiotherapists, for example) are obvious. For a regular member of a sports club the various networks they can tap into – simply by virtue of the commonality of playing golf, tennis and so on – open up several possibilities that someone outside of the club may not have.

Robert Putnam

Putnam's study of Italy in his book *Making Democracy Work* put the concept of social capital firmly on the social scientific map. Putnam built on the influential work of Coleman, taking it a step further in a rather different direction, in particular in his major study of the roots of democracy in Italy. He concluded that civic norms and values were 'embodied in, and reinforced by, distinctive social structures and practices' (Putnam, 1993: 167). Again moving away from Coleman's analysis, Putnam correlates the 'civic-ness' of a given society, gauged by the density of associations and relations of reciprocity, with the performance of local government and its institutions (Box 6.4). A region that has inherited a strong tradition of civic engagement and a high level of citizen participation in civic associations is more likely to 'contribute to the effectiveness and stability of democratic government' (Putnam, 1993: 89).

Box 6.4   Robert Putnam's *Bowling Alone*

Putnam's later work (1995, 2000) saw him turn his attention and analysis towards America and it is these studies that are behind the growth of an effective cottage industry around the topic. If the study of Italy was a catalyst to wider debate and use of the concept of social capital in the social sciences, then Putnam's later work can be seen as spawning a wave of articles, books and debates that transcends the limited field of academia, reaching into public policy and public debates on the role of the state in society. *Bowling Alone* – a metaphor for a citizenry that no longer joins a club to participate and socialize, but rather goes it alone – expands on an article of the same name from 1995 that controversially posited the decline in civic participation among Americans. In his latest work Putnam focuses exclusively on American society and argues that there has been a collapse in honesty and trust among American citizens. The basic premise of Putnam's work is summed up simply: when we bowl together, in clubs, groups and leagues, we have at our disposal a resource that not only teaches us 'civic-ness', but also one that offers us multiple benefits over 'bowling alone'.

Putnam's claims, reinforced by scholars employing his methods and **ontological assumptions**, centre on exogenously generated attitudes and norms, above all, trust and horizontal networks of civic engagement, which in turn facilitate and perpetuate mutually beneficial cooperation between actors. For Putnam, the key source of social trust is to be found in norms of reciprocity and networks of civic engagement, measurable by citizens' membership and participation in associations, ranging from choral societies to rotary clubs. It is here, in clubs and associations, where citizens are inculcated with the rules of compromise and democratic principles. Members of associations tend to be politically and socially more active 'and more supportive of democratic norms' (Stolle and Rochon, 1999: 192). Given the number of sports associations and clubs worldwide, it is clear to see why interest in sport and social capital has grown in the past decade.

Face-to-face relations in such clubs and associations and taking part in meetings hone skills for, and develop interest in, community affairs. Hence the density of such associations in a given society would suggest the extent to which a society possesses a solid stock of trust and reciprocity: in short, social capital. It is this type of capital that 'refers to features of social organization, such as trust, norms, and networks, that can improve the efficiency of society by facilitating co-ordinated actions' (Putnam, 1993: 167). A society with a good stock of social capital would, according to Putnam's research, more probably be well governed and perform better economically. It is this connection between trust, reciprocity and 'civic-ness' on the one hand, and good government and economic performance on the other, that makes social capital research interesting for political scientists, economists, politicians and, especially, policy-makers. The methods used to get at the 'civic-ness' of a society included the use of mass surveys of specific groups, case studies involving in-depth analyses of local press, and analyses of legislation and elite interviews. From these findings a 'civic community' index was constructed, which consisted of turnout in referenda, newspaper readership, associational density in a region and preference voting.

Putnam cites a general decline in community involvement that manifests itself in fewer people willing to volunteer, fewer people voting and fewer social meetings taking place between friends. This decline has spread to a wide variety of associations that have ceased to exist due to a lack of interest (ranging from the Charity League of Dallas to certain chapters of the National Association for the Advancement of Colored People). His major finding is that the decline in civic involvement can be traced to differences between generations of Americans. In brief, people born after 1950 are less likely to engage in civic affairs, join associations and play an active role in social networks (Putnam, 2000: 248–76). Running through all of Putnam's work is the central importance of trust, associations (and citizens' membership therein), networks of reciprocity and the impact these factors have on democracy.

The following sections offer a discussion and critique of the 'Putnam School' approach as this is still the dominant approach in the literature, focusing on the aspects of social capital research that are central to the study of sport. They are, in order:

- A discussion of the concept of *trust*, central to all work on social capital.
- A look at the *types* of secondary associations and organizations that are said to inculcate members with principles of democracy.
- The relationship between '*participation*' in sport and social capital.

All kinds of trust

One of Putnam's central claims is that engagement in associations leads to trust between members/citizens which then impacts positively on society as a whole. As sport is often held up as the arena in which most citizens participate and volunteer, the attraction of promoting sports clubs and associations as social capital generators is obvious. What is clear from Putnam's work, however, is that he fails to differentiate between *types* of trust. Trust is a multifaceted concept that is best divided into several sub-groups for clarity.

There are evidently a variety of types of trust that need to be distinguished in order to lend them any operationalizability (Box 6.5). For example, inter-personal trust is clearly different from trust in institutions or perhaps, more precisely, the actors who populate them (Offe, 1999: 45). Furthermore, the creation of 'generalized trust', that is beyond the individual and group members and extended to strangers, is again different but not necessarily divorced from the above two varieties; furthermore, horizontal trust too between citizens is different from trust between elites and citizens (Offe, 1999: 44).

Trust, as a useful concept, becomes vague and all-encompassing if these categories are not clarified. Putnam's claim that trust generated through face-to-face relations, as in sports clubs and

Box 6.5   Can sports clubs engender trust?

Just as sport is often held up as a panacea for all society's ills, sports clubs and associations could be looked upon as the ideal breeding grounds for active, engaged and democratic citizens. It is not difficult to see why policy-makers are interested in sport and its potential to bond like-minded participants and club members. The problem of 'types' of trust, however, still remains: is the trust that close sports club members develop among themselves automatically transferred to society as a whole (that is, to strangers and those who have nothing to do with their sport)? Much of the 'within-group' bonding that occurs is based on the mutual love of a particular sport, for example, cycling. Often, the intense interest in the minutiae of a sport – for example, the composition of bike frames, measurements of power output and bike wear – is of little interest to the non-cyclist. Additionally, many sports disciplines, for example, triathlon, are dominated by a particular socio-economic group: members are generally White, earn way above the national average and are mostly male (approximately 70 per cent in the UK, for example). Arguably, while very strong 'within-group' social capital is likely to develop, how will this impact on this group and their attitudes to others in society? The assumption of social capital theory is that the trust we gain through being involved in our respective sports networks and clubs, irrespective of discipline, will stand us in good stead in our engagement with wider society.

associations, somehow makes the huge leap to generalized trust beyond the group, club or association is debateable. Even scholars using Putnam's methods admit that: 'Generalized trust involves a leap of faith that the trustworthiness of those you know can be broadened to include others whom you do not know' (Stolle and Rochon, 1999: 182).

Types of associations

The Tocquevillian view of the effect that participation in associations has on individuals and their public spiritedness (Jordana, 1999: 58) is increasing in popularity in America. Debates rage in which proponents of this view urge a return to the virtues of civic engagement of a bygone era (Box 6.6).

Putnam, when correlating the density of intermediary associations with the level of social capital in a given region, fails to clarify three fundamental points.

> **Box 6.6　Are sport associations hubs of 'civic-ness'?**
>
> Given that participation rates in sport are, along with volunteering figures in sports associations, among the highest rates globally, one could argue that sports associations and clubs are hubs of 'civic-ness'. This is based on the social capital argument that engagement and participation in associations impact positively on citizens in terms of how they are likely to engage with the rest of society. This assumes that all sports associations/clubs are similar, when in fact there are a wide variety of types. An all-male golf club may not engender the type of democratic ideals among members that Putnam claims; membership could, in fact, reinforce stereotypical attitudes towards the role of women in society. Equally, it is the quality of people's social networks that comes out of their engagement with clubs and associations, not the clubs and associations themselves. Again, it is not simply the number of 'networks' that a person belongs to, or the 'resources available to and accessed by' (Nicholson and Hoye, 2008) a person, but the quality of relations within these networks that matters.

First, he makes no distinction between *the types* of clubs or associations and their effect on an individual's sense of civic-ness, simply stating that 'participation in civic organisations inculcates skills of cooperation as well as a sense of shared responsibility for collective endeavours' (Putnam, 1993: 90). There are several issues one could raise here in regard to sports clubs and associations. First, there is no 'standard' sports club. Different sports with different histories and traditions have very different modus operandi. Take, for example, an exclusive, men-only golf club and your local jogging club. Both may have 400 members, but they will be governed very differently. The voluntary roles of one will differ greatly from the other. For a start, by definition, an all-men's club will mean members will have little or no face-to-face contact with women. Further, such an environment could actually – tacitly or not – engender a male-dominant discourse and attitude. Arguably a committee made up of both men and women would expose members to a much broader variety of viewpoints, thus contributing to their democratic experience. Equally, sports clubs run by volunteers and amateurs can often lead to the opposite of 'shared responsibility for collective endeavours' as various factions within the club struggle for supremacy. If one takes the definition of 'politics' with a small 'p', outlined in Chapter 1, then sports associations and clubs are highly politically charged environments. Finally, different sports will require different levels of 'teamwork' or 'cooperation' than others, key components considered (simplistically) by governments to be essential for the generation of social capital (see also Nicholson et al., 2011: 3). Civic organizations cover a wide variety of interests, topics and purposes, not all of them with the same degree of importance for the wider community. For example, what kind of civic virtues are to be learnt in a bird watching society? Are these the same as those accrued in a large sports club? How is trust among members of a choral society extended beyond a group with such a narrow focus and how does membership contribute to the stability of democratic government?

Second, Putnam does not elaborate on the fact that, as with all associational activism, the majority of people stem from the middle classes (Stolle and Rochon, 1999: 198; Foley and Edwards, 1999: 153). Sports studies scholars are well aware that the middle class (and the upper class) are far more likely to encourage their children to participate in sport, are far more likely to have the resources to transport them to and from myriad sporting activities and are more likely to be aware of the health benefits of regular sport participation (see Collins, 2008: 81). This bias is coupled with the relevance of education in an individual's propensity to join an association: the more educated people are, the more likely they are to participate in society. As Ken Newton suggests, the spheres of work, school, family and community 'also teach the values of reciprocity, trust, compromise, and cooperation' (Newton, 1999: 16), while accounting for a far wider proportion of citizens than just the middle-class well-educated target group used in traditional social capital research. Equally, and very importantly, the spheres introduced above cover a very wide range of age cohorts and not just the adult population (ibid.). This leads us to one of the problems of causality unresolved in the social capital literature. If people who are more likely to join (sports) associations are the better educated and well to do, they probably become members because they tend to trust others more (as research on trust informs us; see Inglehart, 1999: 89–90; Whiteley, 1999: 30). Thus, Putnam's claim that membership in associations imbues us with the ability to compromise and so on, leading to us becoming more trustful of other people, is a matter of degree. Trustful citizens become even more trustful by mixing with those with similar interests and from similar socio-economic groups. What impact does this have on wider society or on those less privileged groups who are not joining associations? It is obvious that education is a key variable in assessing a citizen's access to a society's stock of social capital (Newton, 1999: 18); it is also a key variable in analyses of access to sporting opportunities. Equally, employment is a fundamental factor to consider when discussing social capital access, for an unemployed person suffers from the classic case of social exclusion, as participation in 'normal' society is usually contingent on citizens having the resources and/or social status to do so. Finally, the extent to which inequality exists in a given society will impact both on the propensity to undertake sport, volunteer and be able to get involved in civic affairs.

Third, Putnam and his followers do not analyse the *quality of relationship* between intermediary groups within society and between associations and government. It is perhaps less the sheer density of (all forms of) civic associations in a given region that characterizes the presence of social capital, but rather the type of association, the cross-section of membership, that is drawing on members from all classes and hence representing society, and the quality of relations between the associations themselves and between them and local government (Stoker et al., 1999).

In addition to the types of association and their members, the fact remains that social capital as a resource is not only positive for society. Putnam pays little attention to negative social capital, for many of the bonds of trust, obligations and commitment that make up a civic community are to be found, in pronounced form, in groups such as the Mafia, which functions on clientelism, prostitution rings, right-wing groups and youth gangs (Poggi, 1983; Portes and Landolt, 1996; Rose et al., 1996: 96–7). However, these groups are by their very nature exclusive and not inclusive. Membership rests on the fact that they are not like others, but the internal rules and procedures are based on an understanding of trust and loyalty. Coffé and Geys (2007: 124) touch on this when they suggest that such

> Strong inward-looking social relations may…generate an us-versus-them way of thinking in which a group develops strong social connections and levels of generalized trust among its members but generally tends to distinguish itself from other groups or even avoid or distrust members from these other groups.

Ethnic groups – and to some extent certain milieu – within society work in a way that means that they offer potential members access to social capital, for example, jobs, financial help, social networks and assistance, that is not open or available to anyone outside of that specific group. Examples of this are respective 'China Towns' in Western countries and the Turkish quarter in Kreuzberg, Berlin, where Chinese and Turkish immigrants respectively gravitate in order to be among a common language and culture and to tap into the networks of social capital available to them. This is not to suggest that these forms of social capital are negative, but rather that they are restrictive, isolated and not accessible to 'outsiders', operating in a not too dissimilar way to our middle-class bird watching club, which would probably be reluctant to have recent immigrants accepted into their ranks.

It is possible that some sports clubs operate in this manner too. If a member of, for example, a rugby club can access the social capital within his/her particular group (that is, among players, players and coach, at the club and so on), what is to say that this extends beyond or is helpful outside the setting of that sport? Much 'bonding' social capital in sports clubs is created and maintained around specific rituals – drinking, certain antics, away matches and so on – that constitute behaviour that is not necessarily in line with what is thought of as beneficial for wider society; thus bonding social capital may lead to exclusion rather than inclusion (see Collins, 2010: 8; Nicholson et al., 2011: 166). Therefore, just as dedicated fans can become imbued with a sense of tribalism around a specific sports team, which can lead to abhorrent behaviour, so too can 'within-group' social capital educate members in practices that are hardly democratic. Interestingly, Brian Moore, an ex-England international rugby player, suggests that: 'Sport is very simple: you win or you lose. There's a comfort in that. But nothing is ever like that again. It's come as a bit of a shock to me: life is not black and white and if you try to live it like that you're going to be in trouble' (*Guardian*, 2013b). The point here that Moore makes is that much of what is learnt in a sports setting cannot necessarily be transferred directly to the life outside sport; social capital scholars, Putnam foremost, suggest that the lessons and skills learnt in *any* associational setting should prove useful beyond that setting. So, trust (see above on this), compromise, dialogue and debate and so on will serve you long after your sporting days are over. There is, of course, a distinction to be made between someone who participates in sport, serves on the club's committee, takes an active role with the association (for example, the finance officer) and someone who simply attends the club to train with others and then goes home. Clearly the former is a 'volunteer', the latter (only) a club member. Another aspect to consider in sport is that between 'competitive' and 'recreational' clubs and associations.

Tonts, concluding his study of social capital and sport in rural Australia in 2005, believes that

> sporting events and clubs can be conceptualised as nodes for local and regional social networks. Such networks form the basis for both the creation and expression of social capital. High levels of participation in sport, together with the considerable time and resources that residents were willing to provide as volunteers or supporters, helps to emphasise the sense of reciprocity and altruism often found in sporting clubs and associations (2005: 147).

Two things of note stand out in Tonts' study: first, he analysed 'competitive' sport; and second, clubs were in a rural area. Both of these factors are likely to impact on the degree to which 'bonding' social capital (or 'within-group') develops. In general, competitive sports are characterized by a 'circuit' of specific events (county, regional, national championships and so on) and the majority of people – parents, competitors – come to know each other relatively quickly. This is very different to the loose ties between two jogging clubs, whose membership rarely if ever compete and remain for the most part 'within-group'. The rural location also adds another dimension to the consideration of sports clubs as sites of social capital development: with far fewer competing distractions and longer distances to travel, it could be argued that the people who do join such clubs invest considerably more resources (time/effort) than those with a club at the end of the road. The point here is that there is not only a need to distinguish between the *type* of association or club under study when discussing social capital, but also *between* different *types* of sports association/club. The task for policy-makers is not how to produce *bonding* social capital, but how to create the conditions under which *bridging* social capital can develop (Woolcock, 2001). That is, social capital that transcends the environment and networks of one sports club to include what Granovetter (1973) termed 'weak ties', for example, people who are not direct family or team mates. Woolcock (2001) identifies a third type of social capital, that of 'linking social capital' which, unlike the other two varieties, has a vertical dimension to it, linking people with institutions and resources that are not available in their community (see also Groeneveld et al., 2012: 10). Conceivably, a sports example could

---

Box 6.7   Types of social capital in sports settings

Two types of social capital have been discussed so far: 'bonding' or what could be termed 'within-group' social capital. This would be the tight-knit rugby team; this type of social capital is also associated with this concept's 'dark side' and is to be found, for example, among groups such as the Mafia; it is exclusive and builds on interests and ties of the established group. 'Bridging' social capital, however, is seen as the connections between groups; this is clearly much harder to establish than 'bonding' social capital, which is natural in a sports club setting. Connections between like-minded organizations – say two different rugby clubs – are likely to be much easier than, say between a rugby club and a darts club. How the 'bonding' social capital of a sports club spills over into wider society is unclear. The notion of 'linking' social capital conceptualizes how people can tap into and draw on resources not found in their usual community. Conceivably, someone who plays sport as part of a team of mixed members with a variety of socio-economic backgrounds may tap into opportunities not usually afforded to them. This is what is behind the age-old maxim: 'it's not what you know, it's who you know'.

---

be a local coach who has links in NSOs of sport and perhaps the Ministry of Sport in the country she/he resides in (see Box 6.7 on types of social capital).

Adams, in his study linking social capital and governance, points out the need to take into account context and be wary of inferring from one level of analysis to another, when he states:

> It is clear that, for some, social capital and its formation through sport organisations is seen as the big idea (Evans, 2009); however, the manner and logic of its incorporation into sport and social policy calls into question whether there is a big idea at all. An important consequence of the apparent strategic policy thrust towards forming democratic social capital outcomes is the apparent acceptance of a hazy logic that insists on societal-level outcomes from individual activity. Indeed, much of what has been written concerning sport and social capital is both under-theorised and lacking in contextual resonance (Adams, 2014: 567).

Indeed, different sports disciplines and different types of sports associations sensitize us to the need to avoid making simple statements such as 'sports clubs = reservoir of social capital'.

Sport participation and social capital

Participation in sport has also been claimed to enhance community cohesion through the development of social capital and social networks that support regeneration and inclusion (see Groeneveld et al., 2012 for an overview). This potential for enhancing social cohesion by bonding social groups is arguably stronger in relation to participation in recreational team sports than in individual sports (Putnam, 2000). As suggested, there may also be a role for sport volunteering in developing civic participation and sports clubs may be able to contribute to social inclusion and development. Community cohesion is also thought to sustain social capital and Coalter (2007: 49) claims that it is this link that underpins a shift in policy from 'developing sport *in* communities to developing communities *through* sport'. However, he argues – rightly – that the use of the concept of social capital in community-oriented initiatives (such as those of Sport England) is vague.

If participation and engagement in associational culture is linked with producing better, more democratic citizens, it is clear why participation in sport and physical activity – with the added health benefits this entails – is thought to be something worth encouraging. As will become clear in subsequent chapters, one of the key motives for staging an SME is to stimulate mass participation in sport and physical activity. In fact, this was *the* key legacy aim of the British government around the London 2012 Olympics. Griffiths and Armour (2013) argue that social capital could be equated with 'legacy' in terms of what the British government set out to generate, in particular among young people; they rightly point out, however, that

> legacy cannot be easily understood as a form of bequest to young people; instead, it has to be understood as an evolving engagement process over which they have some control. From this standpoint, legacy should be a process that enables children and young people to develop a *critical* stance towards sport and the Olympic games (Griffiths and Armour, 2012: 219).

Of interest in relation to a 'participation legacy' from this SME is the fact that the expected 'spike' in interest among youngsters in participating in sport following such spectacles was not met with the requisite resources. Official government figures after the London

2012 Olympics offer an empirical insight into that much quoted phrase 'lies, damn lies and statistics' (attributed to either Disraeli, the former British Prime Minister, or Mark Twain). The UK government celebrated the fact that they are on track with '1.4 million more people playing sport regularly since we won the [Olympic] bid in 2005', while the opposition focused on the overall drop in adults undertaking sport between June 2012 and June 2013 from 10.4 to 10.3 million (*Guardian*, 2013c). There are several issues with both these statements. The data on which they rest – the Sport England Active People Survey (APS) – is not independent, but produced by a government agency; the variables measured within the survey also need to be problematized. An indicative example is that of 'athletics'. The initial results of the survey are very encouraging indeed. In the period 2008–2009, for example, 'athletics' notched up an extremely impressive growth of some 128,000 participants. Club memberships for the same period were less impressive, with the gains in people undertaking 'athletics' not translating into statistically significant numbers joining an athletics club. The link between those taking up 'athletics' as categorized by the APS and those joining athletics clubs is made difficult by virtue of the fact that they are effectively measuring different things: the definition of 'athletics' in published statistics is very broad, including 'jogging' and 'road running', activities for which club membership is not essential. The increase recorded is most likely to come from those people citing 'jogging' and 'road running' as their 'athletics' activity, which in itself is a good thing; however, one needs to be careful not to assume that the 0.27 per cent increase recorded by the APS over the previous survey period (2007–2008) for athletics constitutes a boom for the number one Olympic sport discipline. Despite a drop in figures in athletics participation following the Olympics of around 34,000, this category remains 600,000 higher than the 'base-line' started in 2005/2006 (Sport England, 2015). However, if the majority of these people are not joining clubs, they will effectively be 'bowling alone', that is, pursuing individualized activities that may be good for their health, but are not necessarily linked to social capital generation.

A further point to be made concerning statistics is the 'measuring' of social capital. The problem arises when organizations, governments and academics cannot agree on whether social capital is an 'independent variable' (that is, something that causes or impacts on something else) or a 'dependent variable' (that is, that which is affected by something else; see Grix, 2010b). To put it simply, does the presence of social capital, for example, lead to closer harmonious relationships between members of a group? Or is social capital the outcome of the group in which linkages and networks thrive, in which sporting interests and values are shared, coming together in the first place? This has an impact on how social capital is studied and reported.

Summary

This chapter has set out to introduce the social capital debate in relation to sport and to ask the 'whys and wherefores' behind relationships that appear commonsensical in much literature. Part of the task of this volume is to draw attention to and question the 'givens' that exist in sport policy ('elite sport success inspires mass participation in sport' which in turn 'leads to social capital generation') and so forth. There seems no doubt that sport has a transformative potential; tales of individuals whose lives have been turned around, changed and deeply affected by sport abound. The role that sport has played in breaking down barriers between states on the international stage could be understood as a macro level of social capital; a trust-building exercise between wary partners. It seems commonsensical then to expect an association known for its amateur volunteering to be a focus for generating the social 'glue' that binds society. However, this chapter has attempted to look behind this understanding by going back to the roots of the social capital debate, critiquing the key aspects of it and concluding that there is a need for much more differentiated research on types of sports clubs, sport and their members before scholars can confidently say that engagement in and through sport produces the social capital desired for a fair and democratic society.

Questions

- Why is there so much interest in 'sport' and 'social capital'?
- Why do we need to consider the 'types' of associations and clubs that citizens are members of?
- Ask some of your friends or colleagues who are members of sports clubs/associations whether they belong to any other type of clubs/associations. Compare this with those who are not members of a sports-related club or association.

Further Reading

- Adams, A. (2014) 'Social capital, network governance and the strategic delivery of grassroots sport in England', *International Review for the Sociology of Sport*, 49(5), 550–74.
- Houlihan, B. and Groeneveld, M. (2012) 'Social capital, governance and sport', in M. Groeneveld, B. Houlihan and F. Ohl (eds) *Social Capital and Sport Governance in Europe* (London: Routledge).
- Nicholson, M. and Hoye, R. (eds) (2008) *Sport and Social Capital*. Oxford: Butterworth-Heinemann.
- Putnam, R. (2000) *Bowling Alone: The Collapse and Revival of American Community*. New York: Simon and Schuster.

Chapter 7

The Politics of Performance Sport: Why do States Invest in Elite Sport?

Why should government invest in high performance sport? ... as a driver of the 'feelgood factor' and the image of the UK abroad; as a driver for grassroots participation, whereby sporting heroes inspire participation.

(DCMS/Strategy Unit, 2002: 117)

The quote above encapsulates at least four possible answers to the question posed in this chapter. Much of the thinking behind this volume has been driven by a desire to understand the relatively simple question: 'Why do governments invest in sport?' The current chapter alters this slightly and focuses on 'elite' or 'performance' sport (these terms are used interchangeably, although some prefer 'performance' as it has a less exclusionary ring to it than 'elite'). Policy changes occur often across all policy sectors and while commentators have managed to skilfully outline the contours of an ever-changing sport policy (Houlihan, 1997; Green, 2004, 2006), the simple question as to why governments invest in elite sport in the first place remains inadequately answered. The reason why this is the case lies in the positive discursive nature in which elite sport policy is framed, allowing few possibilities for thinking 'otherwise' (Green, 2004: 367). That is, the question is rarely put, as 'sport' in and of itself is understood as an intrinsically 'good' thing; yet, investments of $55 billion for a Winter Olympics (Sochi, Russia), Australian $100 million in elite sport for the year 2013/2014 (Australian Institute for Sport, 2013) or around £350 million for a three-year period (for example, the 2012–2016 Olympic funding cycle) in the UK (UK Sport, 2014) in any other policy sector would command a great deal of explanation and justification. The late Mick Green pointed to the literature around 'policy as discourse' and the discursive construction of sport policy, whereby certain discourses set the parameters of what is and what is not conceived as possible. He remarks, building on the early literature around the theme of the discursive construction of sport policy related to sports development:

> Taken together, such insights [from the early literature] are useful in that they help sensitise us to the ways in which sport policy has been/is discursively constructed; the argument being that such constructions underlie the privileging of certain interests while marginalising others. (Green, 2004: 376)

The aim is not to suggest that people are simply manipulated by government(s) to believe elite sport is good, 'more that discourse may set the limits to what it is possible to think, and thus the understandings of the choices that can be made' (Newman, 2005: 128). Discursive practices manifest themselves in specific agendas prioritized by government at specific times. Sport policy has witnessed several swift changes and shifts in priority, none more so than the current focus on the elite sport agenda and 'sport for sport's sake' (Collins, 2010) in many advanced capitalist states and increasingly '**emerging**' **states** (see Glossary) too. This agenda has manifested itself in a commitment by governments of all political ideologies and from an array of different regime types to fund elite athletes and to host major sports events (see Grix, 2014b for more on SMEs).

The attempt to answer the question of why governments invest in elite sport unfolds through a discussion of the 'virtuous cycle' of sport. This is an attempt at conceptualizing the discourse behind state intervention in elite sport; importantly, this is *not* what the author *actually* believes takes place, but rather it outlines the causal relationships governments tend to believe in and/or wish others to believe.

Government rationale for investment in elite sport

The majority of (Western) advanced elite sport development systems appear to be based on the premise of a 'virtuous cycle' of sport. This cycle, as an elite policy discourse, has a convincing logic of circularity to it that appears commonsensical. It is such that competing in the global 'sporting arms race' (Collins and Green, 2007: 9) appears to be an unquestionable 'given'. The virtuous cycle of sport touches and builds on phenomena similar to the 'double pyramid theory' as described by Van Bottenburg and by authors in the so-called grey literature (conference papers, in-house papers and so on). The 'double pyramid theory' simply states that 'thousands of people practising sport at the base lead to a few Olympic champions and, at the same time the existence of champion role models encourages thousands of people to take up some form of sport' (Van Bottenburg, 2002: 2; see also Hanstad and Skille, 2010). The notion of a virtuous cycle of sport develops this further, first by presenting the relationship between elite and mass sports as self-reinforcing and circular (see Figure 7.1). The model is embellished with reasons and motives behind investment in elite sport and SMEs by governments (for example, in order to gain international prestige). Moreover, the philosophy underpinning this cycle is believed by the author to be the chief justificatory discourse behind investment in elite sport by states.

In short, the virtuous cycle of sport holds that elite success on the international stage and/or the successful staging of an SME leads to prestige on the international stage; both also contribute to a collective sense of (national) identity; this, then, boosts greater mass sports participation, leading to a healthier populace; this, in turn, provides a bigger 'pool' of talent from which to choose the elite stars of the future and which ensures elite success. The process then starts over again. If one understands elite policy discourse as a virtuous cycle of sport, it helps explain governments' overemphasis on the ability of elite sport success to effect so much change (domestically and internationally).

Figure 7.1   *The 'virtuous cycle' of sport*

1
National elite sport
success/hosting
sports megas

2
International
prestige/collective
sense of national
identity/increased
participation

3
Increased soft
power/health/
wider 'pool' for
talent identification

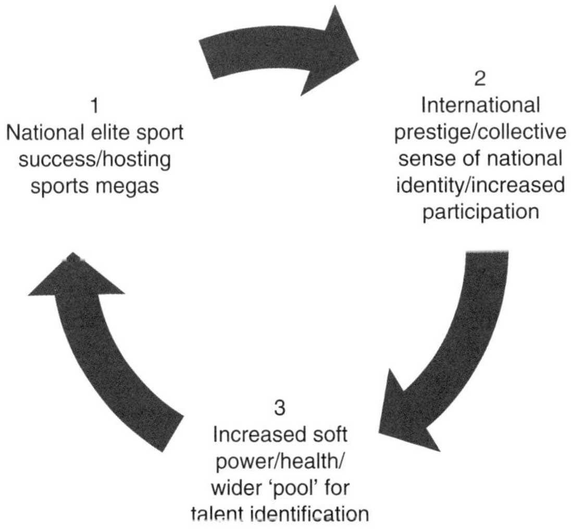

At this juncture it should be made clear that this is simply a conceptualization of how governments act and justify their actions in regard to elite sport investment; the point is not to uphold the implied causality that accompanies this model (see below). In fact, the assumptions that underlie this notion of a virtuous cycle of sport should be problematized.

The starting point for this model is stage one. This is divided into both 'national elite sport success' and 'hosting SMEs'. Some states, for example, the USA, have sought to build a successful elite sport system to produce world-beating athletes *and* to host the largest SME there is, the Olympic Games (1932, 1984, 1996). As discussed in Chapter 10, for many of the future sports mega hosts, the performance of their home teams (be they football, Olympians and so on) is less important than the staging of the event and what is perceived it can do for the hosting nation. Part of the reason for this is that 'emerging' states are increasingly hosting SMEs and they do not possess mature elite sport systems that have received long-term investment. In this chapter the rationale behind both investment in elite sport success and investment in SMEs by states is discussed, as is the hoped-for return on this investment by drawing on historical precedents where appropriate.

Elite sport success

The external rationale for developing and supporting elite sport success – apart from the fact that it is seen today as part and parcel of a nation's national make-up, to be good at least at some sport disciplines – has been shown in the case of East Germany and others (see Chapter 3). Through elite sport success – not the staging of any international SMEs – East Germany was able to force its own *de jure* (in or concerning the law) recognition as an independent state. Instrumental in this process was first and foremost their astonishing global success in sport, but also the role of transnational sporting bodies (see Chapter 8 for more on this) which recognized the GDR as a member of their organizations.

Success in elite sport may equally serve to strengthen the domestic legitimacy of a regime, as the case of the Beijing Olympics in 2008 illustrated (Chapter 10), whereby China's ruling elite not only put on an extravagant globally viewed party, but was also able to top the Olympic medal table to boot. The majority of states which invest vast sums of resources into elite sport appear transfixed by their respective position on the hallowed Olympic medal tables. The Olympic medal table – although the medal table from second-order events is becoming increasingly important too – has become a quasi-barometer of a state's strength and vitality, as rankings are in general linked to the amount of funding invested in elite sport, the size of the competing country's population and its economic strength (Seiler, 2013: 203). That is, they are not linked to the health of a nation or the rate of sports participation among the masses (as seen by the Scandinavian examples given in Chapter 3).

Reasons (or 'assumptions') to invest

The following introduces the key reasons and benefits put forward for investing in elite sport by governments and in SMEs by previous, would-be and future hosts of an event. Interestingly, reasons proffered for staging an event often double as the hoped-for 'legacies' that such events are said to bring to the host nation. Broadly speaking there are five (overlapping) types or categories of legacies or benefits discussed in both academic literature and government and bidding documents, all of which underlie some aspect of economic gain (see Grix, 2012). These will, of course, differ or have different degrees of priority depending on whether the discussion is around elite sport success, on the type of SME under discussion and the type of state hosting or bidding for the event. The broad categories can be understood as assumptions about the legacies that SMEs are thought to deliver:

1. National elite sport success and SMEs can inspire the masses, including youngsters, to take up sport or some form of physical activity, thereby improving their health.
2. Such events are economically lucrative, bringing revenue from, among others, increased tourism.
3. SMEs engender a 'feel-good' factor (or as Crompton, 2001, terms it, the 'psychic income' generated) among citizens of the host nation, which has knock-on effects for their well-being.
4. Much needed urban regeneration is accelerated, improving society and putting cities on the map.
5. States benefit by showcasing themselves internationally; this leads to an increase in international prestige, or how a country and their people are viewed by foreign publics and other states (an increase in so called '**soft power**').

Reason number 5 will be dealt with in much more detail in Chapter 10 because, increasingly, up-coming hosts are focusing more on public diplomacy or the 'soft power' that they seek to derive from sporting events.

Reason 1 – the 'elite sport'–'mass participation' causality

Increasingly, policy discourse – in particular in advanced capitalist states – points to, and revolves around, the ability of elite sport success to drive mass participation, a causal relationship that is difficult to substantiate but one which has gained 'widespread acceptance' (Stewart et al., 2005: 55). For example, there is very little evidence – beyond the anecdotal – to back up assumption 1, which suggests a causal relationship between elite sport (success)/staging a mega-event and the take up of sport or physical activity by the masses. On the surface this sounds eminently sensible and plausible; stories abound about people being 'inspired' by fantastic sporting feats. However, there is no research to confirm that an elite sporting event has had a long-term impact on the sporting behaviour of ordinary people (that is, the 'regular' person). There is some evidence to show that those who already play or have played sport can be re-inspired to return to sport (Weed et al., 2009; Weed, 2014), but these are not the obese or un-sporty that politicians hope to get off the (viewing) couch. Despite the lack of academic data supporting the link between elite sport and mass sport participation, key figures in sport still maintain this is the case. For example, when asked by the chairman of the House of Commons Committee of Public Accounts to explain why GB invested so much public money in supporting elite athletes for the Beijing Olympics in 2008, Liz Nicholl (Director of Performance at UK Sport) summed up the widespread sentiment of the virtuous cycle of sport by stating:

> I would say that between five and nine million people watched Kelly Holmes win a gold medal and Steve Redgrave win a medal and why was there such a fantastic impact when we won the Ashes and the Rugby World Cup? It really does have a huge impact on people in this country in motivating them to participate in sport and compete in sport. That is why we do it. We like winners and that is what we are investing in and success comes at a price. (House of Commons Committee of Public Accounts, 2006; 16)

Some years ago, Goodhart and Chataway (1968: 91–2) wrote about the discrepancy between people wanting to watch sport and undertaking sport themselves:

> Is the British Government edging towards a new pattern of spending and a different set of priorities that make some political sense? A survey carried out...emphasised that for the vast majority of people sport today is an entertainment and not an activity. Over 50% of the sample liked watching football on television...but a mere 5% ever played football. Much the same proportions held true for tennis, cricket and athletics. And the evidence suggests that the number of adults taking part in organized sport is on the decline... More than a playing field or a tennis court down the road, most of the British public may now want a sporting victory on the television.

Given that this was written almost half a century ago, it is striking how it is not too far off describing the situation in Britain and many other advanced capitalist states today.

The essence of the belief in the 'elite sport'–'mass participation' relationship can be traced back, in part, to the spectacular successes of the former Soviet satellite countries, most notably, East Germany, that produced the most Olympic medals per capita of all (Box 7.1). From the outside, the general impression of East German sport was that of a well-oiled and harmonious system that thrived on the mutually supportive relationship between elite and mass sports, providing ample provision for both. East German propaganda fuelled this belief: it insisted that the comprehensive provision of sports facilities and opportunities for the masses was the secret ingredient behind their elite sport success. In reality the East German model was elite-driven and focused on a carefully selected number of sports disciplines with the greatest potential for success at international level, largely at the expense of mass sports provision. Thus, the idea that 'elite sport inspires mass participation' rests partly on a misreading of former communist states and their sport systems (Grix, 2008).

Reason 2 – an economic boon

The second reason relates to the perceived positive economic benefits arising from hosting an SME. In the majority of cases in history, this has proved not to be true, as traditionally SMEs, in particular, the Olympics, have cost hosts dearly. Barcelona 1992 (see Box 10.4 in

Box 7.1   Consequences of an Olympic-driven sport policy

It could be argued that the increasing focus on the Olympic cycle by governments interested in national glory – medallists from the Sochi Winter Olympics, 2014 were showered with cash 'bonuses' from governments across the world – has several undesired consequences. The first is specialization, that is, the narrowing down and focusing on sports disciplines where it is most efficient to 'medal'. This was one of the key tenets of the successful GDR elite sport strategy. Athletes in 1969 woke up to the new 'High Performance Sport Directive', which divided sports into two categories: those that will receive funding and those that will not. Basketball and ice hockey were excluded on the basis of a cost-benefit analysis, as they delivered fewer medals (Dennis and Grix, 2012: 45). Interestingly, UK Sport – the funding body for elite sport in the UK – slashed funding for basketball from £8.5 million to £0 in 2014, because the sport lacks 'medal potential'. The irony here is that basketball has a large and growing number of participants and clearly potential for further growth. Participation, remember, is one of the chief reasons the UK invests in elite sport.

The 'elite investment' = 'mass participation' argument falls a little flat when one considers the Winter Olympics. States spend vast resources on disciplines such as 'skeleton', yet how many inner city, non-sporty children will this inspire to get off the couch? (*Guardian*, 2014).

The consequence of targeting medal-intensive sport only is that other, often more popular, sport will suffer, as resources are skewed towards the former.

Chapter 10) is usually cited along with Los Angeles 1984, as examples of economically successful Games. The 1980s also marks a pivotal point in the commercialization of sport (see Chapter 4), so the 1984 Games need to be understood in the context of the time. The Montreal Olympics (1976) is usually cited as the counter example of economic success. The citizens of Quebec only finished paying off the debts accrued through hosting the Games 30 years after the event. The mayor of Montreal at the time, Jean Drapeau, is credited with suggesting that 'The Montreal Olympics can no more have a deficit, than a man can have a baby' in 1970 (CBC, 2006). To add insult to injury, the grand Olympic stadium is looked upon as an underutilized 'white elephant', a constant reminder of money that was not well spent.

There are usually two factors to consider when assessing whether a sports mega is economically successful or not: first, whether the event made a financial loss or a profit, which is an extremely difficult calculation to make, given the sums of money involved knowing precisely what to measure and the time period over which it is needed to come up with an assessment; second, the impact the event has on tourism, as tourists bring with them investment in to the host city and state, spending money on accommodation, food, entertainment and so on. Often, however, the overambitious expectations of floods of tourists visiting host cities and states are misguided and wrong. In London 2012, for example, there was a 'displacement' of regular tourists who chose not to come to London because of the perceived traffic chaos of the Games. That is, *fewer* tourists than expected visited London around the time of the 2012 Games (European Tour Operators, 2013). The European Tour Operators Association has undertaken research on the last four Olympics which shows that 'the Olympic Games have routinely brought the host countries' tourism industry a catastrophic mix of high expectation and low demand' (ibid.).

Overall then, it is fair to say that the economic benefits that accrue from SMEs are notoriously difficult to measure and differ depending on which event is analysed and who is undertaking the assessment. The FIFA World Cup in Germany – an event far cheaper to stage than the Olympics – appears to have had a positive net impact on Germany's economy through attracting more year-on-year tourism, but also by improving the image of Germany abroad. This latter development is linked with a state's 'soft power' and is dealt with in Chapter 10. The history of staging the Olympics and other SMEs, however, is littered with examples of overinflated budgets, underutilized sporting infrastructure and little sporting legacy.

National elite sport success is another matter. In general, it is very expensive to develop and support an elite sport system over a long period of time (because it needs at least 10 years to mature). This is why 'emerging' states tend to opt for hosting SMEs, rather than investing heavily into elite sport. Some anomalies exist; take Jamaica, for example, the home of 'sprinting' in athletics. There is no doubt that sprinting has put Jamaica on the map and is likely to have contributed to Jamaica's attraction as a tourist destination. However, Jamaica's system of elite sport development would not be held up as exemplary. Other states, however, see the success of their elite sports stars as contributing to their international reputation, which is something closely linked to inter-state trade and ultimately commerce.

Reason 3 – feeling good

The 'feel-good' factor, legacy 3 above, is also an under-researched area with a lot of potential (see Chalip, 2006 for some early work on this

Box 7.2   What is the 'feel-good' factor?

There are several different terms to describe the collective euphoric feeling generated around SMEs. These range from the most common 'feel-good' factor to 'festival effect' in the tourism literature or 'psychic income'. All relate to similar phenomena: the atmosphere of goodwill and heightened mood that accompanies the watching of performance sport and a variety of other events and festivals. It is particularly to be found around the FIFA World Cup and the Olympics, as football is the most popular sport in the world and the Olympics is the biggest festival of sport.

Little research exists on the 'feel-good' factor, although some commentators have begun to study the 'social leveraging' of SMEs (Chalip, 2006). Chalip introduces the terms of 'liminality' and 'communitas' from sociology which seek to explain the exalted collective mood among people, usually around some form of religious ritual. Émile Durkheim (1912/1995), seen as a founding father of sociology, was the first to discover the 'communion of minds' present among worshipers in his in-depth study of religion. Victor Turner (1979) took this work further by developing ideas around 'public liminality': the latter meaning a 'threshold' over which a person passes in terms of their attitudes towards their notion of self and their environment. 'Communitas' is the feeling of 'togetherness' that the 'feel-good' factor alludes to. Momentarily social, religious, racial and gender boundaries are transcended – imagine a group of football supporters celebrating their nation's last minute goal in a vital competition – glossed over until the celebratory mood subsides. *This* is the 'feel-good' factor, something that, hitherto, states have not been able to tap into to effect social change or the longer-lasting breaking down of stereotypes.

area). Despite little research on this phenomenon, there is no doubt that a 'feel-good' factor among certain sections of the population exists during sporting events such as the national football team playing in the World Cup or when national teams participate in the Olympics (Box 7.2).

UK government sports documents have not aided the search for clarity of meaning around this concept. For example, the report 'Game Plan' (2002) informs the reader that although the quantity of medals won at the Olympics is of great importance, one must not neglect the 'quality' of a victory, because:

> 'Quality' can be taken to be the extent to which victory produces the feelgood factor and national pride (as these are the main public benefits of high performance sport). If it is accepted that the more popular the sport, the greater the amount of feelgood which follows, then 'quality' medals are those obtained in the most popular sports. (DCMS/Strategy Unit, 2002: 120–2)

Although this does not explain what the 'feel-good' factor is, it does offer an insight into what the (at the time, Labour) government thought the concept implies. On this reading, the 'feel-good' factor seems to be a variable which can be created and which is able to change in amount over time, and although it is admitted that it is 'difficult to quantify' (DCMS/Strategy Unit, 2002: 14), there seems little room for doubting that it can have a powerful causal effect.

Although no agreed or standard definition of a 'feel-good' factor exists, John Steele (2009), the former Chief Executive Officer of UK Sport, came close to an 'official' definition when he spoke of 'the euphoria of a full Lords Cricket Ground a couple of weeks ago when a single Ashes test was won'. Although the 'feel-good' factor is difficult to pin down, the elite-driven discourse permeating much of elite sport policy gives the impression that its existence is not in doubt. Just because there is no academic evidence of a 'feel-good' factor or no agreed way of capturing or measuring it, does not mean that it does not exist. Collective experiences of sporting achievement have long been thought to 'bind' a nation, albeit temporarily, to the extent that successive UK governments have insisted on a list of 'Crown Jewels' of specific, and nationally important, sporting events that ought to be available on free-to-air television and are protected under the 1996 Broadcasting Act. These include the Summer Olympics, the FIFA World Cup and the European Football Championships, the Grand National, Wimbledon and the FA Cup Final (DCMS, 2009, Independent Advisory Panel: point 170). This panel also recommended that the home and away FIFA qualification matches, cricket's home Ashes test matches and the Open Golf Championship ought to be added to the protected list because of their perceived 'national resonance' (ibid., points 170, 128).

Reason 4 – urban change

Urban regeneration is clearly the most visible of all legacies. London 2012 was a good example of how a landscape can be radically changed through a SME. A former toxic wasteland has been transformed into a well-kept park with several sporting facilities accessible to the public. The Olympic Park in Stratford is unrecognizable from what it was prior to the start of the clean-up and building work. However, such regeneration legacies are no less controversial than all of the others discussed here, for often – as seen in London 2012 – the mass-scale regeneration projects may not be entirely in the best interests of local communities and residents (Grix, 2012). London's East End, one of the poorest areas of the city, has certainly been transformed by this predominantly publicly funded project, but tangible Olympic legacies will be decidedly private: it is open to debate whether, in the long term, the huge (Australian) Westfield Group-owned shopping centre or the Qatari Diar-owned Olympic Village will benefit the locals more than other measures to tackle growing inequality.

Evidence of past SMEs reveals that decisions around previously stalled or rejected urban regeneration have been positively fast-tracked due to the hosting of the event; laws and rules are stretched in an attempt to prepare for the Games or event ahead. Whether the resulting change in infrastructure, housing, roads and so on are better for society than, say, the equivalent investment in non-sports-specific development is difficult to judge. The long drawn-out debate around which *private* football team should receive the *publicly* funded £550 million Olympic Stadium in the UK highlighted the increasingly political nature of SMEs. Of interest is the trend of *failed* bids actually being very beneficial for the would-have-been hosts. New York is a case in point: as a 'loser' of the 2012 Olympics it has now gone ahead with its planned regeneration vision, but *without* the astronomical costs and risks that hosting entails. Hall (2006: 64) correctly suggested that attracting SMEs is a 'key performance indicator in its own right'; this could be extended further to suggest that getting on the shortlist and failing to win may be desirable for states in the future (on New York see PWC, 2012).

More serious issues linked to urban regeneration are the so-called 'social cleansing' strategies of some governments; this refers to the clearing of slums or even people (tramps or those working as prostitutes and so on) to 'clean-up' the area close to and around the sports stadium. The problem is that these 'clean-ups' usually result in the enforced relocation of social problems to a different area of a city; some would argue that the money invested in the one-off sporting bonanza ought to be put to better use by alleviating the social problems that led to the need to 'clean-up' in the first place.

Reason 5 – soft power

Finally, the idea of using SMEs to improve or even alter a state's image is becoming increasingly persuasive (this is discussed in detail in Chapter 10). It is already clear that many states have and do instrumentalize sport to promote their country's image or 'brand' (van Ham,

2001: 2) and attempt to gain prestige, something that is very attractive to states and which works alongside traditional 'material' forces of power such as military might and coercion. Increasingly, the concept of 'soft power' is being used as a macro-level (or 'broad-brush') understanding of the rationale behind a state's decision to use SMEs as part of a package of 'politics of persuasion' or 'politics of attraction' (Manzenreiter, 2010; Horne and Whannel, 2012; Grix and Houlihan, 2013; Grix and Lee, 2013).

Elite athletes are often looked upon as 'diplomats in tracksuits' in the sense that they 'represent' their nation when competing abroad. The discussion in Chapter 3 showed how absurd such a notion is, given that national squads are not necessarily 'representative' of the majority. A new phenomenon since the Cold War, however, has been the development of global sports stars. To return to the Jamaican example of sprinting, it could be suggested that Usain Bolt has single-handedly acted as a positive advertisement for his country. The extent to which such global admiration impacts on inter-state relations, however, is questionable.

Converging elite sport systems?

The section above briefly discussed the return states hope for from investing in elite sport and SMEs and the assumptions that lie behind such investment. The argument of this book is that the 'virtuous cycle' of sport put forward above has led to what Houlihan and Green (2008) term a 'convergence' of elite sport development systems. The belief in the effects of elite sport discussed above, coupled with the outstanding elite sport successes of the Soviet satellite states, the Soviet Union and, above all, East Germany during the Cold War, have led to a convergence of elite sport development systems today. The *structural* roots of modern-day elite sport systems can be traced back to the GDR, as can many of the *ideational* roots too.

Converging ideas

While there are clearly several differences between nations' elite sport development models, the politics of performance sport rests on similar aims and ambitions. Be it hosting a SME or developing elite athletes to achieve international success, there appear to be some common ingredients behind the decisions and systems in place. The vast majority of emerging states hosting SMEs are less interested in – and able to produce – elite sport success; they are bound by a desire to showcase their nations. The most successful nations in elite sport are generally those with a large population and higher GDP. These nations have invested in similar factors: full-time athletes, professional coaching and sport science and so on. On a structural level there is some evidence for a 'converging' of elite sport development systems; the future is likely to see some variation to the dominant elite sport model. As very large emerging countries such as Brazil (almost 200 million inhabitants) develop their own versions of an elite sport system, the variety of models is likely to expand. For example, there is no long tradition of voluntary sports clubs in Brazil; very large private multi-sport clubs, accessible only to those who can afford it, offer state-of-the-art facilities to a section of society. There is also no history of structured, curriculum-based school sport, making the key elements of Brazil's 'sportscape' different to most European countries. The *ideas* behind the different types of systems, however, are very similar. Elite sport success is to be strived for. The answer as to 'why' and what the impact of such success could bring are most likely to be found in the hoped-for 'legacies' discussed above.

The 'convergence' of elite sport development is driven by three broad factors:

1. First, the rapid expansion of transnational capitalism in the past 20–30 years (Nauright and Schimmel, 2005).
2. Second, increasingly states appear to have sports systems underpinned by a notion of a 'virtuous cycle' of sport (see above).
3. Finally, the transfer of policy (broadly defined) and external pressures are behind the convergence of elite sport development systems (Houlihan and Green, 2008).

The accelerated expansion of international capitalism can be understood as the backdrop to the exchange of ideas and policies relating to the development of sport (point one). This expansion brings with it the commercialization and commodification of elite sport. A discussion and clarification of such complex developments goes beyond the scope of this text; suffice to say that the globalization of sport has greatly contributed to points two and three. Point number two effectively sums up the rationale behind modern states' investment in elite sport; point three suggests that the transfer of policy from one country to another and/or from one sub-system to another, whether direct, intentional or otherwise, is in part responsible for the move towards a convergence of elite sport and scientific-technological development. External pressures include the global nature of sport and the processes of governmentalization and commercialization behind the professionalization of elite sport (see Chapter 11; Houlihan and Green, 2008; Grix and Parker, 2011). On this point, a UK Sport-led report which compared six elite sport systems (UK, Canada, Italy, Norway, the Netherlands and Belgium) stated that it is:

> increasing global competition...encouraging nations to adopt... more strategic elite sport policy in order to differentiate themselves from other nations. The net result is an increasingly homogeneous elite sport development system which is ostensibly based around a near uniform model of elite sport development with subtle local variations. (UK Sport, 2006)

The argument put forward here is that the 'near uniform model of elite sport development' cited above resembles, to a large extent, the key characteristics of the East German model.

The politics of performance sport: don't mention the GDR

Ask the key stakeholders involved in elite sport development and they would probably all agree that they do not want to be linked in any way to the former East German model of sport. Look closely at the key characteristics of their sports systems, however, and the undeniable influence of that model on those of today is visible. East Germany produced the highest output of Olympic medals per capita (from 1972) from a tiny population of just 17 million citizens. Sport politics took on a new meaning when the GDR gained external legitimacy and international recognition through the use of elite sport success. The most profound 'legacy' of this elite model of sport (the so-called sports 'miracle') is the influence it has had and continues to exert over the majority of states that excel at elite sport. What was revolutionary in the 1970s is now commonplace. If the belief in a 'virtuous cycle' of sport discussed above is a GDR 'legacy' (in the sense of a 'misreading' of what went on between elite and mass sports), then another and perhaps more profound one is the influence the GDR sports model has had and continues to exert on the majority of states that excel at elite sport (apart from the USA, which depends on its collegiate system).

Most states successful in elite sport do appear to exhibit systems based on the core characteristics of the East German model. Table 7.1 indicates the similarities between modern-day sports systems and the GDR sports system and places them in context by comparing them with a range of different regime types. Of the ten areas of influence listed in the table, the following can be understood as generic characteristics that have stood the test of time:

- A government-led (and Olympic-driven) sport policy.
- Government funding for sport and full-time athletes.
- A system of talent identification.
- The professionalization of coaching.
- The integration of sports science/medicine in attempting to improve athletes' performance.

These core tenets (or 'secret ingredients'; see Box 7.3) of an elite sport development model can be found in, or have been employed in, advanced capitalist states such as Canada, New Zealand, Australia, Norway, the Netherlands and Germany, as well as in China. It is around such tenets that successful elite sport models appear to

---

Box 7.3   Secret ingredients to a successful elite sport model

Is there a secret formula to developing a winning elite sport model of development? 'No' is the short answer. However, there are several key characteristics that most of the more successful share. Although there are clearly nuances in different nations' elite sport policies (Houlihan and Green, 2008), some core components such as 'talent identification' and 'scientific research' appear essential. In a wide-ranging study of 'sport policy factors' that impact on elite sport success in six nations, De Bosscher et al. (2008) drew up nine policy 'pillars' that the state in which the elite sports model is embedded ought to provide to ensure success. All of these 'pillars' can be found at work in East Germany, the most successful sports nation per capita, 40 years previously. These range from the two cited above to 'financial support', 'coaching provision' and 'training facilities'. There is a certain irony here in so far as an authoritarian regime is effectively a 'blueprint' for advanced capitalist elite sport success. The argument that East Germany would not have had such a global impact on elite sport had they not developed the most systematic state-sponsored drugs system ever is hard to maintain, given the advances they made in sports science, coaching, training facilities and programmes and talent identification to name but a few (Dennis and Grix, 2012).

be 'converging' (for earlier comparative discussions of elite sport models and the influence of East Germany on them see also the work of Green and Oakley, 2001; Green and Houlihan, 2005; Collins and Green, 2007).

While De Bosscher et al. have sought to highlight the key sport policy factors that can lead to elite sport success – and thus the things in which nations may wish to invest – Table 7.1 adds a broader dimension to the task of comparison and looks at states' rationale behind investing in elite sport, the 'management' system in place to ensure success, the Olympic-driven sport policy and the broader philosophy underpinning such an approach to elite sport. The point is to signify the similarities between such diverse social and political systems. It also helps highlight the similarities between modern-day sports systems and the GDR sports system and to place them in context across a range of different regime types.

One way of evidencing the convergence hypothesis around the generic model of East Germany is to look at one system clearly influenced by it. The East German model of elite sport has clearly impacted on today's politics of performance sport and states' elite sport systems. The exception, as can be seen from Table 7.1, is the USA and its extremely successful 'collegiate' system of sport which has grown up organically to become the bedrock of another medal 'miracle'. A glance at Table 7.1 reveals clearly that the USA, still the most dominant Olympic superpower, has not been affected by the global developments and trends towards a convergence of elite sports development systems. In fact, Sparvero et al. suggest that the USA has developed elite sport 'amid the chaos' (2008: 260), a reference to the seemingly haphazard and uncoordinated make-up of the sports landscape in the USA.

The next sub-section looks briefly at the UK's current sports model to highlight a system *that has* been profoundly influenced by the key characteristics exhibited in the East German model (see also Green and Oakley, 2001; Green and Houlihan, 2005; Collins and Green, 2007).

The UK's elite sport development model

The UK – and for Olympic purposes, GB – has taken on many of the characteristics of the Australian and East German models of sport. Of note is the fact that the GDR is rarely, and never positively, mentioned in government sport policy documents. Australia, however, is held in

Table 7.1 Key characteristics of select countries' sports models (East Germany, Australia, UK, China and USA)

	East Germany	Australia	UK/GB	China	USA
Regime type	Socialist dictatorship	Democracy	Democracy	Communist dictatorship	Democracy
1. Rationale for investment in elite sport	International prestige; domestic 'feel-good' factor/identity	International prestige; domestic 'feel-good' factor/identity; participation/health	International prestige; domestic 'feel-good' factor/identity; participation/health	International prestige; domestic 'feel-good' factor/identity	International prestige; domestic 'feel-good' factor/identity
2. Policy type	Olympic-driven, government-led sport policy	Olympic-driven, government-led sport policy	Olympic-driven, government-led sport policy	Olympic-driven, government-led sport policy	Distinct lack of government involvement in elite sport; US Olympic Committee drives sport policy
3. Management/ governance type	Technical-rational/instrumental approach ('old' public management)	New public management	New public management	Technical-rational/ instrumental approach	Not applicable
4. Underlying philosophy	Ideologically driven (socialist) professionalism/win at all costs attitude	Ideologically driven (capitalist) professionalism/win at all costs attitude; 'virtuous cycle' of sport	Ideologically driven (capitalist) professionalism/win at all costs attitude; 'virtuous cycle' of sport	Ideologically driven (consumer communist) professionalism/win at all costs attitude	Ideologically driven (capitalist) professionalism/ win at all costs attitude; focus almost exclusively on elite sport in colleges/ universities
5. Talent identification	Systematic talent identification and youth development (initially drawing on USSR)	Well-developed, systematic talent identification programme built on East Germany model	Outline of a talent identification system that draws on Australia and Canada	Systematic talent identification and youth development (similar original roots as East Germany)	Well-developed talent identification systems through professional sports/high school/ universities

6. (Central) State funding for sport and athletes	Athletes effectively full time or given jobs to suit	Athletes offered scholarships and career and education support	Very small group on tiered funding scheme according to their chances to 'medal'	All 'professional' athletes full time and receive wages directly from the state	Funding administered by United States Olympic Committee to national governing bodies. Tiered funding scheme according to national governing bodies' medal success.
7. Coaching and training	Comprehensive system of coaching and coaches; training treated as a science	Funded athletes given access to top-level coaching and training facilities	Funded athletes given access to top-level coaching and training facilities	Comprehensive system of state coaching and training	College/University athletes given access to top-level coaching and training facilities
8. Sports science/ medicine	Advanced and integrated sports science and medicine	Comprehensive system attempting to mesh sports science and medicine	Fledgling system of sports science and medicine	Advanced and integrated sports science and medicine	There is a lack of integrated sports science and medicine programmes
9. Sports facilities and competition	Top-class sports facilities; wide network of sports schools; frequent competition from young age	Network of state-of-the-art facilities	Loose network of English Institutes of Sport based on Australian example	Top-class sport facilities; wide network of sports schools; frequent competition from young age	Top-class and wide-ranging sports facilities; wide network of college and inter-collegiate/university sports; frequent competition
10. Focus on specific sports	1969 decree to split sport into funded and non-funded, crucial to later success	Australian Institute for Sport decision to focus on specific Olympic sports	'Game Plan' discusses the need to focus on 'medal intensive' sports	China remains world leading in specific sports: table tennis, gymnastics; traditionally focused on specific events	Sports leading to professional career favoured

Source: Adapted from Dennis and Grix (2012).

very high regard, even revered. For example, in 'Game Plan' (2002), written shortly after the Sydney Olympics, one passage states that

> We can learn lessons from Australia. Their purposeful pursuit of sporting excellence, sustained by Government in partnership with sporting bodies, has resulted in Australia becoming, on a per capita basis, by far the most successful sporting nation in the world (DCMS, Game Plan, 2002: 7).

Interestingly, Australia's model of sport drew heavily on the East German system for inspiration when setting out on their 'pursuit of sporting excellence' (Dennis and Grix, 2012). A cursory glance at the British cycling team reveals the extent to which an integrated system of sports science, technological advancement, coaching, physiotherapy, sport psychology and research and development have been employed to achieve Olympic success. This approach is reminiscent of that adopted by East Germany over 40 years ago. The UK – along with many states, including emerging nation states in the Balkan and Baltic regions (Bloyce and Smith, 2010: 134) – appears less interested in showing off its political system, than climbing up medal tables, primarily with the intention of enhancing its 'image' abroad and increasing its stock of 'soft power' (see Grix and Houlihan, 2013; Box 7.4).

The UK's new approach to funding athletes, which underpins this shift towards striving for elite sport success, is based on a so-called 'no-compromise' management system clearly linked to an Olympic-driven sport policy. UK Sport, the government 'arm's length' agency charged with distributing elite sport funding, is very clear on how it intends to ensure that all NGBs of sport do not underperform and are held accountable for the monies they receive by publishing a

> series of 'Funding Release Triggers' that will ensure that the planning and governance of all the governing bodies is carefully monitored. *Those not able to meet the criteria over a range of key issues will have performance funding withheld as they modernise their practices and performance systems.* The triggers – which also require performance targets to be achieved – look to set in place a range of sound governance processes...' (author's emphasis; UK Sport, 2008).

Two key points are to be taken from this: first, the manner in which sport is 'managed' – and the discourse in which this is carried

---

Box 7.4   Ideology over reason?

Further evidence of a misreading of Eastern Bloc sporting prowess – and how it impacts on current sport policy – is evident in the dismantling of the successful (English) grassroots School Sport Partnerships (SSP) scheme and the redirection of funding into a School Sports Games, effectively a mini-Olympics for children. The striking parallels with the Soviet and East German *Spartakiade* competitions are hard to avoid. These events were used during the Cold War as high-level competitions to prepare would-be champions for international sports careers. In East Germany, for example, the vast majority of Olympic medallists had been successful at a *Spartakiade* event in their youth.

The Coalition Government's decision to cut £162 million of funding for 450 SSPs in 2010 contradicted directly the number one 'legacy' promise of the London Olympics; that is, to 'inspire a generation of young people to take part in local volunteering, cultural and physical activity'. Research shows that a positive experience of sport in an individual's formative years results in a greater likelihood that they will participate when older. In an era of 'evidence-based' policy this was a decision resting on the assertion that the system of SSPs is 'centralized' and 'bureaucratic', with ministers selectively using statistics to attempt to prop up their case. Long-term statistics reveal that SSPs have had a huge impact on children's participation in sport, rising from 25 per cent undertaking two hours of sport a week, to over 90 per cent in 2010. Interestingly, the common consensus is that SSPs at the coalface have made a difference. This consensus brought forward a wave of protest against the cuts: 75 Olympians and elite athletes wrote to the Prime Minister; 60 head teachers wrote to *The Observer* newspaper stating that this was an 'ignorant, destructive, contradictory and self-defeating decision'.

The decision to cut SSPs is a good example of 'sport politics': it was not based on policy 'evidence' or reason, but rather on political ideology.

---

out – reveals striking similarities with the 'old public management' of the GDR. Target setting, checks and balances, feedback loops, reviews, reassessments and so on are employed to ensure a continuous progression and improvement of the system (see also Bergsgard et al., 2007: 15–16). Second, the elite-driven discourse in sport policy, which underlies and affects most policy decisions, remains unquestioned. Few dispute the underlying logic of the virtuous cycle of sport; few outside academia appear interested in the fact that elite sport success and the holding of SMEs does not appear to be linked to an upsurge in sustained mass participation. Evidence for the long-term effects of elite sport success on participation is hard to come by. A report commissioned by Sport Canada, for example, came to the conclusion that 'there is little empirical evidence to support the anecdotal claims that high performance sport leads to social benefits such as building national pride [...] and encouraging healthy behaviours' (Bloom et al., 2006: ii). The lack of evidence for the 'elite sport–mass sports' causality has not, however, dampened the UK government's appetite for investment into elite sport, as the heavy investment in Olympic sports testifies. Since 1997, consecutive governments have been unequivocal in their emphasis on elite sport as the driver and inspiration for mass sports participation. The coalition government (from 2010) has withdrawn funding from the (English) grassroots SSPs and redirected it into a School Sports Games, effectively a mini-Olympics for children (see Box 7.4).

The belief in the power of elite sport to 'inspire a generation', change the fortunes of a country, improve a state's image and lead to desirable urban generation is what is behind the privileging of elite sport over community or grassroots sport by most governments the world over.

Questions

- What are the three main reasons why states invest in elite sport?
- What does the 'virtuous cycle' of sport actually refer to and how does it help us understand governments and their involvement in sport?
- What are the key characteristics of 'converging' elite sport systems?

Further Reading

- De Bosscher, V., de Knop, P., van Bottenburg, M. and Shibli, S. (2008) *The Global Sporting Arms Race*. Oxford: Meyer and Meyer Sport.
- Green, M. and Houlihan, B. (2005) *Elite Sport Development: Policy Learning and Political Priorities*. London and New York: Routledge.
- Houlihan, B. and Green, M. (2008) *Comparative Elite Sport Development*. London: Routledge.

Chapter 8

Governing Sport: Domestic and International Governance

How can you lose money on an event that lasts for three weeks, rewards its performers with nothing more than a medal tied with a bit of ribbon, and generates billions of dollars of revenue?

(Stefan Szymanski on the role of the IOC)

The 'governance' of sport

There are, of course, many levels at which the 'governance' of sport could be discussed. In this chapter the focus is on the domestic national level of sports governance and the international level of governance. The former concerns itself with how sport policy is delivered, how sport is funded and which type of organizations make up the so-called 'sportscape', including NSOs. International governance of sport concerns itself with those organizations that are responsible for transnational sport, for example, WADA, the International Association of Athletics Federations (IAAF), FIFA and the IOC. Such global organizations set the context within which NSOs operate; decisions made at a supranational level often impact on and directly affect NGBs and their policies. The governance of sport is, therefore, not just a matter for individual nations. Key actors in world politics, for example, the United Nations, and increasingly the European Union and the Council of Europe, have a direct impact on national sport. An example of agenda setting policy at a supranational level is the European Commission's 2007 White Paper on sport, which suggests member states ought to encourage a greater role for equal opportunities in sport. This is likely, in time, to force traditionally gendered sports such as golf to change their archaic policies and practices. Interesting political tension has arisen in the past between national and supranational bodies, for example, around the issue of doping bans, where the NSO has not recognized the ban. For example, Dougie Walker, a GB sprinter, was banned for two years by the IAAF for testing positive for performance-enhancing drugs in 1998, which was subsequently not recognized by UK Athletics (UKA).

Issues around 'governance' have become increasingly important in the last 30 years, as sport has become more politicized and as governments have invested more in sport. With heavy financial investment comes strict accountability and the need to modernize often archaic practices. In the world of sport this has led to several key tensions because sport in many countries has been – and still is to a large extent – run by amateur volunteers. The delivery of sport policy in the majority of advanced capitalist states or advanced liberal democracies runs from government departments via NSOs (in the USA the Olympic Organization distributes monies to NSOs). It is clear to see how increasing levels of government funding and interest can give rise to difficulties in sport policy delivery: as modern technocratic modes of governance meet archaic amateur sports structures there is bound to be friction. Two strands of literature are of interest in helping to understand the manner in which sport is governed at the domestic level: the so-called 'governance narrative' literature and Foucault's ideas about power encapsulated in the concept of 'governmentality'. Why this is of interest to sport politics is also clear: the domestic governance of sports covers key issues such as the funding for NSOs (who gets what, when and how), the mechanisms developed to monitor them (the checks and balances) and the effects such systems have on long-term sport development.

The 'governance narrative'

Sports studies has only very recently begun to draw on the mature debates in political science and public administration concerning the state's changing role in the delivery of public policy, of which sport, of course, is part. Yet, the so-called 'governance narrative' that is slowly becoming the new orthodoxy in political science (Marsh, 2008a), is more often than not presented as *the* key approach to understanding recent developments in public policy in leading textbooks on the subject (see Coxall et al., 2003; Dorey, 2005; Hill, 2009). The 'governance narrative' is a broad-brush approach that can usefully assist in 'framing' particular studies of the sport policy area, ranging from those dealing with issues of meta-governance down to studies involving street-level bureaucrats, or both. The focus of the original work on 'governance' was the 'Westminster style' of government (for example, Australia, Canada and New Zealand), but general principles hold for the majority of advanced capitalist states investing heavily in sport. In particular, how governments fund elite sport, the mechanisms in place to make sports organizations accountable for the funds they receive and the criteria and ideology on which such a system rests.

In a nutshell, the 'governance narrative' suggests a major shift in politics and public policy from 'big' government to governance through networks, a wide array of 'partnerships' and devolved bodies, thereby bringing policy closer to the street level and thus society. 'Partnership' working in particular, especially in sport policy delivery, has been championed strongly. This shift has led to the erosion of central governmental power and with it, the state's ability to determine and deliver policy (Skelcher, 2000; Bevir and Rhodes, 2006, 2008). The diffusion of power moves from a hierarchical, top-down delivery of policy, to one that is sideways, with governance through a series of networks in which a wide variety of interests are represented.

The application of this approach to public policy in the UK has been critiqued for not capturing how the sport policy sector is governed. In particular Goodwin and Grix (2011) and Grix and Phillpots (2011) have shown that sport policy (and several other sectors) is a 'deviant' case and as such does not fit this ideal type. This leads to several very interesting questions that shed light on the most salient aspects of the discussion around domestic governance. For example, why does sport policy (and others) not fit the notion of devolved dispersed power among a variety of actors with increased autonomy from the central executive? After all, there is clearly a trend to 'agencification' in the sport policy area, including arm's length agencies, the rapid growth of 'partnerships', networks, charities, advisory bodies, boards, commissions, councils and other non-governmental bodies. The process described by the 'governance narrative' does not result in a 'hollowing out' of the state but, perhaps paradoxically, rather in an increased capacity for central state control in most mature democracies (see Taylor, 2000). The underlying hierarchical power relations and resource dependence between networks, partnerships and government remain intact. The paradox arises between surface observation (the growth of devolved bodies) and the underlying power relations of networks and partnerships involved in policy-making and delivery. And this surface observation is usually enough evidence to confirm a shift from big interventionist 'government' to more autonomous governance by networks and partnerships (Bevir and Rhodes, 2008; Marsh, 2008b), a central tenet of the 'governance narrative'. Therefore, the 'governance narrative' ideal type does not account for the continuance of 'asymmetrical network governance' (Goodwin and Grix, 2010) between government and resource-dependent actors, which exist in both elite and grassroots policy delivery in the UK (see Newman, 2005, for a critique of elements of the 'governance narrative'). This is an important point and one that has wider significance beyond the UK case. As discussed below, such an understanding of 'governance' – whereby 'devolved' bodies of public policy delivery do not lead to more open democratic processes, but can be read as a state strategy for control – touches on many of the areas central to Foucault's notion of 'governmentality'.

On the surface the 'governance narrative' would appear to correctly characterize the sport policy sector in the UK. There is no doubt that there is a multitude of organizations, committees and charities involved in sport delivery resulting in one of the most 'divided, confused and conflictive policy communities in British Politics' (Roche, 1993: 78) for this very reason. There are a bewildering array of actors – many with overlapping and unspecified roles – involved in the delivery of sport policy, including non-departmental public bodies (for example, the funding agencies for grassroots and elite sport, Sport England and UK Sport), a Sports Minister, an Olympics Minister (at the time of the London Games), a UK Sports Institute, the BOA, 46 NSOs, 49 CSPs and local authorities all working in one way or another together with the government's Department of Culture, Media and Sport to deliver sports-related services. This is further complicated by the fact that there are private actors, charities, not-for-profit organizations, bodies and committees close to government and so on making up the sportscape. However, inherent in this system – depending on how wealthy the NSOs are – are asymmetrical power relationships, mostly driven by dependency on central government resources. This ties in neatly with discussions around 'governmentality'.

Foucault put forward this term – which he coined 'the art of government' (1994, 2001) – as a way of capturing how governments manage to exert power over subjects by using techniques to ensure individuals govern themselves, but in line with the government's aims and objectives. That is, there is no overt use of force, but: 'Increasingly, government seeks not to govern *per se*, but to promote individual and institutional conduct that is consistent with government objectives'

(Raco and Imrie, 2000: 2191). The manner in which this is carried out by governments is to offer autonomy, but with strings attached (Piggin et al., 2009: 89). And this is where sport policy comes in. The UK, Australia, Canada and New Zealand, to name but a few states, have introduced 'modernization' programmes to public policy delivery 'designed (ostensibly) to empower and autonomize NSOs' (Green and Houlihan, 2006: 49). This has been accompanied, however, by a growing regime of centrally set targets, directives and sanctions (Grix, 2009; see Box 8.1 below). Sam (2009: 505) has found similar tendencies in New Zealand sport and states that through 'modernization'

> ...traditional, volunteer 'kitchen table' administration is meant to be replaced with more formalized operations and an adherence to established management practices such as strategic planning, and the use of key performance indicators in monitoring and evaluations.

Thus, 'governance narrative' research on mature democracies and the Foucault-inspired analysis of 'governmentality' point to a sportscape that on the surface resembles a devolved sector, closer to policy delivery and seemingly autonomous from government; under the surface,

---

Box 8.1   The consequences of 'governmentality' for the development of athletics in the UK

In an in-depth study of the effects of the new type of governance apparent in sport policy on the development of athletics in the UK, the author raised several key issues (Grix, 2009):

1. UKA (set up in 1999 after its predecessor went bankrupt) was profoundly influenced by the Labour government's wider modernization agenda, which saw the increasing involvement of central government and its agencies in public policy.
2. Under the new 'governance', UKA has modernized its values, techniques and practices along business lines. This has led its management to develop a narrow, short-term, target-centred approach to athletics.
3. The study argued that the modernization of UKA along 'new managerialist' lines has led to a shift in NSO accountability away from its stakeholders, including the grassroots, and up towards UK Sport.

The effects of 'governmentality' on the longer-term development of sport has yet to be fully researched. However, it is clear that it is likely to be profound.

governments are very much in control of directing policy. In a growing number of states, sport policy is becoming more 'top-down' and government-influenced (see Chapter 3; Harris and Houlihan, 2014).

Establishing that there is a new type of governance at work in several advanced capitalist states is one thing, considering the consequences for the development of sport another. Research into the effects on sport of the 'managerialist' governance described above has begun to show that it can skew sports development towards the aims and objectives of the government (see, for example, Piggen et al., 2009; see Box 8.1 for an example of athletics in the UK). Usually, this means an emphasis on elite sport goals at the expense of both school and community sport. For reasons discussed at length in Chapters 7 and 10, elite sport and elite SMEs tend to be the highest policy priorities for governments.

NSOs (or NGBs) are the guardians of their particular sports disciplines within a particular state (see Box 8.2). They are not wholly autonomous; they enjoy differing degrees of autonomy depending on how wealthy and self-sustaining they tend to be. Thus, professional sports, for example, American football, will be far more autonomous than the governing body for athletics in the UK (UKA; Box 8.1), which is beholden to the will of two funding bodies close to government: Sport England and UK Sport. This is because the UKA received the third highest funding for the Rio Olympic cycle of almost £28 million, behind cycling and rowing (UK Sport, 2014).

Box 8.2   What do NSOs do?

What is an NSO and what does it do? At the point when sport began to be 'rule-bound' and 'codified', that is, the rules of the game were set out and established, there was an obvious need for an organization and officials to govern and uphold them. Several major sports (athletics, boxing, cricket, rugby, soccer) were first established in England in the late nineteenth century; rules were drawn up and the sports were exported – and often adapted – throughout the world. NSOs developed as the 'guardians' of their sport disciplines, ensuring rules were adhered to and altered when necessary. Nowadays NSOs provide the competitions, coaching structures and support services, such as sport science, to their athletes.

The size and complexity of NSOs differ greatly depending on their sports discipline. Athletics NSOs are likely to be – in those states in the top five of the Olympic medal table – of a different order to a nation's boccia NSO (boccia is a game similar to bocce; it is played by competitors who have a physical disability and it requires the use of a wheelchair) in terms of numbers of permanent staff and members associated to it.

In addition to domestic pressure, NSOs are also 'governed' by International Sports Organizations, for example, the IAAF in the case of domestic athletics NSOs. Although technically the IAAF is the umbrella organization for all NSOs, there have been several instances where NSOs have not recognized an IAAF imposed ban on one of their athletes.

International sport governance

In an era of growing politicization and governance of sport it is interesting to note that transnational governing bodies of sport, for example, the IAAF, International University Sports Federation (FISU), the IOC and FIFA, are not accountable to any government in the world. The academic literature tends to lump such bodies together as international non-governmental organizations (INGOs) along with transnational issue groups such as Greenpeace, the Red Cross and so on. Generally, sport INGOs are not the focus of the academic literature on transnational organizations and not considered to be terribly important. This is surprising when one considers the commercial power of the governing body of the world's most popular sport (FIFA) and that of the world's most spectacular global sporting event (the IOC), and the political influence these unaccountable organizations wield. For this reason the following will focus on these organizations, as they possess the power of multinational companies. Organizations such as WADA have as their aim the coordination of anti-doping policy internationally, but responsibility for drug testing is still very much left to the national doping agencies to enforce and oversee.

Consider for a moment the effects that granting the hosting of one of the premier SMEs can have on a state. Apart from the legacy rhetoric that inevitably forms part of a state's acceptance speech after the announcement of, for example, the next Olympic host, there are several profound legacies that remain little discussed. Take, for example, the changes made to a sovereign state's constitution, necessitated and demanded of the host of an SME by the international governing bodies (IOC and FIFA). In Brazil, a 'double host' in the space of two years, a string of constitutional changes were made, first, in order to win the Games, and then later in order to accommodate the demands of FIFA and the IOC. Such changes could be termed '*pre-event* institutional legacies' and should be understood as the changes made to the host country's institutional framework by the host government, ostensibly to be able to stage the event(s) (Toledo et al., 2015). This is an interesting form of 'intervention by invitation', a phrase usually reserved for military intervention in a sovereign state by a foreign state at the request of the former. The gravity of the sporting version of this ought to be pondered: unaccountable, unelected sports organizations grant host status of their showcase, and highly lucrative (for them), events to willing sovereign states, which then have to adapt and change their laws to stage the sports shows. Inevitably, changes to the law can have far-reaching consequences for all citizens (whether sports lovers or not) and the majority of legal alterations made are linked to the deregulation of markets and the liberalization of the host state's economy. For this reason Zirin (2014) suggests that SMEs can be understood as a 'neoliberal Trojan Horse' designed to push through reforms, rush through legislation and deregulate markets: in other words SMEs become a '*de facto* shorthand for regeneration, inward investment, consumption and corporatism' (Silk, 2014).

Houlihan offers a useful classification scheme for international governing bodies (see Table 8.1). Although the IAAF and FIFA may be both classified as 'global, single sport'-led international sports organizations, the similarity stops there. They are of course both umbrella organizations for national athletics NSOs and football associations respectively, but football is the world's most popular sport and the FIFA World Cup is the most viewed sporting event in the world. Athletics is a diverse sport with a very small core fan base. Equally, FISU links university sport globally, but it pales into insignificance next to the most spectacular sporting event in the world, the Olympic Games.

Table 8.1   *Classifying international sports governing bodies*

	Global	*National, regional*
Single sport	International Association of Athletics Federations, Fédération Internationale de Football and so on	Union of European Football Associations and so on
Multisport	International University Sports Federation, International Olympic Committee and so on	Pan American Sport Association, National Olympic Committees and so on

Source: Adapted from Houlihan (1994).

The following sections offer a brief summary of the international sport organizations charged with managing the Olympics (IOC) and the World Cup (FIFA) respectively. The emphasis is on the multisport governing body, IOC, as the political importance of this event is greater that the World Cup, as many states, including the USA and the UK, use the medal index as a quasi-barometer of their 'strength' on the world stage (see van Hilvoorde et al., 2010; Haut, 2014).

The IOC

The French aristocrat, Pierre de Coubertin, usually credited with resurrecting the Olympics (1896), founded the IOC two years before the first Games in the modern era in 1894. De Coubertin was an interesting character who saw in sport a vehicle for improving both the 'physical prowess' of people, but also their 'character'. The lack of the former had contributed, he believed, to the defeat of his countrymen in the Franco-Prussian war (Guttmann, 2002: 8–9).

Both the duality of mind and body and the memory of war are present in the Olympic values that are, in part, about bringing young people together from across the world. The Olympic Charter, for example, states that:

> Olympism is a philosophy of life, exalting and combining in a balance whole the qualities of body, will and mind (IOC, 2014: 11).

It is hard to reconcile this idealistic notion with the modern-day, multi-billion dollar Olympic 'caravan' that rolls on to the next event once the Games have finished (as discussed in Chapter 4). Apart from being the guardian of the jewel in the crown of SMEs, the IOC is officially the umbrella organization for all International Federations and National Olympic Committees (NOCs) (see Box 8.3). The influence and power of the NOC will depend on the country for which it is operating. The IOC organization itself blossomed in the post-War period, gaining in importance and in wealth through caretaking the Olympics, as it moved from a relatively low-key amateur event, to an increasingly competitive and hyper-commercial event at which nations could showcase their athletes, and through them, their nations. The IOC has had just nine presidents in its 120-year history: five from the European nobility (Sage, 2010: 229), with three presidents staying in power for over 20 years each (Chappelet and Kuebler-Mabbott, 2008: 23). This is in part due to the fact that members are elected (by the IOC itself) for a period of eight years

Box 8.3   What do NOCs do?

Interestingly, while NSOs have similar functions throughout the world (the guardians of their sport discipline; up-keeping the rules and so on), NOCs in different countries have differing levels of involvement in elite sport development. All NOCs have a similar mission statement, or a variant of the following: 'To support [name of country here] Olympic and Paralympic athletes in achieving sustained competitive excellence while demonstrating the values of the Olympic Movement, thereby inspiring all [nationality of country here]' (this is the American NOC example).

The American NOC is a good example of a powerful organization: the United States Olympic Committee (USOC) is responsible for 'the training, entering and funding of U.S. teams for the Olympic, Paralympic, Youth Olympic, Pan American and Parapan American Games' (USOC, 2014). At the other end of the spectrum is the BOA. The BOA is 'toothless' in comparison to its American equivalent, mainly because it has nothing to do with the funding of Olympic athletes (this is carried out by a separate organization close to the government, UK Sport; see Chapter 7). The BOA is involved in the selection of athletes for the Olympics (summer, winter and youth), but importantly, they 'work together' with NSOs on this. Also of interest is the fact that the British Olympic Association (BOA) receives no funding from the government or the lottery, but is an independent and privately funded organization.

The Brazilian NOC is a mixture of the styles of both the US and GB committees: it is independent from the government, but is funded by the national lottery; it also invests in schools, university and, mostly, elite sport (BOC, 2014).

initially, with the number of times they can stand for re-election unspecified (Miah and Garcia, 2012: 17). The result of these regulations and structures 'virtually guarantees maintenance of the status quo with members' profound sense of entitlement largely unchallenged' (Lenskyj, 2010: 16). The IOC, based in Lausanne, Switzerland, is made up of several committees, each with a specific remit within the organization. The General Assembly, the highest body in the organization, is the only authority that can change the IOC 'charter', effectively the governing document of the IOC (Box 8.4). The membership of the IOC reads like a who's who of elites from around the world, picked from well-known nobility, ex-top athletes, politicians, leading civil servants and professionals.

The IOC, as the 'manager' of the Olympics, benefitted greatly from the commercialization of sport in general and the Olympics in particular during the 1980s. The appointment of Juan Antonio Samaranch in 1980 – a Spanish Marquess and former minister in Franco's fascist

---

Box 8.4   Salt Lake City scandal

The Salt Lake City scandal is generally referred to when discussing corruption and vote-rigging around the choice of host for the Olympics (in this case, the Winter Olympics). Salt Lake City had made four bids to host the Winter Olympics but to no avail. However, the city's fortunes changed in the bidding process for the 2002 Games in 1995. So, what had made the difference? Apparently 24 of the 114 IOC members accepted a total of around US$1 million in cash and gifts in exchange for their votes (Shepard, 1999). The scandal came to light when a letter from a Salt Lake City Olympic official addressed to the daughter of an influential IOC member surfaced in which details of payments for the woman's tuition fees were discussed. She had received over US$108,000.

As with doping, this major scandal led to expulsions from the IOC membership but also, importantly, policy change. One of the key proposals was that IOC members would no longer be allowed to visit bidding countries. It would appear that IOC members are now trying to overturn this anti-corruption measure by lobbying for such visits to be restored (Reuters, 2014).

---

regime – marks the beginning of the process of turning the Olympics into the ultimate neoliberal corporate event it resembles in the twenty-first century. The Los Angeles Olympics in 1984 are regularly wheeled out as the finest example of partnering a host city/state with private sponsors to (successfully) finance the Games (Tomlinson, 2005). Quite apart from the private capital invested in the Games (see Chapter 4 for a discussion of Olympic sponsorship), the Los Angeles Olympics used and reused existing stadia and sports facilities to cut costs, something new hosts would do well to learn from.

While exact revenue figures are hard to come by – a cursory glance at the IOC's income from the London Olympics offers an insight into the phenomenal earning capacity of this organization: the IOC received a package of US$3.45 billion consisting of, among other things, broadcasting rights and sponsorship which makes up around 90 per cent of the total (*Sports Business Daily*, 2013). The mediatization of the Games, the guaranteed global audience (of approximately 5 billion viewers) and the inelastic nature of demand for the event (that is, there is no alternative that disgruntled viewers can exit to; no 'competitors' in the field) have put the IOC in a rather enviable position. Add to this the growing desire of *all* types of state across the world to host the event and you have a situation that could induce complacency in anybody. The point here is that with *such a demand*, from sponsors, broadcasters and punters, the IOC do not need to change, despite the fact that hosting the Olympics can have a profound negative effect on a state's economy (for example, Montreal, Canada, 1976 and Athens, Greece, 2004).

Thus, an unaccountable organization, in the envious position (from a business point of view) outlined above, which is not dependent on any of its members for its income, and which is not beholden to stakeholders and their capital, will not be 'punished' (in the economic sense again) for undemocratic or corrupt practices.

FIFA

FIFA, the governing body of world association football, was founded in 1904 just 10 years after the IOC and originally shared some similar values: to bring people and nations together regularly for international competition to promote understanding. Currently FIFA has 209 members – these are (usually) the football associations of nation states – and it works together with key regional football federations, such as the Union of European Football Associations (UEFA) and the Confederation of North, Central American and Caribbean Association Football (FIFA, 2015). Interestingly, the United Nations only recognizes 192 members from around the world (UN, 2014).

There are some other striking parallels between FIFA and the IOC (see Box 8.5). Chief among them is the cloak of corruption, accusations of financial irregularity and double-dealing that have accompanied the development of this 'charity', especially since the appointment of Joseph 'Sepp' Blatter in 1998.

FIFA has charitable status under Swiss law which allows for very generous tax exemptions. Like the IOC, FIFA has no 'stakeholders' and no members on which it is reliant for income. In addition, FIFA too benefitted greatly from the rapid commercialization of sport from the 1960s on and was led by an individual in Joao Havelange with a well-developed sense of business acumen, just like Samaranch, discussed above. Thus, the context and climate of the commercialization of sport were able to be exploited by actors such as Havelange. A final similarity between FIFA and the IOC is the showpiece of the World Cup. Arguably, football fandom – and thus the demand for viewing football – is much more inelastic than for viewers of the Olympics. It was estimated that approximately 50 per cent of the world's

---

Box 8.5   Similarities between the IOC and FIFA

Both the IOC and FIFA share some similar founding values, in particular, around bringing people and nations together on a regular basis to promote international understanding. Further, both organizations 'manage' one of the most prestigious, most watched and most lucrative global sporting events ever known. Both too have been accused of corruption on a large scale and the IOC and FIFA respectively are among the richest not-for-profit and charitable organizations that exist.

The IOC and FIFA benefitted greatly from the commercialization of sport from the 1960s on and from the business acumen of specific individuals (Samaranch and Havelange), who were able to take advantage of the unique and enviable economic position of the international governing bodies (see Chapter 4 for more on this).

---

population tuned in to at least 1 minute of the 2010 FIFA World Cup from 'every single country and territory of the Earth, including Antarctica and the Arctic Circle' (FIFA, 2011). FIFA effectively have a locked-in audience who cannot exit the market, cannot choose another World Cup and therefore have to accept FIFA as they are; this makes the World Cup extremely attractive to sponsors and advertisers (Box 8.6). The 'locked-in' nature of demand for the World Cup is explained in Chapter 4.

Thus, FIFA are also in an enviable position of managing the most popular sport in the world and one of the most watched and revered sporting spectacles in the world. This position leads on to the final similarity with the IOC: FIFA is extremely rich with reserves of upwards of US$1.4 billion (FIFA, 2013), making it one of the wealthiest charities in the world. This wealth has led to endemic and systematic corruption over a long period of time. It would appear, however, that the non-transparent and undemocratic FIFA is finally being investigated properly, with several of its top officials arrested by the Federal Bureau of Investigation (FBI), and the long-serving, reform-shy, Sepp Blatter, stepping down in 2015.

While both FIFA and the IOC have grassroots programmes to support the development of sport throughout the world, the vast profits that they and their sponsors generate through the World Cup and the Olympics respectively contrasts sharply with the resource-poor community and school sports organizations that underpin the development of sport from the bottom up. Coupled with the resources regularly

Box 8.6   Deciding the host

One of the most political aspects of FIFA's work – and that of the IOC – is deciding who gets to host the prestigious World Cup every four years. This process has always been politically charged, but recent events have highlighted the inherently political nature of these decisions that go far beyond what happens on the playing field. Take, for example, the judgement of which country was to host the 2018 (and 2022) World Cup back in 2010.

To the outsider, the script reads like a novel: in the driving seat is a (male dominated) organization which exhibits the key characteristics of secrecy, non-transparency, wheeling-dealing, backhanders, under-the-table payments and an aversion to paying tax. At the head is a septuagenarian who rules with an iron fist. This is not a description of the Mafia or East Germany's Politburo, but FIFA. Commentators picking over England's bid in the aftermath of its rejection in favour of 'new lands' (Sepp Blatter), Russia (2018) and Qatar (2022), the smallest country ever to put on the event, pointed the finger of blame directly at the English media. Even the English footballer Rio Ferdinand cited the timing of the BBC's *Panorama* exposé of corruption among FIFA officials as central to the bid's failure.

The English media had flagged up and sought proof for what most people already know: FIFA is, and has been for a very long time, surrounded by accusations of back-stabbing, improper dealing, palm-greasing and profit-seeking. Despite the tendency of the UK media to be insensitive, intrusive and, at times, sensationalist, their investigation(s) into corruption at FIFA have turned out to be well founded.

wasted in hosting the two key global sports events, such monies could and should be used to mitigate and alleviate the serious social problems that the world faces (see Perryman, 2012; Grix, 2014b).

Summary

The purpose of this chapter was to introduce some of the key concepts and debates around the governance of sport. At all levels – be it regional, national or international – sport is 'governed'. As the politicization of sport grows, so too does the need to implement a form of governance to shape and form its development. In states where government investment in sport is high, and systems of schools, community and elite sport are well developed, this is accompanied by governance.

In mature democracies (Australia, Canada, the USA, New Zealand, the Netherlands and so on) this usually translates to a mechanism of state control on its investment. In the name of transparency and accountability, targets are set and aligned with government (sport) policy. Checks and balances are in place to ensure sports organizations are on course. Such a system, a precursor to which is to be found in East Germany some 40 years ago (Dennis and Grix, 2012), can lead to spectacular results (witness GB's rise up the Olympic medal table: 15 medals in Atlanta 1996 – just one gold – to 65 overall and 29 golds at London 2012). As in East Germany, it also leads to a skewing of sports development. That is, a focus on funding specific sport or interventions means a lack of focus and funding for others. A great part of East Germany's success was due to focusing on a limited number of medal-intensive sports, something other states have attempted to emulate. This means that many sports will receive less support and there will be fewer initiatives to promote them to the wider public. On the surface, this would seem sensible. However, given that there is no evidence of a relationship between the number of medals a nation wins and the number of people who participate in sport or who rush out and buy goods, or are more productive at work, or are much happier in themselves as a result of elite sport success, the rationale for investing in moving up the medal table needs to be subject to further analysis. This chapter has shown how sport as a sector tends to defy the so-called 'governance narrative'. While it is easy to relegate such debates to the ivory towers of universities, it is prudent to pause for a moment and think about the real-life effect of concepts such as 'social capital', 'stakeholder society' and, most recently, 'soft power'. Yes, such constructs usually start off as academic, but those that gain traction among the political elites take off on a life of their own. And this is serious because such catchy concepts can become self-fulfilling prophecies.

Domestic governance is one thing, international governance of sport is another. The focus in this chapter was exclusively on the big two: the IOC and FIFA. Both international governing organizations wield great political power, ranging from the ability to grant host status on states to the even more controversial habit of 'recognizing' states that are not recognized by the international community. For example, FIFA recognized East Germany as early as 1952; FIFA's decision helped force the issue of formal *de facto* recognition, albeit 20 years later in 1972 with the signing of the Basic Treaty between West and East Germany. Both organizations tend to behave as if they were major multinational companies, but with the advantage of not being beholden to shareholders. This latter trait, along with being registered as a charity (FIFA) and not-for-profit organization (IOC), makes both organizations unaccountable. The non-transparent nature of both organizations and their undemocratic processes are likely to come under intense pressure to reform in the coming years, given that they reside over, manage and hold sway over the two most popular sporting events on the planet.

Questions

- In what way does the governance of sport matter at the domestic level?
- How does the type of governance in place effect the funding and development of specific sports disciplines?
- Is there anything wrong with the way the IOC and FIFA govern? Who cares?

Further Reading

- Grix, J. and Phillpots, L. (2011) 'Revisiting the "governance narrative": "asymmetrical network governance" and the deviant case of the sport policy sector', *Public Policy and Administration*, 26(1), 3–19.
- Jennings, A. and Simson, V. (1992) *The Lords of the Rings*. London: Simon and Shuster.
- Miah, A. and Garcia, B. (2012) *The Olympics: The Basics*. London: Routledge.

Chapter 9

Doping Matters

This is my body, and I can do whatever I want to it. I can push it; study it; Tweak it; listen to it. Everybody wants to know what I am on. What am I on? I am on my bike busting my ass six hours a day; what are YOU on?

(Lance Armstrong, seven times Tour de France winner and drug cheat)

So long as there have been sporting competitions, some form of doping has taken place in order to enhance participants' performance. Before looking at examples of historical precedents of doping, it is worth noting that in the twenty-first century it is difficult to disentangle the development and proliferation of doping in sport from the globalized nature of sport, the role the media play in sport, the commercialization and professionalization of sport and the politics of performance sport. This holds too for other forms of cheating in sport, for example, match-fixing and spot-fixing games and deliberately injuring opponents, which are clearly akin to doping. Globalization has aided the proliferation of doping in sport with the sharing of 'best practice' crossing international borders; athletes in one country receiving doping substances and advice from people in another. The increased commercialization of sport – linked, as discussed in Chapters 4 and 5, with the development of the media – acts as a driver behind reasons to dope. Lucrative pay-days and careers tempt athletes to cross the rubicon and take performance-enhancing drugs, attempting to gain an advantage in an ever increasingly professional world of sport. The stakes in sport are now much higher. As seen in Chapter 7, performance sport is more political than ever before; never have governments of all regime types been so interested in elite sport performance than in the twenty-first century. These exogenous pressures set the backdrop to current discussions of doping in sport, however, seeking an (unfair?) advantage in sport is nothing new.

Evidence of performance-enhancing substances exists from both Ancient Greece, the birthplace of the modern Olympics, and Rome. Lueschen (2000: 463) offers the example of Galen (130–200 CE), a Greek sports physician who mentioned performance-enhancing substances. Although gladiators, athletes, boxers and many others have taken substances to enhance performance since classical times, objections were not voiced publicly against infringements of fair play until modern times (the 1920s). In fact, up until this time, drugs were relatively widely used. One popular drug, administered to the 1904 Olympic marathon winner in several small doses, Thomas Hicks (USA), was strychnine. Interestingly, this has since been shown to be highly poisonous and would have hindered rather than helped athletes. The use of drugs in sport grew steadily from the 1940s; many drugs were tested in military contexts, for example, on fighter pilots, to help them stay awake longer and remain sharp during battle. The 1960s brought with it a revolutionary change in 'permissive' behaviour which included widespread use of street or recreational drugs. At the same time – especially throughout the Cold War – East European regimes, foremost East Germany, were experimenting and developing performance-enhancing drugs to give their athletes an unfair advantage over others.

Even so, the banning of specific substances by the IOC did not occur until 1967 after a series of scandals in cycling – including the death of British cyclist, Tommy Simpson – surrounding the frequent use of amphetamines and the growing awareness of the systematic use of anabolic-androgenic steroids in strength sports, especially by Soviet and American weightlifters (Box 9.1). The IAAF was among the more active of sports federations in combating drug abuse: in 1972, its Medical Commission placed blood doping and anabolic

---

Box 9.1   What is 'doping'?

But what is doping? The following definition, in 1982, by the IOC Medical Commission embodies the main elements constituting what is widely regarded as doping:

The administration of, or use by a competing athlete of any substance foreign to the body or any physiological substance taken in abnormal quantity or taken by the abnormal route of entry into the body with the sole intention of increasing in an artificial and unfair manner, his/her performance in competition. (in Verroken, 1996: 22)

steroids on its banned list; five years later, doping control became mandatory at its championships (Verroken, 1996; Waddington, 2000; Houlihan, 2002a).

Key terms such as 'foreign' substances, 'abnormal' and 'artificial and unfair manner' are fundamental to definitions of doping devised by many other bodies, yet such terms themselves remain unspecified, which can lead to problems with where appropriate lines ought to be drawn. The IOC, which worked closely with the IAAF was, given the importance of the Olympics, central to the identification and listing of drugs that were regarded as unethical, artificially enhancing and damaging to an athlete's health. The IOC's first classification of doping, issued in 1967, included amphetamines and narcotic analgesics; anabolic steroids were added to the list seven years later after the development of tests able to trace such chemicals in the body (see Box 9.2). Beta blockers and diuretics were listed as banned substances in 1985, probenecid and human chorionic gonadotropin in 1987, and growth hormone and other peptide hormones in 1989. In 1985, classification was extended to encompass pharmacological, chemical and physical manipulation, including blood doping, urine substitution, the breaking of sample seals and the breaching of confidentiality by authorized laboratories (Verroken, 1996: 39–40).

To be effective, classification of banned substances and techniques needs rigorous enforcement. This has proved to be a Herculean task. Only a few of the problems can be mentioned here. Whereas tests for

---

Box 9.2   Broad 'types' of drugs used in sport

1. Anabolic steroids were the East German drug of choice (banned from 1975 onwards. Testosterone was banned as late as 1982); steroids help athletes recover faster and thus enable them to train more often. Steroids also build muscle.
2. Stimulants are used to reduce tiredness and increase alertness, but also competitiveness among athletes.
3. Peptides and hormones; erythropoietin gives athletes more energy by producing more red blood cells. This is favoured by cyclists and distance runners, especially as it does not have to be injected. It was added to the banned list in 1984.
4. Diuretics are used to expel water from the body (for example, for a boxer trying to 'make the weight') and are usually called a 'masking agent', that is, to cover up the fact that an athlete has ingested drugs.

amphetamines were well developed by the 1960s and effective as a deterrent by the mid-1970s, those for the increasingly popular anabolic-androgenic steroids proved far more problematic (Berendonk, 1992). Although the IAAF banned these steroids in 1970 and the IOC in 1974, in anticipation of the Montreal Olympics (Singler and Treutlein, 2008), controls remained inadequate due to the lack of an internationally uniform system of testing and control and the painfully slow development of out-of-competition testing. As the IOC Medical Commission was only too well aware, many substances, including anabolic-androgenic steroids, could not be detected if dosage ceased before the start of competition. This was a strategy adopted to great effect by the GDR: whereas during the 1974 European Athletics Championships in Rome, 17 athletes tested positive as a result of the introduction of a method for identifying anabolic steroids, no GDR competitor was among them due to measures ensuring that dosage ceased 25 days before competition (Spitzer, 1998: 30), but one year later, however, the runner-up in the 100 metres and a member of the sprint relay winning team, Marlies Oelssner (later, Göhr) of the Sports Club Motor Jena, tested positive for anabolic-androgenic steroids at the European Athletics Junior Championships, probably because doctors had exceeded the recommended dosage. Had the transgression been made public by the European Athletics Association, she would have faced a lifetime ban and would have had to return her medals (see Franke and Berendonk, 1997).

Not until the late 1970s and early 1980s did several individual countries, such as Norway and the UK, begin to introduce more effective random out-of-competition testing. Despite the development in the early 1970s of radioimmunoassay for testing for anabolic-androgenic steroids and the establishment in the following decade of a urine test for exogenous testosterone, an effective system of control for drugs was bedevilled by a lack of uniformity between nations and between international sports federations (Dennis and Grix, 2012).

For example, many countries and sports federations turned a blind eye to abuse, doctors and athletes as well as laboratories manipulated test samples, and penalties for proven abuse differed from one national or international sports body to another. Biomedical problems also hindered doping controls. Controllers were – and are – confronted by the difficulty of accounting for athletes who produce naturally above-average levels of hormones and of those who need certain compounds like ephedrine for therapeutic reasons, such as combating hayfever, asthma and other minor ailments. Further intrinsic problems were (and are): the difficulty for controllers to keep abreast of pharmaceutical developments; the lack of firm proof for ergogenicity for many drugs due to methodological problems inherent in medical science; and the variation in the proscription of drugs from sport to sport as compounds do not have a uniform performance impact in each discipline (Verroken and Mottram, 1996). Complicating the whole debate over doping is the ethical issue of the fairness of banning some drugs and techniques but not others in the world of elite sport with its basic logic of, and orientation towards, winning over losing. For example, the gritty middle-distance runner, Peter Elliot, used cortisone – not a banned substance – to overcome an injury and go on to claim a silver medal in the Olympic final at Seoul in 1988. This is compounded by the intrusion into the privacy of athletes by tests, especially those conducted out-of-competition without warning and at any time. Finally, the heavy financial costs of a comprehensive testing regime both at national and international level should be mentioned: over US$1.6 million was spent at the Los Angeles Games on doping controls (Donohue and Johnson, 1986). Given the marginal gains of in-competition testing – for example, out of 6,000 tests at the London 2012 Olympics, only three positives were found – there is a trend towards out-of-competition testing; and costs increase again when a positive test is contested in the courts.

Competing explanations of why doping is so widespread

There are a range of competing explanations attempting to provide an answer to the question of why drugs in sport are so widespread – or, more precisely, what are the drivers behind the use of drugs by athletes – and why some argue that drugs and sport are inextricably linked in the modern era. The reasons range from political pressure by state-sponsored doping schemes, such as that administered by the now defunct East German regime, through to the commercialization of sport and the quest for an allegedly unfair advantage over one's competitors; or the 'levelling' of the playing field by those not born at altitude or the general feeling that 'everyone is on drugs' anyway. Competing explanations can be categorized not only by their level of analysis (the 'state'; the 'athlete'), but also by their type; that is, psychological, historical, political and sociological explanations abound to illustrate why doping appears to be on the increase in sport. The assumption that the banning of drugs in sport would be supported by the majority of academic work on the subject is wrong. Instead, there are many commentators who argue for allowing drugs in sport; the reasons cited range from preventing athletes from having to take untested drugs on the black market, to doubts about whether doping is as harmful as it is often made out to be.

It is fair to say that up until the late 1980s to early 1990s there was not much international cooperation in combating doping. The IOC had begun rudimentary drug testing as early as 1968 at the Mexico Olympics. As often is the case, several crises (in this case concerning doping) prompted policy change. The PAG of 1983 provided the first crisis, as it was the first international sporting event using fairly accurate testing procedures. Some 15 athletes – mostly bodybuilders – failed drugs tests, leading to the onset of sudden injuries among at least another dozen athletes at the Games. The most memorable crisis, however, was the Ben Johnson affair: shortly after storming away from his competitors in the 1988 Seoul Olympic 100 metres final, Ben Johnson of Canada was disqualified for doping. Since then, almost all of the men who ran in that final have either failed a drugs test or been accused of doping. The second case was the near collapse of the 1998 Tour de France by the extent of doping revealed. Houlihan (2009: 386) suggests that four key factors in this case led to major changes in anti-doping policy:

1. The extent of doping discovered during the Tour and the number of riders and officials implicated.
2. The global prestige of the Tour itself.
3. The claims by the international federation of cycling, the UCI, to be the leader in anti-doping campaign.
4. The strength and intensity of intervention by the French government.

The far-reaching implications of this event, the increasing number of drug use cases and international pressure was – following an IOC-organized conference on doping in 1999 – to lead to the establishment of WADA in 1999 (Box 9.3). This was, however, the start of a very long struggle against drugs in sport in which there remain different attitudes towards anti-doping in different sport, different states and differing testing regimes.

Box 9.3   Distinguishing doping

WADA was set up in 1999 against the backdrop of international pressure and several high profile doping scandals. There was clearly a need for international cooperation in the 'fight' against drugs in sport and the creation of WADA (and the national-level anti-doping bodies) has clearly gone some way to clearing up sport. However, dopers appear to always be one step ahead of the testers. Equally, it is extremely difficult to police the list of banned substances with athletes claiming that the 'foreign' substances found their way into their bodies through often unexpected avenues. These range from creams containing diuretics (often used as masking agents; see the case of triple Olympic champion sprinter, Veronica Campbell-Brown, acquitted in 2014; *Athletics Weekly*, 2014), toothpaste containing nandrolone (according to Dieter Baumann, gold medallist over 5,000 metres at the Barcelona Olympics 1992) and excessive sex that led to extremely high levels of testosterone (this was Dennis Mitchell's excuse). Perhaps one of the most comical was Olympic 400 metre champion LaShawn Merritt, who blamed his positive on over-the-counter drugs to enhance his penis. The comical bit was his subsequent statement: 'To know that I've tested positive as a result of the product that I used for personal reasons is extremely difficult to wrap my hands around' (Rowbottom, 2013: 27). In many such cases in track and field non-governmental organizations accept the athlete's explanation, but these can be overturned by the IAAF. The average detection rate for catching drug cheats is said to remain constant at around 2 per cent (ibid.: 21).

Historical precedent and present predicament: the fox and the henhouse

The East Germans produced a state-sponsored doping programme which was the most systematic ever known. The aims of the system were very clear: to give the edge to an already formidable elite sport system (see Chapter 7) and to 'win at all costs'. Ironically, perhaps, elite sport was the only area where the 'capitalist' virtues of competition, winning and individual pursuit of excellence were actively promoted in an otherwise 'collective' authoritarian society. In any other area of life, these virtues would have been frowned on. The doping system affected up to 10,000 athletes (from the mid-1970s to 1989, the GDR's collapse). Some 1,800 athletes were 'top tier', of whom around 80–100 had Olympic medal potential. This group were singled out for 'special' attention by dopers, that is, administered specific dosages of drugs. Anabolic-androgenic steroids were administered to minors from about 12 years of age in athletics, swimming and gymnastics; youngsters of around 14- to 15-years old were doped with hormones in canoeing, kayaking, rowing and some winter sports (Dennis and Grix, 2012).

One of the quirks of the GDR doping system that has relevance today is its doping policy which, clearly, set out with no intention of catching their own athletes. The GDR's Central Doping Control Laboratory (1977) in Kreischa proved crucial in preserving the secrets of the state doping programme. It had two seemingly incompatible functions: on the one hand, it was an IOC-accredited laboratory engaging in international doping controls; on the other, part of its extensive operation was to ensure that there were no positive tests when GDR athletes were competing abroad. This they did so well that GDR officials even toyed with the idea of 'sacrificing' an athlete who had no prospect of an Olympic medal.

The success of East Germany's elite sport had a profound impact on both elite sport development (see Chapters 3 and 7) worldwide *and* doping policy. One could argue that the *dis*-incentive of catching athletes from one's own nation is similar now to what it was then for East Germany. Previous chapters have shown the lengths states – and some sports – go to in order to achieve elite sport success, either through elite athletes or SMEs. The sporting 'arms race' is as competitive as ever and the discourse surrounding elite sport remains positive and upbeat. Equally, states are after burnishing their international image, so putting them in charge of their own doping policy could be likened to putting a fox in charge of the henhouse.

NSOs are well aware that doping scandals are very bad for their sport in terms of sponsors and attracting new members. Where is the incentive to catch dopers? The set-up at present is that WADA currently monitors individual National Anti-Doping Organizations, but does not control them. The IOC and international sports organizations (for example, FIFA) have the power to punish non-compliance to the WADA Code, but the fox guarding the henhouse problem is still an issue (Box 9.4).

In the future it is likely that a separate agency responsible for global testing and code enforcement will be established, as this would prevent the current conflict of interests which is limiting the effectiveness of testing; although this will clearly have resource implications in what already is a very expensive enterprise.

Box 9.4　Fox and the henhouse

Both Jamaica and Kenya could be seen as examples of the fox-henhouse syndrome. Both states have undertaken very little drug testing and, unsurprisingly, have found very few 'positive' cases (Kenya found two positive cases between 2010 and 2012; yet, under pressure from WADA, they managed to find 17 positive cases within a year). Both Jamaica and Kenya have global reputations as *the* place for sprinting and distance running excellence respectively. Both have benefitted from the international exposure that this has brought their nations. Kenya, for example, has a fast-growing trade in distance running tourism, whereby not only top-class athletes flock to the Rift Valley to breathe in the thin air of the distance legends, but normal 'club standard' runners are now taking up 'training' holidays to experience the trails where the world's best log up their miles.

Both Jamaica and Kenya could suffer badly if systematic doping were to be revealed. Both were reprimanded by WADA for a spate of recent drug scandals (Insidethegames, 2013).

It's the money, stupid

The section above considered the actions – or inaction – of the testers as a factor in the proliferation of doping, while this section looks to financial reward as an explanation. The first argument for the widespread use of drugs in sport is simply put: the globalization, commercialization and politicization of sport has combined with their professionalization to create an atmosphere in which the rewards in elite sport are high and the risks associated with taking drugs (getting caught) are relatively low. Sport is now a career, so if athletes 'naturally' cannot make the big-time, they may be tempted to reach for artificial assistance to ensure they do.

Nowadays an Olympic gold medal winner in a wealthy country has a high chance of cashing in on their fame, often becoming a millionaire, especially if they happen to be 'media friendly' and in a popular sport; this usually involves the launch of the athlete's own product (for example, recently retired cyclist, Victoria Pendleton, has her own series of push-bikes for sale).

States have long offered their own premiums for Olympic medals, for example research on the Sochi Winter Olympics 2014 revealed that Olympic committees paid out a total of some US$18 million in 'bonuses' to medal winners (International Sports Press Association, 2014).

Add to this the availability of performance-enhancing drugs (a great deal can be ordered on-line) and you have a recipe for an increase in doping.

Why dope?

Perhaps not surprisingly, there is little research on athletes who have *actually* doped, given that owning up to this almost guarantees a lengthy ban or the cessation of their job or profession. New approaches from sport psychology have led the way in understanding *why* dopers dope and *how* they manage to justify this to themselves. This work has been pioneered by Ian Boardley and colleagues (2014; see Box 9.5) and allows insights into the mechanisms by which individuals are able to morally disengage and continue doping without the usual feelings of guilt, shame or fear. Boardley et al. (2014) built on the mechanisms put forward in Bandura's social cognitive theory of moral thought and

---

Box 9.5   Help from sport psychology

A novel approach to help understand an individual's motivation for doping is Bandura's (1991) social cognitive theory of moral thought and action. Within this theory, Bandura proposes engagement in transgressive activities is normally deterred by the anticipation of negative emotional reactions resulting from such behaviour. Applying this to doping, one would expect athletes to be deterred from doping because they should associate it with unpleasant emotions such as guilt (for breaking the rules), shame (for cheating their opponents and mates) or fear (of being caught). However, Bandura also explains how people can reduce or eliminate anticipation of such emotional reactions by using any of eight psychosocial mechanisms, collectively termed 'moral disengagement'. Moral disengagement allows people to conditionally endorse transgressive acts by cognitively distorting the nature of the act, thereby reducing personal accountability for the act or its consequences. Thus, it is possible that moral disengagement facilitates doping by allowing athletes to dope without experiencing negative emotions that should normally deter their use. One example of a mechanism used by athletes is displacement of responsibility, which occurs when people view their actions as the result of social pressure and not something for which they are personally responsible; use of this mechanism has been supported in past research in which athletes have displaced responsibility for their doping to the presence of successful doping athletes in their training environment (see Boardley and Grix, 2014; Boardley et al., 2014 for empirical examples).

action (1991) by discovering two further mechanisms from the interview data with over 70 English bodybuilders. These are:

1. The 'sliding scale': this notion relates to descriptions reflecting progression from legal supplement use, to initial use of performance-enhancing drugs often in the form of tablets, and finally to serious performance-enhancing drug use such as progression from oral to injectable steroids, use of multiple steroids and/or other substances such as growth hormone. An example from the study of Boardley et al. is:

   > It's like a gradual process, initially you will do the supplements, and then your next step is like to take steroids... then growth hormone.

2. **Family and friends theme**: this relates to bodybuilders making clear distinctions between gym friends, non-gym friends and family when describing who they share knowledge of their performance-enhancing drug use with. Consistent with this theme, most bodybuilders made clear distinctions between people with whom they openly discuss their doping and those they do not. For example, one bodybuilder stated: 'My parents... they don't know I'm on them... my best friend in London doesn't know...'

The value of such research is that it could lead to targeted interventions in doping prevention, if the key mechanisms behind doping by individuals are better understood.

To ban or not to ban?

This section includes a brief discussion of both sides of the argument for and against banning drugs in sport. Surprisingly a fair few commentators are for legalizing drugs or 'creating a level playing field'. It is easier to start with why drugs should be banned.

For a ban – in the red corner: Drugs in sport are intrinsically unfair, as they confer an advantage to whoever consumes them over opponents who do not; equally it is against the rules of sport and – like other rules that differentiate sport from physical activity – one cannot pick and choose. Such an 'unnatural' advantage is not to be compared with the 'natural' advantage of Usain Bolt's long legs or female distance world record holder, Dibaba's, birthplace (Ethiopia;

at altitude); doping goes against the 'ethos' or 'integrity' of sport, that is, sport is supposed to be wholesome and pure, drugs are the opposite: unhealthy and dirty. Further, drugs are seen as an 'easy' route to performing well, which goes against the notion of striving to achieve excellence. Doping and doping scandals are simply bad for business and bad for individual sports disciplines, their reputations, growth and profits. Drugs can, of course, seriously damage the health of an athlete. Finally, sportsmen and women are supposed to be role models for wider society, especially youngsters (see Houlihan, 2009 for more details on some of these arguments). What signal would doping send out?

Against a ban – in the blue corner: First off, there are enough things that confer an 'unfair' advantage to some athletes and not to others. For example, these could be physiological (small calf circumference is apparently a predictor of world-class distance runners), geographical (growing up in the altitude of the Rift Valley is not a bad idea for future marathon runners) and social factors (this relates to class and sport; not too many poor inner city children will turn automatically to polo or horse jumping; socio-economic status also plays a role in introducing children to top-class equipment and training at an early age. For example, Boris Becker, the son of wealthy parents, received high-level coaching from 4 to 5 years of age). Other arguments include the fact that not enough evidence of the impact of long-term steroid use and abuse exists (best not mention this to those former East German athletes suffering serious side-effects of long-term drug abuse; Deutsche Welle, 2006); the state should not be so paternalistic telling people what they should and should not do. Finally, the whereabouts policy (that is, a selected number of top athletes having to stipulate to anti-doping agencies their location at specific times of the day) is both unethical and breaches basic human rights.

Large-scale scandals

Despite the best efforts of a growing network of anti-doping measures and bodies, the dopers are still ahead of the game. It should be noted that 'dopers' refers, in general, to the athletes and the discussion above touched on why and how they cope with doping. What has not been mentioned is that doping does not take place in a vacuum – whereas a bodybuilder may source his or her 'juice' (drugs are rarely if ever named by their real names; this is yet another coping mechanism; euphemisms make drugs sound harmless), do the research on their effects and even administer them to themselves (through injections, for example), doping in professional sport or performance sport usually involves an array of characters. The Bay Area Laboratory Co-operative (BALCO) scandal in the early 2000s contains a cast made up of front men, a chemist, distributors, coaches and the athletes who were doped. In a surprising parallel to the 'sliding scale' above, Victor Conte, the ring leader behind the scandal, set up shop in California selling vitamins. He then opened a shop selling sports supplements and finally, at the other end of the scale, he began work on undetectable performance-enhancing drugs with Patrick Arnold, a chemist (BBC, 2005). Interestingly, the scandal came to light only after a well-known sprint coach sent a syringe with the mysterious drug the 'clear' (due to it not being detectable) to the US national anti-doping agency in 2003.

The implications of this case – apart from prison sentences for Conte and his accomplices – was the realization that doping was rife beyond just athletics. Caught up in this scandal were top basketball and baseball players and American football players. The British sprinter, Dwain Chambers, was also caught out. Since then, he has returned to the sport as an anti-doping spokesperson. The fact that such a large operation, covering many top professional and amateur sports, could remain undetected for so long is something to be concerned about. If the coach of Marion Jones and Tim Montgomery (both Olympic medallists and former world record holders) had not sent off that syringe, BALCO may have continued for many more years.

The second big scandal to shake up the anti-doping world was the case of Lance Armstrong. Armstrong, winner of seven consecutive Tour de France competitions, was a serial denier of any wrongdoing; as it turned out, he was a serial doper. His case has offered further insight into the murky world of doping: not only are the networks of people involved vast, including implications that the cycling world governing body, the International Cycling Union (UCI; or more precisely the Cycling Anti-Doping Foundation – CADF – that deals with anti-doping on its behalf), had been turning a blind eye, but the code of silence (the Omerta) that surrounded the cycling teams prevented anyone from speaking out. The 'Omerta' is usually used in connection with the Mafia: a code of silence to protect criminals; anyone seen to break the code would be in trouble. This apparently stretched as far as journalists covering the cycling competitions. Some, for example, British rider Chris Froome, believe that the scandals rocking the world of cycling have had a positive effect as

> I feel that the omerta has been broken. Anyone now who does [drugs] is not only costing them their career – it is potentially taking down a whole team of cyclists plus the 50-odd support men around them. It is clear that those guys [recent positive tests of two leading cyclists] were acting on their own. They are the minority, the absolute minority and it's great that the tests picked them up (*Guardian*, 2013d).

The newly installed UCI president, Brian Cookson, commissioned an audit of CADF and its practices and the audit team (in March, 2014) 'made a series of recommendation on numerous areas in which it felt improvement or changes needed to be made, with nine of these areas considered "urgent"' (Osborne, 2014).

Summary

Much of the debate around doping in sport ends in more questions than answers: Should drugs be banned? Is there a case to be made for 'levelling the playing field' by allowing drugs? Who is to say what is right and what is wrong? Here lies the difficulty with this topic: it is tied up with ethics and morals and many believe the state should not dictate to citizens what these should be. However, the 'level playing field' idea is equally impractical. Drugs cost money and you need certain resources to have access to them, so even if we got over the fact of allowing drugs in sport – to which the author, an ex-athlete himself, is opposed – people with resources would have a clear advantage over, say, an impoverished athlete from a poor neighbourhood.

Anecdotal evidence from the author's own classes on this topic suggests that there may be a generational aspect to the doping debate. Many students over the years have expressed a relaxed attitude towards doping, even suggesting that it would be interesting to see how fast a human could run (with the aid of performance-enhancing drugs). Allowing doping and standing by as elite sport becomes even more market-oriented than it already is (see Chapter 4), is likely to see sport becoming like 'spectacles' of old.

Questions

- Doping should be allowed to 'level the playing field'. Discuss.
- What is behind the growth of doping and cheating in sport in the past 40 years?
- Should individual states be allowed to run their own anti-doping testing programmes?

Further Reading

- Boardley, I. D., Grix, J. and Dewar, A. (2014) 'Moral disengagement and associated processes in performance enhancing drug use: a national qualitative investigation', *Journal of Sport Sciences*, 32(9), 836–44.
- Houlihan, B. (2003) *Dying to Win: Doping in Sport and the Development of Anti-doping Policy*. Council of Europe.
- Verroken, M. (1996) 'Drug use and abuse in sport', in D. Mottram (ed) *Drugs in Sport* (London: E & FN Spon).

Chapter 10

Public Diplomacy, Soft Power and Sport

Sport has often been used by states as part of their foreign policy objectives (see for example Merkel, 2008; Manzenreiter, 2010). Both elite sport performance and the staging of SMEs are seen as two potential sources of international prestige for states. Evidence suggests that international sporting success, whether by national teams and athletes competing abroad or by the effective staging of a SME, provides arenas for the deployment of soft power through which states seek to 'attract' others with their values and culture. States also seek to persuade the outside world to want what they want by projecting a specific 'image' to foreign publics and by creating 'a favourable impression and increase[ing] understanding among foreign audiences' (Potter, 2009: 51). This chapter introduces the use of SMEs by states as a public diplomacy tool. It does so by discussing the concept of 'soft power' which acts as a prism through which to grasp why states vie to host ever more expensive sports events. The concept of 'public diplomacy', nation 'branding' and 'soft power' all need some explanation as they are key to unpicking the rationale why states are prepared to invest scarce and finite resources into what often amounts to a few weeks of sporting action.

Sport and soft power

If there is a growing literature around international relations and sport in general (see Chapter 2), scholars who have focused on states and their strategic use of SMEs and linked this with the concept of 'soft power' are few and far between (see Cornelissen, 2010; Finlay and Xin, 2010; Manzenreiter, 2010; Grix et al., 2013; Brannagan and Giulianotti, 2014). This section looks at how Joseph Nye's (1990) soft power concept can help us better understand states' structural motivations behind bidding for and hosting SMEs and what they hope to achieve through such actions (see Box 10.1).

Box 10.1   What is an SME?

While a consensus regarding the definition of a 'mega-event' has yet to emerge there is substantial support (from Horne, 2007; Kellett et al., 2008; Matheson, 2009) for Roche's definition that mega-events are

> large-scale, cultural (including commercial and sporting) events which have a dramatic character, mass popular appeal and international significance. They are typically organised by variable combinations of national governmental and international non-governmental organisations and thus can be said to be important elements in 'official' versions of public culture (1994: 1).

For Nye the changing nature of international relations after the end of the Cold War, and the risk attached to deploying traditional military forms of power, has led to 'intangible power resources such as culture, ideology, and institutions' becoming more important in inter-state relations (Nye, 1990: 167). This should not be taken, however, to mean that Nye advocates replacing traditional 'hard power' with 'soft power' in international relations, but rather that states ought to make far more use of the latter; preferably in combination with the former (so-called 'smart power'; Nye, 2004: 32). Nye distinguishes between power to 'influence the behaviour of others to get the outcomes one wants' (coercive power) and the ability to 'attract and co-opt them to want what you want' (soft power; Nye, 2004: 2). Thought about in this way, a nation's soft power is its ability to make itself more 'attractive' to others. In this sense attraction, rather than coercion, is the essence of soft power and it resides in the ability to shape the preferences of others and align those preferences to your own. As such it is similar to Lukes' 'third dimension' of power, 'the power to shape, influence or determine others' beliefs and desires, thereby securing their compliance' (2007: 90) and also to the Habermasian notion of legitimation and persuasion in relation to explanations of domination within democracies (Habermas, 1979). The sources drawn on by a state to exert such soft power are very different to those of traditional 'hard' power and are primarily, though not exclusively, discursive and ideational. Justin Morris, for example, lists the English language, Greenwich Mean Time, the 'Westminster Model' of government (see Chapter 8), English Law and the BBC World Service among other 'soft power' assets belonging to Britain (Morris, 2011: 332–3). Together, these aspects of British life influence foreign publics' view of Britain.

Sport and diplomacy

Sport has been used as a soft power resource in several different diplomatic contexts. For example, the oft quoted 'ping-pong' diplomacy of the 1970s can be read as an 'ice-breaker' role for sport, in which initial sporting contacts between the USA and China led to more formal discussions and negotiations, following a basketball competition between the two countries one year later. The fact that the Chinese were clearly superior in table tennis, and the USA clearly superior in basketball, was designed to rob sport temporarily of one of its core attractions: its unpredictability. There is a difference between sports diplomacy and using sporting success to garner international prestige or to increase inward (foreign) investment and boost the tourist sector. It is clear that different states will have different reasons to draw on and use soft power and will also aim at different audiences. The USA is increasingly trying to win over the 'hearts and minds' of foreign publics, as well as opinion leaders, as an alternative to direct military intervention, and increasingly so after their image abroad was effected negatively following the Iraq War in 2003 (Grix and Himpler, 2007). Those states burdened with negative national images and national stereotypes that impact on others' perception of them deriving from, among other things, particular historical events, human rights issues or poverty – for example, the Holocaust and the Germans – appear to have much more to gain from mobilizing soft power to (positively) change their image. The governments of Germany, South Africa (2010 FIFA World Cup); China (2008 Olympic Games), India (2010 Commonwealth Games) and, in the future, Qatar (2022 FIFA World Cup) are, and will be, attempting to use SMEs to persuade the governments, businesses and the public in other countries to alter the often negative stereotypes they hold. Such is the interest in utilizing the resource of soft power that Kurlantzick went as far as to say that 'China's growing soft power has emerged as the most potent weapon in Beijing's foreign policy arsenal' (2007: 5).

Public diplomacy which, since '9/11' (that is, the terror attacks on the twin towers in New York, 11 September 2001), has grown in importance among the majority of states throughout the world, is an 'instrument governments use to mobilize...[soft power] resources to communicate with and attract the publics of other countries' (Nye, 2008: 95). It should be noted that it is not only the concept of soft power that is contested; 'public diplomacy' itself is a contested term and there are several competing definitions, some of which (see Signitzer and Coombs, 1992 for example) give greater emphasis to the role of private individuals and groups in the practice of public diplomacy (see Gilboa, 2008 for a fuller discussion). Public diplomacy studies differentiate between the 'old' modus operandi via 'hierarchical state-centric structures' on the one hand and the 'new' model of a 'network environment' in which several actors, of which the state is but one, undertake public diplomacy (Melissen, 2005: 12; Hocking, 2005: 72). However, the state, usually the Foreign Ministry, still plays a central role managing the network and funds of many of the 'arm's length' organizations of which it is made. This mirrors debates in political science literature on 'governance' discussed in Chapter 8. Governance scholars have highlighted a shift from big government to governance by and through networks; this can be seen in the trend to 'agencification', including arm's length agencies, the rapid growth of 'partnerships', networks, charities, advisory bodies, boards, commissions, councils and other parastatal bodies involved in policy deliberation and delivery (Bevir and Rhodes, 2006; Marsh, 2008a, 2008b). The 'new' public diplomacy (see Signitzer and Coombs, 1992) is consequently seen as involving an array of non-state actors including sporting bodies such as FIFA and the IOC at the international level and NSOs at the national level. As Chapter 8 discussed: both the IOC and FIFA are not beholden to national governments and cannot be 'controlled' and 'managed' in the same manner as those dependent on state resources, such as NSOs. It is not only the number of transnational contacts made through such non-governmental bodies, but also their number that is increasing (see also Nye, 2004: 90).

Nation 'branding'

Public diplomacy, of course, uses traditional diplomatic channels and is generally understood as a tool for securing foreign policy interests, whereas 'branding' has turned to the tools of marketing to project a state's image abroad. There appears to be some overlap of the 'old' and 'new' types of public diplomacy, blurring the role of the state in public diplomacy and branding. Many states now appear to have internalized the language of 'soft power'. They are equally at ease with the use of such marketing-related terms as 'nation branding' and national 'image'. While the lines between 'nation branding' and 'public diplomacy' are less clear cut than perhaps they were previously, the central role of the state in manipulating sport to achieve non-sporting goals is apparent in the vast majority of cases.

Australia, as suggested in Chapters 3 and 7, projected a national image before, during and after the Sydney Olympics in 2000 of a 'sporting nation'. According to the Australian Tourist Commission the result of a successful Olympics (in terms of hosting and Australian athletes) and the boost to their national image was the 'accelerated development of Brand Australia by 10 years' (Australian Tourist Commission, 2001: 3; see Manzenreiter, 2010 for China's use of the Beijing Olympics and image management). This 'image management' is important if soft power is to be leveraged to shape international relations through affecting external perceptions of a country, although, it must be stated at this stage, a country's 'image' must rest on something recognizable (for example, a reputation for producing reliable products) other than simply good public relations (see also Anholt-Gfk Roper, 2010). This becomes more pertinent when 'emerging states' with difficult pasts attempt to project their new burnished image through an event that appears to offer a 'coming out party' in which countries are guaranteed a global audience for their 'brand' (Kuper, 2011).

In an age of global media audiences and global communications, many more structurally weaker actors can seek to influence world politics using soft power strategies. As Mattern (2005: 590) suggests 'soft power is available to any actor that can render itself attractive to another'. South Africa, for example, was able to enhance its agency in world politics with a successful soft power strategy of communicating their 'attractive' democratic values in the post-apartheid era, not least through the politics of attraction embodied in Nelson Mandela, South Africa's first post-apartheid president (for a detailed analysis of South Africa's influence on world politics see Lee et al., 2006). And in so doing they were able to legitimately claim a place at the top table of multilateral summitry such as the G8 meetings and join the other emerging powers in extending their agency beyond their regional base.

The rapid development of relatively cheap information technology has facilitated the habitual use of soft power by a whole range of state and non-state actors and the extensive development of public diplomacy strategies by governments and non-state actors suggests widespread recognition of the value of soft power as a tool for agency in international politics (Hayden, 2012).

Utilizing SMEs for public diplomacy

If the last 30 years have witnessed the growing political salience of sport, then special note should be made of how a wide range of governments of advanced and emerging economies have focused on elite sporting success and the hosting of SMEs. In general, in relation to sport, only the Olympic Games and the football World Cup qualify as mega-events, with other events such as the Cricket and Rugby World Cups and the EUFA Champions League defined either as second tier, second order, major events or as regional events (O'Brien and Gardiner, 2006; Black, 2008, 2014; Walters, 2008). It is the international significance of SMEs, the global captive audience they command and the involvement of governments in bidding for and hosting them that makes such events politically interesting.

From the very first 'modern' Olympics in 1896 in Athens, states have sought through these events to signal their modernity to the external world on the one hand, and to appease or 'deflect domestic tensions' away from more pressing concerns on the other (Tomlinson and Young, 2006: 1; see Chapter 1). Guttmann's summary of the reasons why states wish to bid for and host such global events is difficult to improve. He suggests they are simply seeking 'the twin suns of prestige and profit' (2002: 175). While there are of course a variety of reasons put forward by cities and states for hosting, 'prestige' and 'profit' are among all potential hosts' wish lists, irrespective of regime type (see Chapter 7).

The discussion on SMEs unfolds as follows. Of the key reasons and benefits put forward by previous, would-be and future hosts of SMEs for bidding for and staging such an event (see Chapter 7), the final category – international prestige and 'soft power' – is the focus of the rest of this chapter. In discussing the political use of SMEs it is fruitful to talk of both 'legacies' and 'leveraging' and understand how they are linked.

Replaces 'hoped-for' legacies

Much of the discourse around 'legacies' from SMEs is, as seen in previous chapters, based on hope, not evidence (see Preuss, 2007, 2014). According to a recent meta-review of sports tourism research, the nascent literature around the strategic 'leveraging' of SMEs for specific purposes represents a welcome 'shift' from a dominant focus on measuring post-hoc (that is, after the event) impact assessments

(Weed, 2009: 621). Scholars at the forefront of this work (Chalip, 2004, 2006, 2014; O'Brien, 2007) have sought to focus attention on the strategies employed by host cities and states in 'leveraging' opportunities from SMEs through long-term and carefully planned, pre-event activities. 'Leveraging' is generally taken to mean 'those activities...which seek to maximize the long-term benefits from events' (Chalip, 2004: 228) and take the form of a series of interventions with this aim in mind.

In recent years there has clearly been a major shift from advanced capitalist states (USA, Australia, Canada and so on) to 'emerging' or even 'small' states competing to put on a SME. Table 10.1 indicates this trend.

While it is useful to note a trend away from advanced to emerging and small states as hosts of SMEs, this is only part of the story. Four of the seven events above, for example, are arguably not first and foremost about the performance of the host nation's team (apart from China, 2008, the Brazilian football team at the 2014 World Cup and the Russians in Sochi, 2014). Previously, it was essential that the host state's team finish high on the Olympic medal table or were among the finalists in the World Cup; for the new group of hosts, it is hosting that matters. Given the doubts expressed above about many of the expected outcomes and legacies from SMEs, it would appear that 'image' leveraging is crucial to these new hosts.

Increasingly, 'emerging' states are focusing on this aspect of SMEs, attempting to use them to put themselves on the international map (Box 10.2).

Table 10.1   *Recent and upcoming sports mega-events in emerging states*

Year	Event	Country
2008	Olympic Games	China (Beijing)
2010	Commonwealth Games	India (Delhi)
2014	Winter Olympics	Russia (Sochi)
2014	FIFA World Cup	Brazil
2016	Olympic Games	Brazil (Rio de Janeiro)
2018	FIFA World Cup	Russia
2022	FIFA World Cup	Qatar

Box 10.2 'Legacy' or 'leveraging'?

A 'legacy' (see Glossary) is usually something that is left behind or bequeathed to someone. It is a concept that has a multitude of meanings and in combination with 'SME' or 'Olympics' it does not become any clearer (see Preuss, 2007). Nowadays it tends to be shorthand for the answer to the question: What are we going to get for our investment in a sports mega? What will remain *after* the event has packed up and moved on to the next city, region and nation? What will change *as a result of the event*, that is, if it had not taken place, what would not have changed? 'Leveraging', however, is a pre-event strategy, in which the city, region and state attempt to get as much as possible out of the event through specific campaigns and interventions. These take place prior to, during and can continue after the event (see below for an example of excellent event 'leveraging' by Germany in hosting the 2006 FIFA World Cup. The 'legacy' was a more confident nation and enhanced image abroad; see Grix, 2013a).

In recent years the potential positive impact on the nation's image or brand has moved from being a welcome consequence to a significant justification for investing in hosting SMEs. One consequence is that many states have instrumentalized sport to promote their country's image. More recently even small Gulf states, such as Qatar and Bahrain, have also become interested in staging SMEs, with Qatar scheduled to host the 2022 football World Cup (*Time*, 2011).

'Image' leveraging via SMEs

Leveraging is a deliberate strategic tactic as opposed to haphazard and hopeful handling of large-scale events. Such a strategy is usually targeted at something specific, be it economic, urban regeneration or, increasingly, 'image'. This could be taken a step further by suggesting that many would-be hosts seek actively to alter their image, especially if they have had a troubled history, poor national image or low international prestige. Germany is the obvious example here with an image abroad tainted by memories of Nazism and atrocities against Jews in the Second World War; all of the states listed in Table 10.1 have reason to improve or enhance their international image. An enhanced image on the global stage would make the process of diplomacy easier and improve the likelihood of good inter-state relations. A few examples will suffice. Qatar has a poor reputation for upholding human rights and wishes to project an image of a modernizing, sport-friendly state, especially in preparation for the 'post-oil' period (that is when the oil, the source of its immense wealth, dries up; see Brannagan and Giulianotti, 2014). Russia and Russians are not blessed with a positive world image (BBC, 2010). By hosting the Winter Olympics in Sochi in 2014 and the FIFA World Cup in 2018 it will want to change – or at least alter slightly – this image, paving the way, no doubt, for a bid to host the summer Olympics in the future. The Russian case is not straightforward, admittedly, as a nation it appeared unperturbed by the international uproar surrounding Russia's intervention in the Ukrainian crisis during the Sochi Winter Olympics in 2014 (see Box 10.5 below for more on this). Although, as will become clear, hosting a sports mega is clearly a double-edged sword and may not end in the enhanced global image and prestige for which many states hope.

Before introducing the mini case studies of China (Olympics, 2008), South Africa (FIFA World Cup, 2010) and Brazil (FIFA World Cup, 2014; Olympics, 2016), a discussion of the potential for diplomatic damage through event hosting is outlined.

The double-edged sword of hosting

While this type of 'politics of attraction' is becoming popular, inviting the global media to scrutinize in detail the host state, government, politics and policies during a sports 'mega' can lead to unintended consequences. Some examples from history (see Box 10.3) and the recent examples below are indicative of where an event turned out to be a double-edged sword:

- **2010 Commonwealth Games in Delhi, India.** This event was supposed to be a precursor to an Indian Olympic bid, but instead turned into an unprecedented disaster for India and its global reputation. The intense focus of the world's media was partly to blame for quashing India's ambitions of hosting an Olympics after the debacle surrounding the preparations for the Commonwealth Games. Images and reports of crumbling building work, wild monkeys, child labour, dengue fever and corruption were beamed across the world. Just two years later, the Indian Olympic Committee was banned by the IOC for corruption (December 2012), leaving potential Indian Olympic athletes to compete under the IOC flag, if this debacle cannot be resolved by the Rio Olympics in 2016 (see Baviskar, 2014).
- **European Football Championship in 2012 (Euro 2012).** Ukraine – as co-host with Poland – was similarly faced with an unprecedented

level of media scrutiny. A British BBC *Panorama* exposé on racism among Ukrainian football fans started a fierce debate about whether England's multi-ethnic supporters should heed former England player, Sol Campbell's, warning to stay at home, just prior to the start of the event. Further media scrutiny focused on the treatment of the former Prime Minister, Yulia Tymoshenko, who at the time of the event was languishing in jail on charges many believe 'trumped up'. Overall, Ukraine attracted the kind of attention that can lead to a deterioration of their image abroad rather than the positive boost for which they were hoping. The constant stream of bad press, the threats of boycotts (the UK government suggested, rather optimistically, that they would 'boycott' the final, should England get through), and the media gaze gave rise to questions about the democratic legitimacy of the Ukrainian regime and concerns around racism among a population who have previously lived under dictatorial conditions and, like many former communist states, experienced little multiculturalism in their society.

Box 10.3   Negative Olympics?

1972: the Munich Olympics is remembered for terrorists, murder and mayhem. The tragic killing of 11 Israeli Olympic team members and 1 West German policeman by the Palestinian group Black September (five of their members were also killed) is the abiding memory of this event.

1976: the Montreal Games are often used as the prime example of a debt-ridden Games that took the taxpayers 30 years to pay off. Also, the Montreal Olympic stadium is a classic example of an underutilized 'white elephant'.

2004: much more recently the Athens Olympics very likely contributed considerably to Greece's major financial and economic problems and many of the facilities became 'white elephants' not long after the Olympic circus rolled on.

2008: the Beijing Games was the most expensive Olympic bonanza at the time (since eclipsed by the Sochi Winter Olympics). The opening ceremony alone cost an estimated £64 million (as opposed to Danny Boyle's well-received £27 million effort to launch London 2012); moreover, the Games clearly highlighted the issue of human rights and the Chinese treatment of Tibetan Monks.

2012: London 2012 has been described as the apex of the neoliberalization of the Olympics. It was by far the most commercialized (and 'securitized') Games to date, boasting the largest McDonald's outlet in the world. This could be understood as a negative development, taking the event further away from sport and nearer to that of a business fair.

In the Western press, the Beijing (Olympics, 2008) and the 'second-order' events of Delhi (Commonwealth Games, 2010) and Ukraine (2012 co-host of the Euro 2012 UEFA Football Championship) are examples where a soft power strategy can have the opposite to its intended effect.

Successful 'megas'

By contrast, there have been SMEs that can be considered an unmitigated success. In fact, most events – apart from those above – are by general consensus considered successful once the sport begin.

Providing the scandals uncovered by the media are not far reaching, the media coverage and scrutiny of sports megas follows a startlingly similar pattern: in the years leading up to the event, reports are few and far between, but as the event approaches, attention is drawn to any possible cause of a scandal, usually around facilities not being finished in time (for example, Athens 2004), the politics of the host nation (Euro 2012), any potential protests or uprising around the event (2012 Bahrain Grand Prix) or deteriorating roads and outfaced private security firms, which required the publicly funded army to provide the security of the Games (London 2012). In general, however, once an SME starts, sport take centre stage and the mistakes made in the run-up are quickly forgotten in a 'manufactured consent' (Herman and Chomsky, 1988) that surrounds such big events. Even years after an event, little discussion takes place about mistakes made. In the wake of the Greek financial crises from 2012 one would have expected more probing questions into the implications of 'Greece [hosting] a party that cost 5 per cent of its annual revenue...' (Szymanski, 2009: 161) back in 2004. Barcelona is usually cited as the best example of a successful SME (see Box 10.4) both in terms of image enhancement for

---

Box 10.4   Barcelona: a success story?

The case of the Barcelona Olympics (1992) is usually drawn on when discussing a 'successful' Games. Dubbed the 'regeneration Olympics', the £11 billion investment transformed a rundown area in the east of the city into a vibrant new marina with dozens of restaurants and 2,000 new flats. The success appears to lie in the fact that Barcelona was able to benefit from their initial investment through increased tourism and the long-term viability of the sports facilities they built for the event. Also, unlike Montreal (1976), Barcelona had neither 'white elephants' (facilities underutilized) nor massive financial debt. Some suggest, however, that the main stadium has not been fully utilized.

the city, balanced books and wider legacy (Standard, 2011). A more recent important example of a successful SME was Germany's hosting of the FIFA 2006 World Cup. This event revealed what long-term planning and a focused approach to SME hosting could achieve. It is fair to say that this sports 'mega' really was an unmitigated success. As a country that had suffered from a poor image abroad for over 60 years, Germany set out to use the FIFA World Cup to improve it on a global scale. Three essential parts of the Germany strategy were employed to achieve this end:

1. Long-term (pre-event) campaigns.
2. A fan-centred approach to staging the FIFA World Cup.
3. The (unintended) creation of a 'feel-good' factor around the four weeks of the event (see Grix, 2013 for a full study).

Post-event it is clear that Germany's attempt to alter its negative national image was successful. Although international attitudes towards Germany had begun to improve in the years prior to the FIFA World Cup – including the notoriously difficult British media – there has been a marked improvement in the manner in which Germany is now perceived by foreign publics. Inbound tourism rose before, during and after the event and has continued to rise – some two million visitors came to Germany for the FIFA World Cup in 2006 – and here lies the rub: one of the most important factors in improving a state's image, apart from a trouble-free event, is to have people visit your country, return home happy and spread the word (Box 10.5).

States with unsavoury pasts or images they wish to see corrected or enhanced have far more to gain from a successful global SME, but a great deal to lose if things do go wrong. Qatar's sense of excitement at winning the right to host the 2022 FIFA World Cup is likely to have diminished with the unprecedented media scrutiny of its cultural practices, especially around its treatment of construction workers and domestic staff. Qatar's problems have been exacerbated by the extremely long 'run-in' to the actual event (12 years between the announcement and the event) which has intensified media interest: before Qatar, Russia will host the 2018 FIFA World Cup.

It is with the notion of a 'double-edged' sword in mind that the next section turns to three key examples of 'emerging' states: China, South Africa and Brazil, of which the former two have already hosted key

Box 10.5   Sochi Winter Paralympics – a 'third way'?

So far this chapter has discussed 'successful' and 'unsuccessful' SMEs. Could there be a third category, negative from the outside, but positive from the point of view of the host?

From the 'outside': The Sochi Paralympics (2014) became the latest in a long list of sports events to be marred by politics; enough to have had the founding fathers of the birthplace of the Paralympics, Stoke Mandeville, turning in their graves. The last Olympics in Russia (then the USSR) in the 1980s are best remembered for the boycotts of the US team and 64 others in protest against the invasion of Afghanistan; the Moscow Olympics are little remembered for the fact that the (summer) Paralympics did not take place there but were moved to the Netherlands because, as a Soviet official put it: 'we do not have anyone with impairments here'. So, when the new International Paralympic Committee President, Sir Philip Craven, stated in March 2014 – in reference to Russia's de facto military takeover of the Crimea – that 'we will leave global politics to the politicians', this was simply a variant of the tired refrain that 'sports and politics do not mix'. There are some parallels between the 1980 Olympics and Sochi: the UK Prime Minister, David Cameron, ordered a boycott of the Paralympics by British Ministers, and Prince Edward, patron of the Paralympics, stayed away.

The intense media scrutiny is simply one of the by-products of hosting and the longed-for recognition may not be quite what was intended. Qatar (hosts of the 2022 FIFA World Cup) has learnt the hard way by having its treatment of construction and domestic workers examined closely. This could be a case of accidental democratization: the decision to award Qatar the event was political, made by an undemocratic unelected and non-transparent organization, yet the outcome may be improved conditions for workers in Qatar.

From the 'inside': Shortly before the Sochi Games, Russia announced its controversial anti-gay laws; shortly after, it mobilized troops in response to the growing crisis in the Ukraine, let off warning shots and provocatively tested a ballistic missile amid the tension. The Sochi Winter Olympics and the 2018 FIFA World Cup are more than just showcasing events for Russia. Hosting the most expensive Olympics of all time (including summer events) is part of the growing confidence of a state which sees itself returning to its former glory after two decades of difficult economic and social transition. Such events can be used to send signals externally to the international community of the strength of the host; internally they can aid the process of binding the nation's citizens around a common cause.

Russia appears to be testing the boundaries of global opinion and the Sochi Olympics and Paralympics have ensured everyone is paying attention. In the run up to the 2018 FIFA World Cup, the showcase event of the world's most popular sport, Russia as a (re-)emerging state is likely to be at the forefront of debates on the changing face of global power.

SMEs. All can be grouped under the broad label of 'emerging' states; however, there are great differences between them in terms of political regime, demographics, history and sports culture.

Case study of SMEs and three 'emerging' states

2008 Beijing Olympic Games: China's coming out party?

One of the strategies states adopt to make an impact via sport is investing heavily into elite sport and into hosting SMEs in order to top the Olympic medal table and put on a show for the world, thereby bolstering domestic and international prestige. China did just this by using the 2008 Beijing Olympic Games to enhance its image on the world stage and as a domestic tool for its own internal credibility (see Tomlinson, 2010: 14; Cull, 2008: 134).

The example of the Beijing Games is instructive in indicating the risks involved in hosting SMEs or the Janus-faced nature of hosting. That is, on the one hand, if a state suffers from a poor image based on the past, poor human rights or undemocratic governance, then a major sports event could be the best way to re-socialize others towards a more positive image. On the other hand, however, show-casing a nation to a global audience – Beijing's cumulative television audience reportedly topped four billion (IOC Marketing Report, 2008) – and the intense media scrutiny that comes with it may not be quite the 'Olympic effect' (deLisle, 2008: 45) sought and may not be the best way to improve an image and increase a state's influence on the world stage. China, although a more 'closed society' than most, still operates in a 'world of the internet and global satellite news' that means that the nation will be 'known as it is, not as it wishes to be' (Cull, 2008: 137), leading to a constant stream of bad press around human rights issues (see Brannagan and Giulianotti, 2014, and their concept of 'soft disempowerment' which captures a similar sentiment).

China, as the host for the 2008 Olympic Games, was the first of seven emerging states (from 2008–2022) to host SMEs and repre-sents a bold move on behalf of the IOC, signalling the international 'acceptance' of this one-time pariah state. While the IOC would maintain it is simply being fair by shifting the Olympics to what the then head of FIFA, Sepp Blatter, referred to as 'New Lands'

(Blatter, 2011), it is very clear that the idea is to extend and spread the Olympic (and FIFA) corporate brand to new and large markets. China, just as East Germany and the Soviet Union before it, adopted sport and sporting glory to assist domestically in validating its own political ideology, with several commentators arguing that the Beijing Games was more about propping up domestic support than showcasing the nation to the wider world (see Brownwell, 2008; Collins, 2008). Scholars have argued, however, that there is little doubt that China used the Olympics to promote its rise as an emerging power and aid its integration and agency in the international system (see Lee et al., 2010: 132). If one accepts Cull's notion of the Olympic project itself 'as an exercise in public diplomacy' (2008: 119), then it is clear that China, more than most hosts, used the Beijing Games in search of the politics of attraction and the soft power that comes with this (Cull, 2008: 134; see also Tomlinson, 2010: 144).

Beijing's opening ceremony offered a mix of ancient tradition and the new modern nation, and can be read as an attempt to project China's power to a global audience (the difference in style and funding of the opening ceremony to London 2012 – £64 million as opposed to £27 million – could not have been starker). Weixing Chen (2010: 815) offers a gushing description of China's use of the event which 'through the imposing opening ceremony of the Beijing Games...displayed to the world a Chinese-style narrative, highlighting the theme of harmony'. Brownell offers a much more sober reflection of what the Games mean for the most populous nation in the world and the one 'farthest from the political centres of the West both geographically and culturally...' (2009: 1; see also, 2008). Brownell, a sinologist, has shown how the attempt to understand China through the 'Western liberal orthodoxy' has led to several misunderstandings and misinterpretations. For example, Brownell cites the mechanics of the important '...host–guest relationship...':

> In accord with the Confucian tradition, hosting the Olympic Games was said to be similar to inviting a guest to one's home: the host's hospitality should help forge a relationship of trust that facilitates an honest exchange of opinions afterwards...Only an uncivilized guest would start criticizing the host before he even arrived, and this was how many Chinese people viewed the Western criticism of China during the lead-up to the games (2012: 310).

The successful bid to host the 2008 Olympics itself needs to be understood as part of China's rise in prominence in recent years. It is clear that Beijing has done for China what elite sport success achieved for another authoritarian regime, East Germany: international recognition (see also Xu, 2006: 104; Dennis and Grix, 2012).

China's hosting of the Olympics could be read not as an attempt to present a changed nation to the international community, but rather one that has arrived. China is not attempting to be part of a 'core', occupied as it is by advanced capitalist states, but rather an emerging alternative power to those in the West, as is clearly evident in its interventions in Africa and its dealings with foreign visitors hungry for Chinese trade. Nevertheless, domestically the Chinese authorities described the Olympics as their 'coming out party' (Cha, 2009: 3).

2010 World Cup: South Africa (and Africa's) renaissance

Although many commentators expressed surprise at the awarding of the 2010 World Cup to South Africa, Pretoria had been applying for, and hosting, what Black termed 'second' and 'third' order events (Black, 2007: 2014) for many years. Shortly after becoming a democracy in the post-apartheid era (1994), South Africa played host to the very successful 1995 Rugby World Cup – along with symbolic and iconic photographs of Nelson Mandela sporting the victorious Springbok's colours – the 1996 African Cup of Nations, the 1999 All-Africa Games and the 2003 Cricket World Cup (Black and Van Der Westhuizen, 2004; Cornelissen, 2004, 2010, 2011; Knott et al., 2012). Like China, success in bidding for these events signalled the international credibility of this once-pariah state, providing a platform for the exercise of the politics of attraction.

The difference between all the events above and the World Cup is its global reach (media coverage of the event reached an estimated 46 per cent of the world's population; FIFA, 2013). After controversially losing out to Germany in the bid to host the 2006 World Cup amid accusations of bribery and racism (Cornelissen, 2008), South Africa was awarded the event in 2004 in what, it now transpires, was another bidding process mired in corruption. Following in the footsteps of the World Cup in Germany was particularly difficult, as the 2006 event was a spectacular success in all manner of ways, ranging from the lack of violence, the innovative use of 'fan miles', to a very efficient transport infrastructure (see Grix, 2013a). The crucial difference was that Germany is an advanced and very wealthy state with little (recent) history of high crime and poverty; South Africa is an emerging state with a long history of both. The similarities between these two states, however, lay in one of the key motives behind hosting the event: the attempt to use it as a form of public diplomacy to improve the image of their nation among foreign publics abroad.

Whereas Germany's image was tarnished by the Nazi past – other, less important, negative stereotypes include 'dull', 'boring' and (ruthlessly) 'efficient' (Grix and Lacroix, 2006) – Lepp and Gibson (2011) point to a host of images that encompass the whole of Africa, of which South Africa is part. These include social, political and economic instability, war, terrorism, corruption, (violent) crime, disease, poor healthcare facilities and so on (2011: 213; see also Donaldson and Ferreira, 2009: 7) which embody the unattractive nature of African politics to others.

Scarlett Cornelissen rightly sees South Africa's hosting of the World Cup in part as an exercise in post-apartheid state-building in which the state used the event for both internal state-building and external showcasing. She suggests: 'South Africa's bid to host the 2010 FIFA World Cup reflected the meshing of sport, politics, diplomatic ambitions and domestic developmental objectives' (Cornelissen, 2014). South Africa framed its bid and the event itself as 'pan-African'; that is, it represented the African continent (Cornelissen et al., 2011; see also Ndlovu-Gatsheni, 2011). If state-building was one key goal, reimaging South Africa and Africa more generally was the other. This was the politics of African attraction by the continent's leading power.

South Africa's 2010 World Cup legacies

There is no doubt that South Africa took a risk in inviting the world's media to scrutinize its country for four weeks. With 49 per cent of the population living under the poverty line, 25 per cent of its population unemployed, an 18 per cent HIV/AIDS infection rate and an extremely high crime rate, it is easy to understand the misgivings of the world media that South Africa was even considered for the World Cup (Harris, 2011: 408). Despite these concerns, consensus among commentators is that this event has definitely put the new democratic South Africa on the map, fulfilling one of their central foreign policy goals of presenting itself as a 'global middle power' (Cornelissen, 2011: 485). Several studies evidence this successful socializing of others, reporting changing perceptions among visitors to South Africa from negative to more positive

(Donaldson and Ferreira, 2007, 2009; Holtzhausen and Fullerton, 2013). Some 309,000 visitors came to South Africa for the World Cup (South Africa Information, 2011). The vast majority were in South Africa just for the sport, with some 51 per cent suggesting that they would never have thought of visiting had it not been for the Finals (Knott et al., 2012). Controversy around overinflated budgets, unnecessary extravagance – especially in building the picturesque Green Point stadium, an ultramodern football stadium in Cape Town – remain.

Despite this, there is, therefore, some evidence to show that South Africa has been able to socialize foreign publics as the first African state to hold a global SME and that it was successful in practising the politics of attraction through hosting the 2010 World Cup.

2014 World Cup and 2016 Olympic Games: Brazil's shift from regional to global power

Brazil has, since Stefan Zweig's prognosis of Brazil as the 'Land of the Future' in 1941, struggled under a sense of burden of expectation (Rohter, 2012). It would appear that finally Zweig's prescient notes on his adopted homeland are coming to fruition because Brazil, perhaps more so than any other BRICS country, is at the forefront of the new 'emerging powers' discourse. Already the world's fourth largest democracy, towards the end of 2011 Brazil overtook the UK to become the world's sixth largest economy, thereby underlining the claim to the title of emerging power. While wider debates rage about the ways in which Brazil will exercise its newly found power in the international system (see Vieira, 2012), the hosting of the two largest SMEs in the world within two years has received far less scrutiny. Brazil is no novice at showcasing itself through large-scale events: the successful staging of the 2007 PAG was clearly a precursor to winning the right to host both the 2014 World Cup and the 2016 Olympic Games (see Curi et al., 2011). This was followed by the successful hosting of the global Rio+20 United Nations Conference on Sustainable Development in 2012. It is clear that the rationale behind wanting to stage the two biggest sporting events in the world is simply an extension of this global exposure. The vast majority of emerging states use SMEs to announce their arrival on the world stage as major players, as a so-called 'coming out' party (Kuper, 2011) or 'to signal their "graduation" to the status...of advanced state' (Black and Van Der Westhuizen, 2004: 1206); however, in Brazil's case, it is not simply to announce that it is ready to join the advanced Western capitalist states (that is, move from the so-called 'periphery' to the 'core'), but to indicate its shift from a regional actor to a global actor in international affairs (see Vieira, 2012). As suggested, SMEs are just part of a package of measures used by emerging states to express and enhance their soft power; however, sport has a universal appeal and an ability to cross deep cleavages in society, which makes them attractive to event hosts, but also to a global audience and are an essential factor in the politics of attraction exercised by hosting states.

Winning the bidding process for the Olympics or the World Cup usually sends out several positive signals of inclusion and acceptance in the international system: being chosen for two in short succession suggests that the IOC and FIFA have enough trust in Brazil to put on successful events and a belief that it can put its historical in-fighting to one side, streamline its culture of opaque *bureaucracy* and clamp down on the rampant corruption linked to its political elite (Rohter, 2012); that is, refashion the unattractive political and social elements. The latter is reflected in Brazil's 72nd spot in the 2013 'corruption index' put together by the non-governmental organization Transparency International, joint with South Africa and eight places above China. This position appeared justified when, in March 2012, Ricardo Teixeira, a long-term stalwart in FIFA and the head of Brazil's Football Confederation, was forced to resign following allegations of corruption (*Guardian*, 2012). As mentioned above, using SMEs in an attempt to socialize others as part of a soft power strategy is a double-edged sword and can backfire, notably due to the intense media focus so central to these events. While both events are likely to be 'mediated', that is, camera angles and media coverage will avoid the favelas, traffic problems and the like (see Curi et al., 2011: 145), the presence of foreign journalists and the availability of social media will mean that Brazil will be seen and known as it is.

If, however, both events are successful, staging these events will be another step on the way to becoming an embedded regional, and global, power. Brazil's 'rise' is clearly not just economic; this is likely to be matched by political influence as witnessed with the examples of China and South Africa, both of whom are, post-event, established participants in multilateral summits such as the G8.

Summary

Public diplomacy through sport has long been part of a state's foreign policy armoury. This chapter set out to discuss the trends in the development of this area of study. Several new trends were noted, in particular the shift away from established advanced democracies using SMEs to showcase their nations towards the rise of so-called 'emerging' states as hosts. The concept of 'soft power' from IR was also introduced with which to understand the rationale behind states' desire to host sports megas. Such soft power strategies by states must be understood in the changed, post-9/11 environment of world politics.

Elite sport and sports megas are part and parcel of state soft power strategies: the attempt to showcase nations, alter tarnished national images and, generally, improve a nation's standing in the international order. This, in turn, it is thought, will improve diplomatic relations and trade relations between states.

It is quite clear that states with images in need of improvement are attracted to SMEs like moths to a light; however, as has been shown, inviting the world's media to scrutinize your state affairs is a risky business and may not result in the hoped-for legacies some states seek in return for their (usually very high) investment. What impact hosting an expensive mega event actually has on a state's diplomatic standing on the world stage is difficult to calculate; it is clear, however, that states think that hosting is generally beneficial. This is despite a long list of examples where hosting has led to what Brannagan and Giulianotti term 'soft disempowerment' (2014), that is, the opposite to what most hosts want from staging these expensive events.

Questions

- What are the 'legacies' that states hope to achieve through putting on an SME?
- What is 'soft power' and how do SMEs fit with this strategy?
- What is meant by the 'double-edged sword' of hosting sports megas?
- Why do you think 'emerging' states are interested in hosting SMEs?

Further Reading

- Fan, Y. (2006) 'Branding the nation: what is being branded?', *Journal of Vacation Marketing*, 12(1), 5–14.
- Grix, J. (ed) (2014) *Leveraging Legacies from Sports Mega-Events: Concepts and Cases*. Basingstoke: Palgrave Pivot.
- Horne, J. and Manzenreiter, W. (eds) (2006) *Sports Mega-Events: Social Scientific Analyses of a Global Phenomenon*, Sociological Review Monograph Series. Oxford: Blackwell.

Chapter 11

The Future of Sport Politics

The intention is not to offer a blow-by-blow summary of the preceding chapters. Rather, a discussion of the overarching and often overlapping themes should aid understanding of the processes that have led to sport becoming even more political than it has been in the past. Simply put, this text is an introduction to understanding why sport has become more politicized in the past 30–40 years. In doing so, it is hoped that any doubts as to whether sport is political, or whether sport and politics 'mix' in the real world, should have been put to one side. The following broad-brush categories are a way of attempting to capture the wider processes influencing sports development. Houlihan and Green (2008: 9), in discussing factors that have impacted on the convergence of elite sport systems (see Chapter 7), suggest that 'globalization, commercialisation and governmentalization' are central. Each state is subject to similar pressures, yet not all react to them in a similar fashion. There is little doubt, however, that these three overlapping 'pressures' play a part in the **politicization** of sport. Globally, states now compete to host elite sport events or to showcase their nation through elite sport success; even effectively 'buying-in' foreign nationals and naturalizing them instantly, so that a Kenyan citizen, for example, can represent Qatar at distance running almost overnight. The global reach of sport is unprecedented with football clubs in the English Premier League attracting millions of fans in places as far, and as dense in population, as India and China; star teams of the NFL in the USA are now making regular appearances at the sacred 'soccer' grounds of Wembley in England and also Europe.

The commercial potential of such untapped markets adds to the commodification of sport, a process that has accelerated since the mid-1980s. As sport become more lucrative for athletes, players and sponsors, the motives for taking part, the manner in which sport is delivered and consumed will change too, especially as social media and the internet as platforms for consuming and disseminating sport develop. The concept of 'governmentalization', discussed in Chapter 8, refers to both the increasing government involvement in sport and the process by which sport is governed. If governments of advanced capitalist states, 'emerging' states and even 'small' states are scrambling to host SMEs or achieve 'national' elite sport success, then the process by which governments involve themselves in sport is set to continue unabated.

The seven themes below represent just some of the broad topic areas that are likely to play a major role in sport politics in the future.

Themes likely to define sport politics in the future

The 'mainstreaming' of sport as an area of study

Over time it is likely that the political study of sport will begin to do what was called for in Chapter 2: there will be a reverse-flow of ideas from sports-related cases back to main academic disciplines, refining their concepts, theories and perspectives in doing so. Equally, the study of sport for political scientists and IR scholars is no longer likely to be simply understood as a 'hobby', and thus this topic will not be left to historians and sociologists to tackle, but rather it is likely to become a veritable Aladdin's cave for analysing phenomena that transcend the boundaries of the subject matter (Grix, 2010c). The role of sport in society is only just being understood; the 'feel-good' factor around SMEs and sporting occasions – discussed below – is clearly more than just ephemeral entertainment. How is it that rational educated citizens become irrational and narrow-minded once their team takes to the field? What is it about sport that can turn reason to irrationality? It is the same substance that prevents 'loyal' fans from exiting the sporting market, even when merchandise and ticket prices become overinflated; this, together with the unpredictable outcome of sport, plays into the hands of those who control sport (the agents, the owners, the sponsors, the major international governing bodies, such as FIFA and the IOC).

Within sports studies more broadly several nascent developments in the area of concept shaping have taken place. For example, here are just some of the concepts that have been employed extensively in sports studies:

- soft power
- social capital
- partnerships
- governance/governmentality.

The origins of these concepts are from IR, sociology, policy analysis and political science/sociology respectively. This is indicative of the magpie nature of sports studies: key concepts are drawn from a wide range of disciplines and sub-disciplines. Most concepts have a developmental history that needs to be taken into account, if they are to be applied correctly (Grix, 2010b); yet there is no reason why concepts cannot be developed and shaped when applied to the subject matter of sport. There is a burgeoning sports literature on each of the concepts listed above. In part, these debates play out in sports-related journals, which tend to have less impact and limited appeal. There is a trend, however, in which sport-focussed analyses, taking central themes such as those listed above, are making their way into 'mainstream' academic journals. Such a development translates into a wider audience for sports-related analysis which, in the long run, could enhance the reputation of the study of sport and will have an impact on the development of concepts back in the 'mainstream' disciplines.

Inherent 'tensions' in sport

There are several significant inherent tensions in sport, some of which have been around for over 100 years. When seeking to understand how sport politics is likely to develop, it seems prudent to reflect on the most persistent 'tensions' in sport. The following is a shortlist of just some of the most pressing:

A. Governments tend to support elite sport over both community and schools sport.
B. Amateur versus professional (business-like) delivery of sport policy/top-down government-led policy versus bottom-up street-level policy delivery.
C. The essence of sport versus its commodification and commercialization.

Elite versus community and schools sport

While policy priorities in states tend to oscillate frequently, sport policy has tended to focus on either 'sport for sports sake' or 'sport for development'. The former is linked to growing and improving sport *per se*, the latter to the broader social use of sport, that is, improving health and communities.

The demand for nations to achieve elite sport success and to stage large-scale expensive sports events appears to be increasing, therefore, it is likely that the sporting 'arm's race' is set to continue. This brings with it a policy focus on elite athletes, elite sport development and those elements of community and schools sport thought to be linked to the development of future elite sport stars. Despite a lack of research that indicates a causal relationship between elite sport success and the hosting of SMEs and an increase in mass participation in sport or physical activity, governments across the world continue to act *as if* this were the case.

Amateur versus professional (business-like) delivery of sport policy

The macro developments outlined at the beginning of this chapter have led to the professionalization of sport. In a sector dominated and serviced by volunteers this has and will lead to tensions. Once government monies are invested in sport, then clubs, organizations, policy delivery units and so on, become accountable; accountability brings with it a complex system of monitoring, checks and balances. Many volunteers are neither trained nor willing to engage with the process of 'governmentality' that attends modern government involvement in sport and seeks to control the conduct of those who work in this (still) overwhelmingly voluntary sector.

The clash between the professionalization of sport and volunteerism may not be new, but it will have a long-term impact on the development of individual sport (for example, athletics; see Chapter 8) and sport as a whole, for, if governments are selecting certain sports over others to support – usually in the hope of international glory – then this will clearly impact on citizens' access to and engagement with those sports over time.

The essence of sport versus its commodification and commercialization

This tension runs through many of the points made in this final chapter. The hyper-commercialization of sport is becoming far removed from the origins and joy surrounding sport in the first place. While there are heart-warming stories of UK Premier League footballers sending home wages to keep hundreds of relatives in developing countries, this does not detract from the fact that the average Premier League footballer earns more in a week than the UK national average wage of £26,500 per year (BBC, 2012). The irony is that such unbelievable wealth in one sports discipline does not seem to have a 'trickle down' effect to the grassroots of the game, just as elite sport success will not of its own accord 'trickle down' and inspire people to be active.

Sport and physical activity as a public good (sport as 'medicine')

Although there is widespread disagreement about whether humans are facing an 'obesity' crisis or not, there is clear research evidence to suggest that chronic disease is the main cause of death that people face. Research shows that non-communicable diseases kill 38 million people globally per annum. These diseases share the following risk factors: tobacco use, an unhealthy diet, alcohol abuse and physical inactivity (WHO, 2015). Given that physical inactivity is the fourth leading risk factor for mortality, it is very likely that interventions to raise physical activity among populations will become even more of a priority than they already are. Another factor driving physical activity is the soaring costs of health systems; logically, a fitter and healthier citizenry will put less of a strain on, and require less resources from, a nation's health care system.

The hyper-commercialization of elite sport and SMEs (see below) appears to be increasing along with levels of physical inactivity. This then is likely in the future to lead to a switch in funding away from 'white elephants' and underused and underutilized sporting facilities and stadia, towards longer-term investment in structural and environmental planning to encourage a more physically active citizenry. Clearly this will differ from state to state and their economic development. Many advanced capitalist states already have the infrastructure in place to host a major sports event. For example, Germany's hosting of the 2006 World Cup involved updating a few stadia and slight improvements to a road system already the envy of a majority of countries in the world. Many advanced capitalist states are slowly becoming wary of the hollow 'legacy' promises of SMEs, as the list of spectacular 'no' votes to bidding for the 2022 Winter Olympics testifies (this included Germany, Sweden, Norway, Poland and Switzerland; Wetzel, 2014).

Rather than spending upwards of £10 billion on a bombastic Olympics (London 2012) or US$55 billion on a Winter Olympics (the most expensive Olympics ever, Sochi 2014), governments are more likely to introduce free swimming or gym use to large sections of the population, especially as this is seen, in the long run, to ease pressure on a state's healthcare system. A report in the UK claimed that if motorists swapped their cars for bicycles for just five minutes per day, this could save the National Health Service some £250 million per annum due to its contribution to inactivity-related illnesses (British Cycling, 2014). However, the UK's infrastructure has a long way to go before it is deemed safe by many to tempt them to begin cycling. Painting a thin white line on the side of the road is unlikely to inspire confidence among frightened would-be cyclists. If sport and physical activity are to increase, investment in urban design and planning needs to take place to encourage people to walk, cycle and be active. A visit to several European countries where cycling is second nature would reveal, quickly, that designated cycle lanes instil confidence in cyclists and increases their numbers exponentially.

Social 'leveraging' and the 'feel-good' factor

Ironically, perhaps, one of the possible sources of good that could come from sport and SMEs is also the least researched and understood. Rather than remaining an empty politician's slogan or simply a well-cited but little understood notion of something that accompanies SMEs, the 'feel-good' factor is likely to become the object of serious study. As part of the 'social leveraging' of SMEs and other significant public events, more sustained research will determine what it constitutes, how and whether it can be enhanced, and what purpose it may serve in society beyond simply entertainment. The 'feel-good' factor needs to be studied alongside other concepts employed to capture the excitement surrounding sporting events such as the 'carnivalesque' in sport. The latter is

...a blanket term that refers to those traditional, historical and enduring forms of social ritual, such as festivals, fairs and feasts, that provide sites of 'ordered disorder'. (Crabbe and Blackshaw, 2004: 53)

In terms of sport, 'carnivalesque' has often been used to describe crowd behaviour in which people lose themselves in the collective moment. This has close parallels with several early studies, which offer a starting point for an analysis of the phenomenon that clearly exists among citizens and spectators prior to, during and shortly after major sporting events. Chief among these is Durkheim's study of religion (1912/1995) in which he focused on ritual and developed the concept of 'collective effervescence' to describe the sense of 'we-ness' among worshippers who experienced strong emotions and 'psychic exaltation' (Olaveson, 2001: 97). Importantly, Durkheim understood such collective gatherings as vital for society, for: 'It is through them that the group affirms and maintains itself...Thus a rite is something other than a game; it belongs to the serious side of life' (1995: 386). This work, together with Turner's (1968) very similar notion of 'communitas' (effectively a 'communion of minds'), offers a launching pad for an investigation into the ritual that attends SMEs. Central to this is the belief that the 'feel-good' factor is an essential part of community bonding – local and national – as witnessed by the public outpouring of emotion around 'royal weddings, civic parades [and] remembrance gatherings' (Giulianotti, 2005b: 6). That is, while necessarily an ephemeral phenomenon, vanishing gradually after the event, it may well serve a greater purpose in society. Similar studies need to be undertaken around the Paralympics and the 'feel-good' factor attending the amazing feats of Paralympic athletes. There has been much talk about such events being able to change attitudes towards disability in society more widely; there has been less sustained research, however. Interestingly, governments bidding for SMEs talk confidently in terms of a 'feel-good' factor, despite a lack of clear conceptual and empirical work to base this on.

The notion of 'communitas' has been applied in sports studies to the 'rituals' carried out by football fans (Bromberger, 1995) and even hooligans (Armstrong, 1998), yet there is a lack of work on the collective experiences of (general) spectators and SMEs. For example, many of the spectators caught up in the 'communitas' experienced in the specially designed 'fan miles' outside the football stadia at the German 2006 World Cup were not ardent football fans (Grix, 2013a: 15). Recent studies of the brain have highlighted the neurons associated with empathetic and social behaviour; indications are that the sense of shared belonging humans experience around such mass events as sport serves an important social purpose (Keysers, 2013).

Thus, along with refocusing SMEs towards the spectacle of sport away from a commercial fair (see below), a sustained effort to leverage social benefits for citizens ought to be central to such undertakings.

Sport and (national) identity

Representative sports have always been bound up with national identity and this is likely to remain unchanged. What is changing, however, is the pace at which states are 'buying' up teams and athletes to represent their adoptive countries. This is especially the case in cash-rich but – in terms of sport – performance-poor nations, such as Qatar. Qatar has been blessed with immense reserves of 'liquid gold' (oil), but has a very small population with few home-grown champion athletes or sports stars. On the face of it, drafting in someone from a foreign country to represent another nation with which they have no cultural, historical or linguistic connection sounds farcical, but this trend is on the increase. Wilson Kipketer, a Kenyan by birth, broke Sebastian Coe's long-standing 800 metres world record while wearing the vest of Denmark; Bernard Lagat, still competing at world-class-level athletics into his forties, made the news when, after winning a 3,000 metres indoors race in Britain, the organizers belted out 'Born in the USA' on the arena public address system. Lagat is also a Kenyan by birth (*Athletics Weekly*, 2014).

It is not just small states seeking international recognition that are involved in 'adopting' athletes from other countries, often on spurious grounds. One of the most political cases was that of Zola Budd, a South African, who was granted British Citizenship in a rushed – and clearly politically expedited – process to allow her to compete for Britain at the Los Angeles Olympics in 1984, given that her home country was banned. A campaign led by the right-leaning *Daily Mail* and premised on the fact that Budd's grandfather was British, saw, for the first time, protests at the blue-ribbon English National Cross Country Championships in 1984, in which protesters against South African apartheid rushed onto the course and stopped Budd from continuing a race she was tipped to win (*LA Times*, 1984). Things went from bad to worse, for at the Olympics in the 3,000 metres and under intense media scrutiny Budd not only failed to bring home a medal (she wore a British vest, but South African sport was fully behind her), she tripped up (accidentally) America's golden girl, Mary Decker, who was the favourite to win gold at her home Olympics (see also Guelke, 1986: 140).

Despite the fact that it is increasingly difficult to speak of a 'nation' with a particular 'national identity', the trend towards using representative sport to portray a nation shows no signs of abating.

Securitization of sport

One of the clear legacies of SMEs is that of security. A cottage industry has grown up around this subject area, especially following London 2012 and the Sochi Winter Olympics, both of which took the securitization of sport to new levels.

One clear and unintentional legacy from London 2012 is that of a 'security' Olympics. Events like those in Munich in 1972 haunt organizers; security concerns since '9/11' have seen Olympic security grow in both scale and complexity. This process was compounded by the July 2005 London bombings which took place the day after the announcement that London would host the Olympics in 2012. It is relatively clear why terrorist groups would target the Olympic Games: it is the largest sporting event in the world, attracts a (cumulative) global audience in excess of 4 billion (in Beijing, for example; Horne, 2010: 29), with over 200 nations present, and it represents the most potent and symbolic arena in which many states attempt to increase their national prestige through winning medals and their position on the medal table. There is also unprecedented 24-hour media coverage of the event through a wide variety of media, social media and the internet. London, then, will be remembered as the most 'securitized' summer Games to date, with some commentators referring to the event as 'lockdown London' (Milne, 2012: 31; see also Coeffee, 2012). The mantle of the most 'securitized' Games ever has now shifted to Sochi after Russia effectively cordoned off the area around the Olympics to prevent any terrorist attacks, similar, for example, to the suicide bombers who struck in Volgograd shortly before the start of the Games, killing 16 people and injuring 50 others (*Guardian*, 2014a).

There is a clear 'risk' in staging SMEs, as the threat of a terrorist attack or similar is never far away. The logistics involved in securing an Olympic Games in Britain, for example, has been described as the biggest military and security operation in British peace-time history. The global security firm, G4S, failed to secure the London 2012 Olympics. This private firm, employed to secure the Games, admitted that it would not be able to provide the requisite number of staff needed on time and so the British army were, quite literally, sent in to secure the event. The scandal around the private security firm, G4S, raises central questions for those interested in politics. There is a sense of delicious irony in the strategy of outsourcing security to a private firm that then has to be brought back on track by public services (police and army) which, at the same time, were undergoing major cuts in their budgets, in order to reduce public spending to allow the employment of more 'efficient' private sector providers. It is quite clear that issues around security threaten to ruin an SME. In London, for example, measures taken to prevent a security risk included: surrounding the Olympic park with an 11 mile (17,700 metres), £80 million, 5,000-volt electric fence and providing more British troops than those employed at war (at the time) in Afghanistan (approximately 13,500). The UK even stationed anti-aircraft missiles on residential roofs close to the Olympic park and positioned a Navy vessel on the River Thames.

Much of the expense for the Sochi Winter Olympics was due to security. A 'wall of security' surrounded the city, with the one road leading into it guarded heavily, and some 40,000 security personnel involved in securing the Games (BBC, 2014b). The geopolitical position of Sochi is clearly a contributing factor, as it lies close to the North Caucasus, a notoriously volatile region. Nonetheless, the sums are breath-taking: US$55 million for a Winter Olympics which has a far smaller following than its Summer cousin and in sports disciplines that are very unlikely to inspire the masses to turn to physical activity to get fit.

The increasing securitization of major sporting events runs in parallel to their unstoppable growth in terms of size and commercial value. Fans of sports events – while wishing to remain safe – are not the beneficiaries of such continual expansion. Commerce more broadly and security-related firms more specifically are set to profit handsomely from the 'inevitable' growth of SMEs.

The hyper-commercialization of sport: the tipping point

It is hard to see an end to the spiralling costs of hosting SMEs or the increasing resources states invest in elite sport. At the time of writing, the Sochi Olympics entered the record books, mostly for the wrong reasons. It was the most expensive Olympics ever (see the 'securitization of sport'), not the most expensive Winter Olympics, but the most expensive of all Olympics. For those who baulked at London's £10 billion plus, US$55 billion plus must be incomprehensible. To remain unmoved by this type of expenditure on a group of very niche sports is difficult. The trend of pouring resources into sports events, facilities, security and the festivals that attend them is likely to continue, as long as the demand to host SMEs remains high and the key international governing bodies remain unaccountable.

There are some signs that a 'tipping point' is being reached, at least in advanced capitalist states who have already hosted events or have looked carefully at the broken promises and unfulfilled legacies of a majority of previous SMEs. Clearly different states at different stages of development have diverging opinions about the ability of elite sport and SMEs to bring them the prestige they crave. Brazil, for example, has no recognizable elite sport system to systematically nurture and produce world-class talent in sport. However, they are hosting the Olympics in 2016 and their nation will probably finish in the 20s on the coveted medal table. This may trigger a 'critical juncture' in the national sporting consciousness and lead to a major investment in an elite sport system, as has been the case in many other nations. The point here is the inevitability of the upward trajectory of elite sport performance and states' desire to obtain this; coupled with the inevitable trend towards bigger and more bombastic SMEs, turning over more revenue than ever before, attracting more sponsors and wealth than ever before, it appears that SME hosting is moving to a point of hyper-commercialization that is producing a backlash among citizens who would like to see taxpayer's money being invested in more socially relevant areas.

The referendum of citizens of Bavaria and St Moritz in which they voted 'no' to their region bidding for the 2022 Winter Olympics is the first example: both are very wealthy regions who see the negative side of hosting SMEs. Environmental damage and the non-transparency of the IOC were behind the Germans' 'no'. According to Ludwig Hartmann, a Green Party member of the Bavarian state legislature:

> The vote is not a signal against the sport, but against the non-transparency and the greed for profit of the IOC (International Olympic Committee)... I think all possible Olympic bids in Germany are now out of question. The IOC has to change first. It's not the venues that have to adapt to the IOC, but the other way around (Mackay, 2013).

The sentiment in Bavaria is clear: reform of the IOC and a return to sport are what people want, not more of the same. Interestingly, Brazil, an 'emerging' state, provides a second example. The demonstrations surrounding the 2014 World Cup and 2016 Olympics are, to a large extent, motivated by similar sentiments to that of Bavaria and St Moritz: Why is Brazil spending precious resources on incredulous investments when their health and education systems are in desperate need of finance? Riots in Rio de Janeiro were squarely aimed at the government, especially after an announcement in January 2014 of rising public transport costs, which sparked demonstrations in which people cried 'FIFA pay my fare' and a journalist was killed by a 'homemade explosive device' (BBC, 2014e). Such demonstrations could indicate a 'tipping point' in public opinion and a need for SME hosts to stop operating in an 'evidence-free' zone and finally take notice of the outcome of dozens of previous SMEs across the world.

Thus, it is possible that there may be a return to the roots of sport, for much of what has been discussed – from the 'feel-good' factor to 'nation branding' – is not achieved through fancy stadia, but rather through the sports action on the field or in the arena.

Given the above, it is highly likely that cheating in sport will continue apace. Cheating ranges from doping in sport (see Chapter 9), match-fixing, unsporting behaviour (on the field) and any form of attempting to alter the outcome of a sporting event by a means not allowed by the rules of the game in question.

Conclusion

Throughout the preceding volume the discussion has rarely, if much at all, focused on sport *per se*. This was not a deliberate choice or conscious decision, but rather the nature of the subject matter: sport politics. If one adopts the 'arena' understanding of politics, outlined in Chapter 1, then all social relations could be construed as political. The reader should by now be left in no doubt that sport is inherently political; that sport is becoming increasingly political; that states are becoming increasingly interested in manipulating sport for non-sporting ends; that government involvement with and investment in sport – from all political ideologies – is on the increase; that alongside the politicization of sport, their commodification and commercialization are also intensifying. At the same time, citizens around the world are dying from the opposite of physical exertion and prowess: physical inactivity. Sedentary lifestyles and poor diets – once restricted to rich capitalist states – are affecting populations as far apart as India, the USA, Qatar, Australia and China, making no discrimination against political views or ethnic backgrounds. It would appear that the higher the levels of physical inactivity and the associated illnesses that accompany it, the more states wish to invest in elite sport athletes and host SMEs in the hope of reversing the trend, despite the lack of evidence to substantiate such a causal claim.

The purpose of this book was to introduce the reader to sport politics, to familiarize the reader with the debates, concepts and themes covered by this emerging sub-discipline, to prepare the reader for further, in-depth study of some of the topics introduced, skirted over or touched on. Further, the aim was to equip the reader with the introductory knowledge necessary to grasp how and why sport can be understood as political and to encourage them to look beyond the gloss and spin often associated with sport at all levels, be it as a cure for society's ills or for national 'glory'.

Glossary

The following glossary of terms lists the words marked in bold throughout the main text. Most of the following words are either explained in the main text or their meanings are obvious from the context in which they have been used. The best idea is to look at both the Glossary *and* the word or term in the text to get a better understanding of it.

Cold War: this 'war' was unusual in that there was no actual fighting; the 'war' was carried out along ideological lines, in the main between 'capitalist' and 'communist' states, beginning a few years after the end of the Second World War. Historians do not agree on the exact dates, but a rule of thumb would be 1947 to 1991: the first is two years after the total surrender of Germany; the latter the end of Soviet rule. In summary, the 'war' was really a state of political tension between the USA (and its allies) on the one hand and the Soviet Union (and its allies) on the other. Over a period of more than 40 years many instances occurred that almost led to military conflict between the 'communist' Soviet side and the 'capitalist' USA side. As tensions built up, so too did each side's arsenal of weapons, which led them to engage in what was termed an 'arm's race'. The latter is said to have contributed considerably to the Soviet downfall in 1991, as scarce resources were poured into ever more sophisticated weapons and deterrents. The term 'Cold War' has been attributed to George Orwell in the late 1940s, who went on to write the best-selling novels *Animal Farm* and *Nineteen Eighty-Four*, which looked critically at the misuse of power under dictatorial rule. For this volume it ought to be noted that international sporting success was seen as one of the key ways to showcase a state's socio-economic system during this period; thus, 'success' on the sports field often equated to the 'success' of either communism or capitalism.

Commercialization of sport: this process is understood in the present volume as one that is bound up with the professionalization and politicization of sport. Also, to relate the story of sports commercialization without reference to the role of the media would be impossible (see Chapters 4 and 5). Generally, the mid-1960s is cited as the start of the commercialization of sport, although it differs from sport to sport. The Los Angeles Olympics of 1984 could be looked upon as the turning point in the history of sport, after which the pace of commercialization has increased dramatically. The London 2012 Olympics was the most commercial Games to date: the overlapping interests of the media, sponsors and international sports organizations have combined to turn the Olympics into a multi-billion dollar extravaganza. Many bemoan the fact that commerce has stripped the soul out of sport and that many of the dubious decisions made around staging sports mega-events and constructing underutilized sporting facilities are driven by an elite who benefit the most from the event at the expense of the tax-paying citizens in the hosting state. In part, the International Olympic Committee's (IOC) '2020' agenda is about attempting to put a brake on the inexorable drive towards commercialization that characterizes today's Olympic events; it remains to be seen whether future IOC events return to a focus on sport or continue their journey towards ever greater commercial gains for stakeholders, sponsors and the IOC respectively.

Communism: communism is a socio-economic system that is premised on the notion that there is no private ownership and no social class system. The following captures the essence of a communist regime type by stating that communism is:

> An economic and social system envisioned by the nineteenth-century German scholar Karl Marx. In theory, under communism, all means of production are owned in common, rather than by individuals. In practice, a single authoritarian party controls both the political and economic systems (Dictionary Reference, 2015).

The distinction between 'theory' and 'practice' is well made. On paper communism appears a very fair system that cares for all; in practice, however, the way in which 'communism' has often been implemented has led to dictatorships akin to those described by George Orwell (see Cold War) in which a small elite prosper at the expense of the majority. For this volume it is useful to note that communist regimes (the Soviet Union and its satellite states) were among the most successful in sport during the Cold War and beyond. There is little need for political compromise and consensus in dictatorships, so – as in East

Germany – unprecedented resources can be poured into producing champion athletes without discussion.

Community sport: while it is relatively easy to distinguish between performance and elite sport on the one hand and recreational sport on the other, the category of 'community sport' is often lumped together under 'grassroots' sport. Grassroots sport tends to refer to amateur sports participation played for fun, not involving any payment and with participants not necessarily striving to become better at the event in which they are taking part. As with all definitions, there will be, of course, exceptions. All Olympic athletes will have to start somewhere, such as a taste of football in the park or dabbling in athletics at school; grassroots sport is where every future champion begins her or his career. The term 'community sport' overlaps with grassroots sport, but can be taken to mean *more organized* sport, either through local authorities, private and public sports facilities, private and community clubs, sports centres and so on. It is fair to say that 'community sport' is not as attractive to governments as 'elite sport' and it can be looked upon as its poor cousin. The support that community sport attracts will differ, of course, from state to state. Brazil, for example, appears to have a less developed system of state-funded community sport than the UK.

Emerging states: this term is usually reserved for states that are seen as up-and-coming in the economic, but also political sense. The 'BRICS' acronym (Brazil, Russia, India, China, South Africa) flagged up the next group of states where fast growth and rising power was likely to take place. Interestingly, all of the BRICS states have used or are in the process of using sports mega-events to consolidate their arrival on the world stage. Having said that, some states, such as India, are unhappy with the notion of an 'emerging' state because they view themselves as already 'emerged'. Equally, some 'emerging' states, for example, Brazil, do not see themselves as attempting to become an advanced Western state (this lies behind the implication of 'emerging'), but rather see themselves developing from a regional into a global power in their own right. Sports megas appear to belong to this journey, as all of the BRICS states have staged one. The latest acronym of 'emerging' states is 'MINT': that is, Mexico, Indonesia, Nigeria and Turkey. It remains to be seen whether the latter three will ever stage an Olympic Games (Mexico did in 1968) or a Fédération Internationale de Football Association World Cup.

Epistemology: derived from the Greek words *episteme* (knowledge) and *logos* (reason), epistemology is the theory of knowledge. Epistemological considerations depend on beliefs about the nature of knowledge. Also, assumptions about forms of knowledge, access to knowledge and ways of acquiring and gathering knowledge are epistemological issues (Holloway, 1997: 54). All of the above impact on the research process and, importantly, data collection and analysis. Epistemology refers to the 'strategies through which a particular theory gathers knowledge and ensures that its reading of phenomena is superior to rival theories' (Rosamond, 2000: 7, 199).

Government to governance: the notion behind the shift from 'government' to 'governance' is a devolving of power from top-down 'big' government towards more democratic delivery of public policy (including sport policy) that is nearer to the end-user, the public. This debate, carried out in and about mature democratic states, has led to a reconceptualization of the 'Westminster' style of government prevalent in Australia, New Zealand and, of course, the UK. Many commentators have shown, however, that sport policy – especially since governments have become much more interested in it – is still very much government-driven. This has led – and is leading – to several developments in those sports disciplines dependent on state funding, as the Olympic cycle steers policy towards sport in which the chances of a medal are highest, rather than where developmental needs are greatest.

Legacy: the term 'legacy' is much used in relation to sports mega-events (SMEs) and can be fruitfully understood in connection with 'leveraging' strategies (see below). Many states 'hope' their expensive sporting spectacle brings them what they desire (for example, economic wealth in the shape of foreign tourists, inward direct investment and so on); the thinking here is the event itself will act as a catalyst to achieve the desired 'legacy'. At its most basic, a 'legacy' is generally what is left after an event or a person's term of office (for example, a political legacy) has finished. Its use and overuse in the SME literature and by SME 'boosters' (that is, SME advocates and supporters) has rendered it hollow, to the point where a 'legacy' of an event is simply a given. However, recent research on 'leveraging' has pointed to the (fairly simple) fact that without a pre-event strategy to 'leverage' a legacy (that is, get the most out of an event through specific and precise interventions), 'legacy' is likely to remain a hope. The majority of touted 'legacies' from major SMEs remain unsubstantiated, contested and underanalysed.

Legitimacy: a legitimate state is one which is recognized by other legitimate states in accordance with (international) law; those that lack such legitimacy have often sought to use sport to gain it. International governing bodies of sport have been involved in precipitating such recognition by welcoming would-be states into the sporting fraternity, in particular, the Fédération Internationale de Football Association (FIFA) World Cup and the Olympics. Interesting, perhaps, is the fact that both FIFA and the International Olympic Committee are not 'legitimate' in the democratic sense of being both accountable to the public or a government representing a public or of representing the voice of those who have voted them in office.

Leveraging: this term is inextricably bound up with 'legacy' (see above) and refers, simply, to a pre-event strategy to attempt to gain the most out of a major sports event rather than simply 'hoping' a legacy will happen. It is clear that would-be hosts ought to learn from past events – especially those that have managed to 'leverage' a legacy from a sports mega-event (SME) – and implement long-term leveraging strategies with which to derive the most societal benefit as possible from their one-off event. Alas, to date 'social' leveraging – obtaining the most from an event for the host's citizens – does not appear to be high on the agenda. It is astonishing how long the list is of wasted opportunities for leveraging strategies to be put in place around SMEs. Even the Brazilian Fédération Internationale de Football Association World Cup of 2014 learnt little from the past, with the vast majority of football stadia built for the event chronically underused and draining much needed, scarce resources within a year of the event. This is another case where a lack of leveraging strategies gave way to fanciful legacy rhetoric for short-term gain for some individuals at the expense of the majority.

Ontology/ontological assumptions: ontology is a branch of metaphysics concerned with the nature of being. The first part of the word comes from the Greek verb equivalent to the English 'to be'. It can be understood as the basic image of social reality on which a theory is based. It can, however, be better understood as the way in which we view the world; it is our starting point in research, upon which the rest of the process is based. Ontological claims are 'claims and assumptions that are made about the nature of social reality, claims about what exists, what it looks like, what units make it up and how these units interact with each other. In short, ontological assumptions are concerned with what we believe constitutes social reality' (Blaikie, 2000: 8). Your 'ontological position', whether you know it or not, is implicit even before you choose your topic of study. We all have views on how the world is made up and what the most important components of the social world are.

Politicization (of sport): throughout this volume the politicization of sport has been discussed as a modern development. This is only partially correct, given that sport has been used and manipulated for political ends for a great number of years. What is meant by the more recent developments in the politicization of sport is the increase in interest that governments of all regime types have shown in sport, be it elite sport, sport policy initiatives for the masses or hosting sports mega-events. The 'magic' of sport has always been present; its alleged ability to cure several of society's ills, however, has come of age in an era of obesity, physical inactivity and increasing wealth. This joins a longer list of ailments for which sport offers a relatively quick and cheap cure: social exclusion, violent behaviour, extreme poverty, breaking down ethnic barriers to name but a few. While sport is a unique social phenomena enjoyed by millions of people across the world, the key structural features that lead to the societal cleavages touched on above need to be addressed before sport can work their magic.

Politics: generally, there are two ways of understanding 'politics'. First, it refers to the formal institutions of government (parliament, government departments, ministers, the president or prime minister and so on) and the ideologies that underpin different political stances. Second, a much broader understanding of the 'political' includes everything to do with power, power relations, and the distribution and origin of power. So, wherever there are power relations in society, 'politics' is said to exist. For some, this latter definition is too broad, however, this volume adopts such an understanding of 'politics' because the narrow definition of politics as the locus of state power reveals little about the way in which power is exercised and resources distributed outside the (limited) confines of political institutions. Much of what comes under 'sport politics' – as discussed in Chapter 2 – would not be included if such a narrow definition of politics were adopted.

Soft power: this is the latest in a long line of concepts that lend themselves to bandwaggoning: that is, authors pick up on a concept and employ it without knowledge of its origins, heritage and meaning. A similar process took place with 'social capital', a relatively new recruit to sports studies. Soft power, however, could be looked upon as a useful lens through which to understand the motives for investing in elite sport and elite sport events across a wide range of regime types. Soft power – as opposed to guns, bombs and coercion – is the business of persuasion and attraction; through sport, language, music, tourism and culture the idea is to influence foreign publics' view of a state; that is, influence their image abroad. Germany's hosting of the 2006 Fédération Internationale de Football Association World Cup was one of the most successful examples of just such a soft power strategy of which the hosting of a sports mega-event (SME) was part. Other states, however, may not achieve the same level of success, especially if they have skeletons in their closets because hosting a SME brings with it the very close scrutiny of the world media, as Qatar is finding out, the hard way.

Sport: as discussed in Chapter 1, this is not an easy term to define. At its root (*desporter*), sport refers to a diversion, yet this does not clarify much if commentators equate 'sport' with 'physical activity' and 'exercise'. One way of defining 'sport' is to take a rule-bound understanding of the term. Thus, 'sport' can generally be seen as physical activity that is governed by hard-and-fast rules, that is, set codes of behaviour and rules that have to be adhered to; this element also makes sport and sporting competitions comparative across continents, as all follow the same rules. A key difference between 'sport' and the other terms is that, in general, the former is competitive or contains at least an element of competition, whereas 'exercise' and 'physical activity' do not. Equally, sports are rule-bound activities in which there are (usually) clear winners and losers, which is one of the reasons why international sport appear so interesting (we cheer on our 'national' side or 'national' athlete but see Chapter 3 for some of the problems with equating a 'national' squad with a nation). Of note is the fact that there has been little take-up of the idea of international competitions in 'exercise'.

Sports mega-events: sports mega-events (or SMEs) is a term given to any large sporting event. In the literature, there is generally a distinction made between major SMEs (the Olympics and the Fédération

Internationale de Football Association World Cup) and 'second order' events such as the Pan American Games or the Commonwealth Games, that do not attract the same kind of global audience as the major SMEs, but do, however, have much in common with them. The literature on SMEs is relatively new. The motives behind wishing to stage SMEs, the benefits (or 'legacies') they are said to deliver and the leveraging strategies that are best used to achieve such legacies are contested. It is clear, however, that most event hosts tend to ignore what happened in previous events, thus proceeding to make similar mistakes in terms of overinflated expectations, underutilized sports facilities and going over budget. Each SME has its advocates – mostly drawn from the ranks of politicians, ex-sportspersons, international governing sports organizations, business and media elites – whose discourse combined provides a 'manufactured consent' around the benefits of the sports spectacle. A new development in SMEs – albeit only in democratic states – has been the introduction of plebiscites (that is, asking the electorate of potential hosts to vote) on whether to apply to host an event or not. Such a referendum is not available in some of the so-called 'emerging' states (see above); thus, the mistakes of the past discussed above look set to continue.

Bibliography

Adams, A. (2014) Social capital, network governance and the strategic delivery of grassroots sport in England, *International Review for the Sociology of Sport*, 49(5), 550–74.

Anderson, B. (1983) *Imagined Communities*. New York: Verso.

Andranovich, G., Burbank, M. J. and Heying, C. H. (2001) Olympic cities: lessons learned from mega-event politics, *Journal of Urban Affairs*, 23(2), 113–31.

Anholt-GfK Roper. (2010) *Nation Brand Index 2007–2011* [online]. Available at: http://www.gfkamerica.com/practice_areas/roper_pam/nbi_index/index.en.html [Accessed 01.02.15].

Allison, L. (ed) (1986) *The Politics of Sport*. Manchester: Manchester University Press.

Allison, L. (ed) (1993) *The Changing Politics of Sport*. Manchester: Manchester University Press.

Allison, L. (1998) Sport and civil society, *Political Studies*, 46(4), 709–26.

Allison, L. (2000) Sport and Nationalism, in Coakley, J. (ed) *Handbook of Sport Studies*. London: Routledge.

Allison, L. (ed) (2005) *The Global Politics of Sport*. London and New York: Routledge.

Armour, K. and Jones, R. (1998) *Physical Education Teachers' Lives and Careers: PE, Sport and Educational Studies*. Basingstoke: Falmer Press.

Armstrong, G. (1998) *Football Hooligans: Knowing the Score*. Oxford: Berg Publisher Ltd.

Athletics Weekly. (2014a) Dip finish, December 18th.

Athletics Weekly. (2014b) *Putting Family First Pays Off for 'Supermum' Jo Pavey* [online]. Available at: http://www.athleticsweekly.com/featured/putting-family-first-pays-supermum-jo-pavey-9494/ [Accessed 01.04.15].

Australian Commission. (2013) *Women's Sport* [online]. Available at: https://secure.ausport.gov.au/clearinghouse/knowledge_base/organised_sport/sport_and_government_policy_objectives/womens_sport [Accessed on 20.02.15].

Australian Institute for Sport. (2013) *Annual Report* [online]. Available at: http://www.ausport.gov.au/__data/assets/pdf_file/0011/552269/Annual_Report_2012-13_PDF_Version.pdf [Accessed 24.03.15].

Australian Tourist Commission. (2001) *Australian Tourist Commission Olympic Games Tourism Strategy* [online]. Available at: http://full text.ausport.gov.au/fulltext/2001/atc/olympicreview.pdf [Accessed 23.03.15].

Bailey, R., Collins, D., Ford, P., MacNamara, A., Toms, M. and Pearce, G. (2010) Participant development in sport: an academic review, *Sports Coach UK*, 4, 1–134.

Bairner, A. (2001) *Sport, Nationalism and Globalization: European and North American Perspectives.* Albany: SUNY Press.

Bairner, A. and Molnar, G. (eds) (2010) *The Politics of the Olympics: A Survey.* London and New York: Routledge.

Bandura, A. (1991) Social cognitive theory of self-regulation, *Organizational Behavior and Human Decision Processes*, 50(2), 248–87.

Barnes, S. (2006) *The Meaning of Sport.* London: Short Books.

Baviskar, A. (2010) Spectacular Events, City Spaces and Citizenship: The Commonwealth Games in Delhi, in Anjaria, J. S. and McFarlane, C. (eds) *Urban Navigations: Politics, Space and the City in South Africa.* New Delhi: Routledge.

Baviskar, A. (2014) Dreaming Big: Spectacular Events and the 'World-Class' City: The Commonwealth Games *in Delhi*, in Grix, J. (ed) *Leveraging Legacies from Sports Mega-Events: Concepts and Cases.* Basingstoke: Palgrave.

BBC. (2005) *Balco Boss Begins Jail Sentence* [online]. Available at: http://news.bbc.co.uk/sport1/hi/athletics/4350810.stm [Accessed 30.03.15].

BBC. (2010) *Russia's Drive to Improve Its Image* [online [10th June]]. Available at: http://www.bbc.co.uk/news/10285389 [Accessed 24.05.13].

BBC. (2012) *Average Earnings Rise by 1.4% to £26,500, Says ONS* [online]. Available at: http://www.bbc.co.uk/news/business-20442666 [Accessed 30.03.15].

BBC. (2014a) *Price of Football: Ticket Increases Outstrip Cost of Living* [online [15th October]]. Available at: http://www.bbc.co.uk/sport/0/football/29614980 [Accessed 20.02.14].

BBC. (2014b) *Volleyball Woman Ghoncheh Ghavami Out of Iran Prison* [online [23rd November]]. Available at: http://www.bbc.co.uk/news/world-middle-east-30170752 [Accessed 03.02.15].

BBC. (2014c) *UK Sport: Funding Policy Could be Recognized* [online [28th October]]. Available at: http://www.bbc.co.uk/sport/0/olympics/29791277 [Accessed 02.02.15].

BBC. (2014d) *Russia's Olympic Wall of Security Surrounds Sochi* [online]. Available at: http://www.bbc.co.uk/news/world-europe-25985678 [Accessed 30.03.15].

BBC. (2014e) *Brazil: Rio Protest Over Transport Fare Rise Ends in Violence.* Available at: http://www.bbc.co.uk/news/world-latin-america-26077374 [Accessed 25.05.15].

Beamish, R. and Ritchie, I. (2006) *Fastest, Highest, Strongest: A Critique of High-performance Sport.* Abingdon: Routledge.

Berendonk, B. (1992) *Doping – von der Forschung zum Betrug.* Reinbek: Rowholt.

Bergsgard, N. A., Houlihan, B., Mangset, P., Nødland, S. I. and Rommetvedt, H. (2007) *Sport Policy: A Comparative Analysis of Stability and Change.* Oxford: Butterworth-Heinemann.

Bevir, M. and Rhodes, R. A. W. (2006) *Governance Stories.* London: Routledge.

Bevir, M. and Rhodes, R. A. W. (2008) The differentiated polity as narrative, *British Journal of Politics and International Relations,* 10(4), 729–34.

Billig, M. (1995) *Banal Nationalism.* London: Sage.

Black, D. (2007) The symbolic politics of sport mega-events: 2010 in comparative perspective, *Politikon: South African Journal of Political Studies,* 34(3), 261–76.

Black, D. (2008) Dreaming big: the pursuit of "second order" games as a strategic response to globalisation, *Sport in Society,* 11(4), 467–80.

Black, D. (2014) Megas for Strivers: The Politics of Second-Order Events, in Grix, J. (ed) *Leveraging Legacies from Sports Mega-Events: Concepts and Cases.* Basingstoke: Palgrave.

Black, D. and Van Der Westhuizen, J. (2004) The allure of global games for 'semi-peripheral' polities and spaces: a research agenda, *Third World Quarterly,* 25(7), 1195–1214.

Blaikie, N. (2000) *Designing Social Research.* Cambridge: Polity.

Blatter, S. (2011) *Russia, Qatar Take World Cup to New Lands* [online]. Available at: http://in.reuters.com/article/2010/12/02/idINIndia-53307220101202 [Accessed 20.07.12].

Bloom, M., Gagnon, N. and Hughes, D. (2006) *Achieving Excellence: Valuing Canada's Participation in High Performance Sport.* Ottawa: The Conference Board of Canada.

Bloomberg. (2013) *Sports Revenue to Reach $67.7 Billion by 2017, PwC Report Says* [online]. Available at: http://www.bloomberg.com/news/articles/2013-11-13/sports-revenue-to-reach-67-7-billion-by-2017-pwc-report-says [Accessed 20.02.14].

Bloyce, D. and Smith, A. (2010) *Sport Policy and Development: An Introduction.* London: Routledge.

Boardley, I. D. (2013) Can London 2012 inspire mass participation in sport? – An application of popular sport motivation theories, *International Journal of Sport Policy,* 5, 245–56.

Boardley, I. D. and Grix, J. (2013) Doping in bodybuilders: a qualitative investigation of facilitative psychosocial processes, *Qualitative Research in Sport, Exercise and Health,* 6(3), 422–39.

Boardley, I. D., Grix, J. and Dewar, A. J. (2014a) Moral disengagement and associated processes in performance-enhancing drug use:

a national qualitative investigation, *Journal of Sports Sciences*, 32(9), 836–44.

Boardley, I. D., Grix, J. and Harkin, J. (2014b) Doping in team and individual sports: a qualitative investigation of moral disengagement and associated processes, *Qualitative Research in Sport, Exercise and Health* (ahead-of-print), 1-20.

BOC. (2014) *About Cob* [online]. Available at: http://www.cob.org. br/en_[Accessed 30.03.15].

Brannagan, P. M. and Giulianotti, R. (2014) Soft power and soft disempowerment: Qatar, global sport and football's 2022 World Cup finals, *Leisure Studies*, online-first, DOI: 10.1080/02614367.2014.964291.

Bramham, P., Hylton, K., Jackson, D. and Nesti, M. (2001) *Sports Development: Policy, Process and Practice*. London: Routledge.

British Cycling. (2014) British Cycling launches 10-point plan to transform Britain into a true cycling nation. Available at: http:// www.britishcycling.org.uk/article/cam20140207-British-Cycling-launches-10-point-plan-to-transform-Britain-into-a-true-cycling-nation-0. [Accessed 23.03.15].

Bromberger, C. (1995) Football as world-view and as ritual, *French Cultural Studies*, 6(18), 293–311.

Brownell, S. (2008) *Beijing's Games: What the Olympics Mean to China*. Lanham, MD: Rowman and Littefield.

Brownell, S. (2009) Western-centrism in Olympic studies and its consequences in the 2008 Beijing Olympics [working paper]. *Fluminense Federal University* [online]. Available at: http://www.uff.br/esportesociedade/pdf/es1203.pdf [Accessed on 20.09.12].

Brownell, S. (2012) Human rights and the Beijing Olympics: imagined global community and the transnational public sphere, *The British Journal of Sociology*, 63(2), 306–27.

Browning, B. and Sanderson, J. (2012) The positives and negatives of Twitter: exploring how student-athletes use Twitter and respond to critical tweets, *International Journal of Sport Communication*, 5(4), 503–21.

Business Insider. (2014) *NBA Tops All Sports Leagues With Highest Average Salary For Players* [online]. Available at: http://www.businessinsider.com/chart-nba-average-salary-2014-4?IR=T [Accessed 20.02.15].

Butler, N. (2014) *Exclusive: Kipketer Warns of Dangers of Athletes Switching Nationality*. Available at: http://www.insidethegames. biz/articles/1023133/exclusive-middle-distance-legend-kipketer-warns-of-dangers-of-athletes-switching-nationality [Accessed 25.05.15].

Carlisle Duncan, M. and Messner, M. A. (2000) The Media Image of Sport and Gender, in Wenner, L. A. (ed) *MediaSport*. London: Routledge, 170–85.

Carlson, M. (2008) *From GDR to GBR. A New Perspective on Britain's Olympic Success* [online [20th August]]. Available at: http://www. mcarlson-andoverhere.blogspot.co.uk/2008/08/from-gdr-to-gbr-new-perspective-on.html [Accessed 08.01.15].

Carter, T. F. (2012) The Olympics as Sovereign Subject Matter, in Sugden, J. and Tomlinson, A. (eds) *Watching the Olympics. Politics, Power and Representation.* London and New York: Routledge.

Cashman, R. and Darcy, S. (2008) *Benchmark Games.* Petersham: Wallawalla Press.

Cashmore, E. (1982) *Black Sportsmen.* London: Routledge and Kegan Paul.

Cashmore, E. (2003) *Making Sense of Sport.* London: Routledge.

Cashmore, E. (2010) *Making Sense of Sports* (5th edition). London: Routledge.

CBC. (2006) *Quebec's Big Owe Stadium Debt is Over* [online [19th December]]. Available at: http://www.cbc.ca/news/canada/montreal/quebec-s-big-owe-stadium-debt-is-over-1.602530 [Accessed 14.11.14].

Cha, V. D. (2009) *Beyond the Final Score: The Politics of Sport in Asia.* Chichester and New York: Columbia University Press.

Chalip, L. (2004) Beyond Impact: A General Model for Host Community Event Leverage, in Ritchie, B. and Adair, D. (eds) *Sport Tourism: Interrelationships, Impacts and Issues.* Clevedon: Channel View Publications.

Chalip, L. (2006) Towards social leverage of sport events, *Journal of Sport & Tourism*, 11(2), 109–27.

Chalip, L. (2014) From Legacy to Leverage, in Grix, J. (ed) *Leveraging Legacies from Sports Mega-Events: Concepts and Cases.* Basingstoke: Palgrave.

Chappelet, J. L. and Kuebler-Mabbott, B. (2008) *The International Olympic Committee and the Olympic System.* London and New York: Routledge.

Chen, W. (2010) The communication gesture of the Beijing Olympic Games, *Sport in Society*, 13(5), 813–18.

CNN. (2015) *"Soldiers Without Weapons": Palestine Football's Painful Journey* [online [5th February]]. Available at: http://edition.cnn.com/2015/01/11/football/palestine-asian-cup-japan-football/ [Accessed 20.02.14].

Coakley, J. (2007) *Sports in Society: Issues and Controversies* (9th edition). New York: McGraw-Hill.

Coakley, J. (2009) *Sports in Society: Issues and Controversies* (10th edition). New York: McGraw-Hill.

Coakley, J. (2003). *Sport in Society: Issues and Controversies.* New York: McGraw Hill.

Coalter, F. (2007) *A Wider Social Role for Sport. Who's Keeping the Score?* London: Routledge.

Coalter, F. (2013) *Sport and International Development: What Game are We Playing?* London: Routledge.

Coeffee, J. (2012) Policy transfer, regeneration legacy and the summer Olympics: lessons for London 2012 and the future, *International Journal of Sport Policy and Politics*, 5(2), 295–311.

Coffé, H. and Geys, B. (2007) Toward an empirical characterization of bridging and bonding social capital, *Nonprofit and Voluntary Sector Quarterly*, 36(1), 121–39.

Collins, M. (2008) Public Policies on Sport Development: Can Mass and Elite Sport Hold Together?, in Girginov, V. (ed) *Management of Sports Development*. Oxford: Butterworth-Heinemann.

Collins, M. (2010) From 'sport for good' to 'sport for sport's sake' – not a good move for sports development in England?, *International Journal of Sport Policy*, 2(3), 367–79.

Collins, S. and Green, M. (2007) The Australian Institute of Sport, *Journal of the Academy of Social Sciences in Australia*, 26(2), 4–14.

Coleman, J. S. (1988) Social capital in the creation of human capital, *American Journal of Sociology*, 94, 95–120.

Cornelissen, S. (2004) Sport mega-events in Africa: processes, impacts and prospects, *Tourism and Hospitality Planning & Development*, 1(1), 39–55.

Cornelissen, S. (2008) Scripting the nation: sport, mega-events, foreign policy and state-building in post-apartheid South Africa, *Sport in Society*, 11(4), 481–93.

Cornelissen, S. (2010) The geopolitics of global aspiration: sport mega-events and emerging powers, *The International Journal of the History of Sport*, 27(16–18), 3008–25.

Cornelissen, S. (2011) Mega event securitisation in a third world setting: glocal processes and ramifications during the 2010 FIFA World Cup, *Urban Studies*, 48(15), 3221–40.

Cornelissen, S. (2014) South Africa's 'Coming Out Party': Reflections on the Significance and Implications of the 2010 FIFA World Cup, in Grix, J. (ed) *Leveraging Legacies from Sports Mega-Events: Concepts and Cases*. Basingstoke: Palgrave.

Cornelissen, S., Bob, U. and Swart, K. (2011) Towards redefining the concept of legacy in relation to sport mega-events: insights from the 2010 FIFA World Cup, *Development Southern Africa*, 28(3), 307–18.

Coxall, B., Robins, L. and Leach, R. (2003) *Contemporary British Politics*. Basingstoke: Macmillan.

Crabbe, T. and Blackshaw, T. (2004) *New Perspectives on Sport and 'Deviance': Consumption, Peformativity and Social Control*. Abingdon: Routledge.

Crompton, J. L. (2001) Public Subsidies to Professional Team Sport Facilities in the USA, in Gratton, C. and Henry, I. P. (eds) *Sport in the City: The Role of Sport in Economic and Social Regeneration*. London: Routledge.

Cull, N. J. (2008) The Public Diplomacy of the Modern Olympic Games and China's Soft Power Strategy, in Price, M. E. and Dayan, D. (eds) *Owning the Olympics: Narratives of the New China*. Ann Arbor, MI: University of Michigan Press, pp. 117–44.

Curi, M., Knijnik, J. and Mascarenhas, G. (2011) The Pan American Games in Rio de Janeiro 2007: consequences of a sport mega-event on a BRIC country, *International Review for the Sociology of Sport*, 46(2), 140–56.

Daily Telegraph, The. (2001) *Forlorn Albania Welcomes England*. Available at: http://www.telegraph.co.uk/sport/football/teams/england/3001766/Forlorn-Albania-welcomes-England.html?mobile=basic [Accessed 25.05.15].

Darby, P. (2002) *Africa, Football, and FIFA: Politics, Colonialism, and Resistance*. London: Routledge.

DCMS (Department for Culture, Media and Sport). (2002) *Game Plan, a Strategy for Delivering Government's Sport and Physical Activity Objectives*, produced by the DCMS and the Strategy Unit.

DCMS (Department for Culture, Media and Sport). (2008) *Playing to Win: A New Era for Sport*. London: DCMS.

DCMS (Department for Culture, Media and Sport). (2009) Independent Advisory Panel. *Review of Free-to-air Listed Events* [online]. Available at: http://webarchive.nationalarchives.gov.uk/+/http:/www.culture.gov.uk/images/consultations/independentpanel-report-to-SoS-Free-to-air-Nov2009.pdf [Accessed 30.03.15].

DDR-Wissen. (2013) *DDR-Lexikon. Sport*. Online. Available at: http://www.ddr-wissen.de/wiki/ddr.pl?Sport [Accessed 11.11.13].

De Bosscher, V., de Knop, P., van Bottenburg, M. and Shibli, S. (2008) *The Global Sporting Arms Race*. Oxford: Meyer and Meyer Sport.

deLisle, J. (2008) "One World, Different Dreams". The Contest to Define the Beijing Olympics, in Price, M. E. and Dayan, D. (eds) *Owning the Olympics. Narratives of the New China*. Ann Arbor, MI: University of Michigan Press.

Deloitte. (2015) *Football Money League* [online]. Available at: http://www.slideshare.net/deloitteuk/deloitte-football-money-league-2015-commercial-breaks [Accessed 22.02.15].

Dennis, M. (1988) *The German Democratic Republic: Politics, Economics and Society*. London: Pinter.

Dennis, M. and Grix, J. (2012) *Sport Under Communism: Behind the East German 'Miracle'*. Basingstoke: Palgrave.

Deutsche Welle. (2006) *FWC Reports* [online]. Available at: http://www.dw-world.de [Accessed 02.03.12].

Dictionary Reference. (2015) *Entry for 'Communism'* [online]. Available at: http://dictionary.reference.com/browse/communism [Accessed 30.03.15].

Donaldson, R. and Ferreira, S. (2007) Crime, perceptions and touristic decision-making: some empirical evidence and prospects for the 2010 World Cup, *Politikon*, 34(3), 353–71.

Donaldson, R. and Ferreira, S. (2009) (Re-)creating urban destination image: opinions of foreign visitors to South Africa on safety and security, *Urban Forum*, 20(1), 1-18.

Donohue, T. and Johnson, N. (1986) *Foul Play: Drug Abuse in Sports.* Oxford and New York: Basil Blackwell.

Dorey, P. (2005) *Policy-making in Britain: An Introduction.* London: Sage.

Downes, S. and Mackay, D. (1996) *Running Scared: How Athletics Lost its Innocence.* Edinburgh: Mainstream.

Dunning, E. (1999) *Sport Matters: Sociological Studies of Sport, Violence and Civilization.* London: Routledge.

Durkheim, E. (1912/1995) *The Elementary Forms of Religious Life.* Oxford: Oxford University Press.

Elias, N. (1939) *The Civilizing Process: Sociogenetic and Psychogenetic Investigations* (trans. Edmund Jephcott). Blackwell, Oxford.

Espy, R. (1979) *The Politics of the Olympic Games.* Berkeley, CA: University of California Press.

Etymology Dictionary. (2014) *Sport* [online]. Available at: http://www.etymonline.com/index.php?term=sport [Accessed 04.03.14].

European Commission. (2007) *White Paper on Sport* [online]. Available at: http://eur-lex.europa.eu/legal-content/EN/TXT/?uri=CELEX:52007DC0391. [Accessed 23.03.15].

European Tour Operators. (2013) *London Tourism Rates Plunge During 2012 Olympics.* Available at: http://www.etoa.org/media/all-news/news-item/london-tourism-rates-plunge-during-2012-olympics [Accessed 20.03.15].

Evans, J., Penney, D. and Bryant, A. (1993) Theorising implementation: a preliminary comment on power and process in policy research, *Physical Education Review*, 16(1), 5–22.

Evans, M. (2009) Gordon Brown and public management reform – a project in search of a 'big idea'?, *Policy Studies*, 30(1): 33–51.

Fan, Y. (2006) Branding the nation: what is being branded?, *Journal of Vacation Marketing*, 12(1), 5–14.

Federal Archives of Germany, Berlin (1987) DY/30/IV/2/2.039/250, p. 175, '*Grundlinie für die perspektivische Entwicklung des Leistungssports der DDR bis zum Jahre 2000*'; from Krenz to Günter Mittag, Economics Minister; 15 July 1987.

Federal Government (Germany). (2006) 2006 FWC. *Final Report by the Federal Government.* Berlin: Federal Ministry of the Interior.

Federal Ministry of the Interior (Germany). (2006) *Die Welt war zu Gast bei Freunden – Bilanz der Bundesregierung zur Fußball-Weltmeisterschaft 2006.* Berlin: Federal Ministry of the Interior.

FIFA. (2011) *Almost Half the World Tuned in at Home to Watch 2010 FIFA World Cup South Africa™* [online]. Available at: http://m.fifa.com/newscentre/news/newsid=1473143/ [Accessed 30.03.15].

FIFA. (2015) *About FIFA* [online]. Available at: http://www.fifa.com/aboutfifa/organisation/confederations/index.html [Accessed 30.03.15].

FIFA. (2015) 2010 FIFA World Cup South Africa. Available at: http://www.fifa.com/mm/document/affederation/tv/01/47/32/73/2010fifaworldcupsouthafricatvaudiencereport.pdf [Accessed 25.05.15].

Financial Times. (2011) *Olympic Sponsors Seek Podium for Brands* [online [3rd September]]. Available at: http://www.ft.com/cms/s/0/edb08c4e-ce71-11e0-b755 00144feabdc0.html#axzz3UGGEELhM [Accessed 22.02.15].

Finlay, C. J. (2008) Toward the Future: The New Olympic internationalism, in Price, M. E. and Dayan, D. (eds) *Owning the Olympics: Narratives of the New China*. Ann Arbor, MI: University of Michigan Press.

Finlay, C. J. (2011) *Between Leverage and Legacy: Producing the 2012 London Olympics in a Global New Media Environment* (Doctoral dissertation, University of Pennsylvania).

Finlay, C. J. and Xin, X. (2010) Public diplomacy games: a comparative study of American and Japanese responses to the interplay of nationalism, ideology and Chinese soft power strategies around the 2008 Beijing Olympics, *Sport in Society*, 13(5), 876–900.

Foley, M. W. and Edwards, B. (1999) Is it time to disinvest in social capital? *Journal of Public Policy*, 19(2), 141–73.

Forbes. (2014) *The World's Highest Paid Athletes* [online]. Available at: http://www.forbes.com/athletes/list/ [Accessed on 23.03.15].

Foreign and Commonwealth Office. (2010) *FCO Public Diplomacy: The Olympics* [online]. Available at: http://www.publications.parliament.uk/pa/cm201011/cmselect/cmfaff/581/10111002.htm [Accessed 08.02.13].

Foucault, M. (1994) Governmentality, in Faubion, J. (ed) *Michel Foucault: Power, Essential Works of Foucault 1954–1984*, Vol. 3. London: Penguin.

Foucault, M. (2001) The Political Technology of Individuals, in Faubion, J. (ed) *Essential Works of Foucault 1954–1984*, Vol. 3. London: Penguin.

Fowler, R. (2001) *Language in the News. Discourse and Ideology of the Press*. London: Routledge.

Franke, W. W. and Berendonk, B. (1997) Hormonal doping and androgenization of athletes: a secret program of the German Democratic Republic government, *Clinical Chemistry*, 43(7), 1262–79.

German Tourist Board. (2007b) *The Importance of Tourism* [online]. Available at: www.germany-tourism.de [Accessed 07.07.11].

Gilboa, E. (2008) Searching for a theory of public diplomacy, *The ANNALS of the American Academy of Political and Social Science*, 616(1), 55–77.

Gilchrist, P. and Holden, R. (eds) (2011) *The Politics of Sport: Community, Mobility, Identity.* London: Routledge.

Giulianotti, R. (1999) *Football: A Sociology of the Global Game.* Cambridge: Polity.

Giulianotti, R. (2002) Supporters, followers, fans, and flaneurs: A taxonomy of spectator identities in football, *Journal of Sport & Social Issues*, 26(1), 25–46.

Guilianotti, R. (2005a) Playing an Aerial Game: The New Political Economy of Soccer, in Nauright, J. and Schimmel, K. S. (eds) *The Political Economy of Sport.* Basingstoke: Palgrave.

Giulianotti, R. (2005b) *Sport: A Critical Sociology.* Cambridge: Polity.

Giulianotti, R. (2015) *Sport: A Critical Sociology* (2nd edition). Cambridge: Polity.

Goethe Institute. (2015) *About Us* [online]. Available at: http://www.goethe.de/enindex.htm [Accessed on 23.03.15].

Goodhart, P. and Chataway, C. (1968) *War Without Weapons.* London: W.H. Allen.

Goodwin, M. and Grix, J. (2011) Bringing structures back in: the "governance narrative", the "decentred approach" and "asymmetrical network governance" in the education and sport policy communities, *Public Administration*, 89(2), 537–56.

Granovetter, M. S. (1973) The strength of weak ties, *American Journal of Sociology*, 78(6), 1360–80.

Grant, W. (1982) *The Political Economy of Industrial Policy.* London: Butterworths.

Grant, W. (2007) An analytical framework for a political economy of football, *British Politics*, 2(1), 69–90.

Gratton, C. and Taylor, P. (2005) *The Economics of Sport and Recreation.* London: Routledge.

Gratton, C. and Tice, A. (1989) Sports participation and health, *Leisure Studies*, 8(1), 77–92.

Green, M. (2004) Changing policy priorities for sport in England: the emergence of elite sport development as a key policy concern, *Leisure Studies*, 23(4), 365–85.

Green, M. (2006) From "sport for all" to not about "sport" at all? Interrogating sport policy interventions in the United Kingdom, *European Sport Management Quarterly*, 6(3), 217–38.

Green, M. (2007a) Governing under advanced liberalism: sport policy and the social investment state, *Policy Science*, 40(1), 55–71.

Green, M. (2007b) Olympic glory or grassroots development? Sports policy priorities in Australia, Canada, and the United Kingdom 1960–2006, *International Journal of the History of Sport*, 24(7), 921–53.

Green, M. (2009) Podium or participation? Analysing policy priorities under changing modes of sport governance in the United Kingdom, *International Journal of Sport Policy,* 1(2), 121–44.

Green, M. and Houlihan, B. (2005) *Elite Sport Development: Policy Learning and Political Priorities.* London and New York: Routledge.

Green, M. and Houlihan, B. (2006) Governmentality, modernization, and the "disciplining" of National Sporting Organisations: an analysis of athletics in Australia and the United Kingdom, *Sociology of Sport Journal,* 23(1), 47–71.

Green, M. and Oakley, B. (2001) Elite sport development systems and playing to win: uniformity and diversity in international approaches, *Leisure Studies,* 20(4), 247–68.

Griffiths, M. and Armour, K. (2013) Physical education and youth sport in England: conceptual and practical foundations for an Olympic legacy? *International Journal of Sport Policy and Politics,* 5(2), 213–27.

Grix, J. (2000) *The Role of the Masses in the Collapse of the GDR.* Basingstoke: Macmillan.

Grix, J. (2009) The impact of UK sport policy on the governance of athletics, *International Journal of Sport Policy,* 1(1), 31–49.

Grix, J. (2010a) Introducing "hard interpretivism" and "Q" methodology, *Leisure Studies,* 29(4), 457–67.

Grix, J. (2010b) *The Foundations of Research* (2nd edition). Basingstoke: Palgrave.

Grix, J. (2010c) From "hobbyhorse" to mainstream: using sport to understand British Politics, *British Politics,* 5(1), 114–29.

Grix, J. (2010d) The governance debate and the study of sport policy, *International Journal of Sport Policy,* 2(2), 159–71.

Grix, J. (2012) The politics of sports mega-events, *Political Insight,* 3(1), 4-7.

Grix, J. (2013a) 'Image' leveraging and sports mega-events: Germany and the 2006 World Cup, *Journal of Sport and Tourism,* 17(4), 214–34.

Grix, J. (2013b) Sports politics and the Olympics, *Political Studies Review,* 11(1), 15–25.

Grix, J. (2014a) Germany and Sport Politics, in Colvin, S. (ed) *Handbook of German Studies.* London: Routledge.

Grix, J. (2014b) *Leveraging Legacies from Sport Mega-Events: Concepts and Cases.* Basingstoke: Palgrave.

Grix, J. and Carmichael, F. (2012) Why do governments invest in elite sport? A polemic, *International Journal of Sport Policy and Politics,* 4(1), 73–90.

Grix, J. and Cooke, P. (eds) (2002) *East German Distinctiveness in a Unified Germany.* Birmingham: University of Birmingham Press.

Grix, J. and Himpler, N. (2007) *German and British Media Representation of America and Iraq*, European Research Institute Working Paper Series, No. 17, February, 2007, University of Birmingham. Available at: http://www.eri.bham.ac.uk/research/working-papers.shtml

Grix, J. and Houlihan, B. (2013) Sports mega-events as part of a nation's soft power strategy: the cases of Germany (2006) and the UK (2012), *British Journal of Politics and International Relations,* 16(4), 572–96.

Grix, J. and Lacroix, C. (2006) Constructing Germany's image in the British Press: an empirical analysis of stereotypical reporting on Germany, *Journal of Contemporary European Studies,* 14(3), 373–92.

Grix, J. and Lee, D. (2013) Soft power, sports mega-events and emerging states: the lure of the politics of attraction, *Global Society,* 27(4), 521–36.

Grix, J. and Parker, A. (2011) Towards an explanation for the decline in UK athletics: a case study of male distance running, *Sport in Society,* 14(5), 608–24.

Grix, J. and Phillpots, L. (2011) Revisiting the "governance narrative": "asymmetrical network governance" and the deviant case of the sport policy sector, *Public Policy and Administration,* 26(1), 3–19.

Grix, J., Brannagan, P. M., and Houlihan, B. (2015). Interrogating states' soft power strategies: A case study of sports mega-events in Brazil and the UK. *Global Society,* 29(3), 463–479.

Groeneveld, M., Houlihan, B. and Ohl, F. (eds) (2012) *Social Capital and Sport Governance in Europe*. London: Routledge.

Guelke, A. (1986) The Politicisation of South African Sport, in Allison, L. (ed) *The Politics of Sport*. Manchester: Manchester University Press.

Guttmann, A. (1978) *From Ritual to Record*. New York: Columbia University Press.

Guttmann, A. (2002) *A History of the Modern Games*. Urbana and Chicago, IL: University of Illinois Press.

Guttmann, A. (2003) Sport, politics and the engaged historian, *Journal of Contemporary History,* 38(3), 363–75.

Habermas, J. (1979) *Communication and the Evolution of Society,* Vol. 29. Boston, MA: Beacon Press.

Hall, C. M. (2006) Urban entrepreneurship, corporate interests and sports mega-events: the thin policies of competitiveness within the hard outcomes of neoliberalism, *The Sociological Review,* 54(2), 59–70.

Hall, N. (2014) The Kardashian index: a measure of discrepant social media profile for scientists, *Genome Biology,* 15, 424.

Hall, S. (1992) The Question of Cultural Identity, in Hall, S., Held, D. and McGrew, T. (eds) *Modernity and its Futures*. Cambridge: Polity.

Hampton, J. (2009) *The Austerity Olympics: When the Games Came to London in 1948*. London: Aurum.

Hanstad, D. V. and Skille, E. A. (2010) Does elite sport develop mass sport? A Norwegian case study, *Scandinavian Sport Studies Forum*, 1, 51–68.

Hargreaves, J. A. (1994) *Sporting Females: Critical Issues in the History and Sociology of Women's Sport*. London: Routledge.

Hargreaves, J. A. (2000) *Heroines of Sport: The Politics of Difference and Identity*. London: Routledge.

Harris, H. A. (1972) *Sport in Greece and Rome*. New York: Cornell University Press.

Harris, L. (2011) Mega-events and the developing world: a look at the legacy of the 2010 Soccer World Cup, *South African Journal of International Affairs*, 18(3), 407–27.

Harris, S. (2013) *An analysis of the significance of the relationship between CSPs and NGBs in the community sport policy process*, PhD Thesis, Loughborough University.

Harris, S. and Houlihan, B. (2014) Delivery networks and community sport in England, *International Journal of Public Sector Management*, 27(2), 113–27.

Haut, J., Prohl, R., & Emrich, E. (2014) Nothing but medals? Attitudes towards the importance of Olympic success. *International Review for the Sociology of Sport*, DOI: 1012690214526400.

Hay, C. (2002) *Political Analysis*. Basingstoke: Palgrave.

Hayden, C. (2012) *The Rhetoric of Soft Power: Public Diplomacy in Global Contexts*. Lanham: Lexington Books.

Herman, E. S. and Chomsky, N. (1988) *Manufacturing Consent: The Political Economy of the Mass Media*. New York: Pantheon.

Hill, C. (1992) *Olympic Politics*. Manchester: Manchester University Press.

Hill, J. (2003) Introduction: sport and politics, *Journal of Contemporary History*, 38(3), 355–61.

Hill, J. (2011) *Sport in History. An Introduction*. Basingstoke: Palgrave.

Hill, M. (2009) *The Public Policy Process* (5th edition). Edinburgh: Longman.

Hilton, C. (2008) *Hitler's Olympics: The 1936 Berlin Olympic Games*. Gloucester: Sutton Publishing.

Hilvoorde, I. V., Elling, A. and Stokvis, R. (2010) How to influence national pride? The Olympic medal index as a unifying narrative, *International Review for the Sociology of Sport*, 45(1), 87–102.

Hirschman, A. O. (1970) *Exit, Voice, and Loyalty: Responses to Decline in Firms, Organizations, and States*. Cambridge, MA: Harvard University Press.

Hitler, A. (1926) *Mein Kampf* (trans. Manheim, R., 2001). New York: Houghton Mifflin.

Hoberman, J. M. (1984) *Sport and Political Ideology*. Austin, TX: The University of Texas Press.

Hocking, B. (2005) Rethinking the "New" Public Diplomacy, in Melissen, J. (ed) *The New Public Diplomacy. Soft Power in International Relations*. Basingstoke: Palgrave Macmillan.

Holtzhausen, D. and Fullerton, J. (2013) The 2010 FIFA World Cup and South Africa: a study of longer-term effects and moderators of country reputation, *Journal of Marketing Communications*, online first, DOI: 10.1080/13527266.2012.740065.

Holzweissig, G. (1981) *Diplomatie im Trainingsanzug. Sport als politisches Instrument der DDR in den innerdeutschen und internationalen Beziehungen*. Munich: Oldenbourg Press.

Holzweissig, G. (2005) Sport – Gesellschaftliche Rolle und politische Funktion, *Horch und Guck*, 51, 1–9.

Horne, J. (2007) The four 'knowns' of sports mega-events, *Leisure Studies*, 26(1), 81–96.

Horne, J. (2010) The Politics of Hosting the Olympic Games, in Bairner, A. and Molnar, G. (eds) *The Politics of the Olympics: A Survey*. London and New York: Routledge.

Horne, J. and Manzenreiter, W. (eds) (2006) *Sports Mega-Events: Social Scientific Analyses of a Global Phenomenon*. Oxford: Blackwell.

Horne, J., Tomlinson, A. and Whannel, G. (2005) *Understanding Sport: An Introduction to the Sociological and Cultural Analysis of Sport*. London: E & FN Spon.

Horne, J., Tomlinson, A. and Whannel, G. (2006) *Understanding Sport: An Introduction to the Sociological and Cultural Analysis of Sport*. Oxon: Spon Press.

Horne, J. and Whannel, G. (2012) *Understanding the Olympics*. London and New York: Routledge.

Houlihan, B. (1991) *The Government and Politics of Sport*. London: Routledge.

Houlihan, B. (1994) *Sport and International Politics*. London: Harvester-Wheatsheaf.

Houlihan, B. (1997a) *Sport, Policy, and Politics: A Comparative Analysis*. London: Routledge.

Houlihan, B. (1997b) Sport, national identity and public policy, *Nations and Nationalism*, 3(1), 113–37.

Houlihan, B. (2002a) *Dying to Win: Doping in Sport and the Development of Anti-doping Policy* (2nd edition). Strasbourg: Council of Europe Publishing.

Houlihan, B. (2002b) *Sport, Policy and Politics: A Comparative Analysis*. London: Routledge.

Houlihan, B. (2002c) Sport and Politics, in Coakley, J. and Dunning, E. (eds.) *Handbook of Sports Studies*. London: Sage.

Houlihan, B. (2005) Public sector sport policy developing a framework for analysis, *International Review for the Sociology of Sport*, 40(2), 163–85.

Houlihan, B. (2006a) Sporting excellence, schools and sports development: the politics of crowded policy spaces, *European Physical Education Review*, 6(2), 171–93.

Houlihan, B. (ed) (2006b) *Sport and Society: A Student Introduction.* London: Sage.

Houlihan, B. (ed) (2008) *Sport and Society: A Student Introduction* (2nd edition). London: Sage.

Houlihan, B. (ed) (2009) *Sport and Society: A Student Introduction* (2nd edition). London: Sage.

Houlihan, B. and Giulianotti, R. (2012) Politics and the London 2012 Olympics: the (in) security games, *International Affairs*, 88(4), 701–17.

Houlihan, B. and Green, M. (2006) The changing status of school sport and physical education: explaining policy change, *Sport, Education and Society*, 11(1), 73–92.

Houlihan, B. and Green, M. (eds) (2007) *Comparative Elite Sport Development.* London: Routledge.

Houlihan, B. and Green, M. (2008) Comparative Elite Sport Development, in Houlihan, B. and Green, M. (eds) *Comparative Elite Sport Development: Systems, Structures and Public Policy.* Amsterdam: Butterworth-Heinemann.

Houlihan, B. and Green, M. (2009) Modernization and sport: the reform of Sport England and UK Sport, *Public Administration*, 87(3), 678–98.

Houlihan, B. and White, A. (2002) *The Politics of Sports Development: Development of Sport or Development Through Sport?* London: Routledge.

House of Commons Committee of Public Accounts. (2006) *Examination of Witnesses (Questions 1-19)* [online [6th February]]. Available at: http://www.publications.parliament.uk/pa/cm200506/cmselect/cmpubacc/898/6020602.htm [Accessed 13.12.14].

Huizinga, J. (1955) *Homo Ludens: A Study of the Play-Element in Culture.* Boston, MA: Beacon Press.

Huntington, S. P. (1993) The clash of civilizations?, *Foreign Affairs*, 72, 22–49.

Hutton, W. (2015) *Football is Just One Example of the Inequalities that Bedevil Us* [online [15th February]]. Available at: http://www.theguardian.com/commentisfree/2015/feb/15/football-one-of-the-inequalities-that-bedevil-us-premier-league [Accessed 15.02.15].

Hylton, K. (ed) (2001) *Sport Development: Policy, Process and Practice.* London: Routledge.

Hylton, K. (2008) *'Race' and Sport: Critical Race Theory.* London: Routledge.

Hylton, K. and Bramham, P. (2008) Models of Sports Development, in Girginov, V. (ed) *Management of Sports Development*. Oxford: Elsevier.

Infratest Tourist Survey Results. (2006) Available at: http://www. reisen-experten.de/reiseinformationen/reise-news/news/newsartikel/fussball-wm-befluegelt-image-des/index.html. [Accessed on 21.09.12].

Inglehart, R. (1999) *Trust, Well-Being and Democracy*, in Warren, M. E. (ed) *Democracy and Trust*. Cambridge: Cambridge University Press.

Insidethegames. (2013) *Kenya Latest Country Blasted by WADA over Doping Problems* [online]. Available at: http://www.insidethe games.biz/news/1016727-kenya-latest-country-blasted-by-wada-over-doping-problems [Accessed 30.03.15].

International Olympic Committee (ed). (1968) *The Speeches of President Avery Brundage*. Lausanne: IOC.

International Olympic Committee. (2012) *IOC Marketing: Media Guide* [online]. Available at: http://www.olympic.org/Documents/IOC_Marketing/London_2012/IOC_Marketing_Media_Guide_2012.pdf [Accessed 22.02.15].

International Olympic Committee. (2014) *Olympic Charter* [online]. Available at: http://www.olympic.org/Documents/olympic_char ter_en.pdf [Accessed 30.03.15].

International Sports Press Association. (2014) *Breaking the Bank: Almost 18 Million USD Spent on Sochi Medal Bonuses* [online [6th March]]. Available at: http://www.aipsmedia.com/index. php?page=news&cod=13223&tp=n [Accessed 06.03.14].

Jarvie, G. (1993) Sport, Nationalism and Cultural Identity, in Allison, L. (ed) *The Changing Politics of Sport*. Manchester: Manchester University Press.

Jarvie, G. and Reid, I. A. (1999) Sport, nationalism and culture in Scotland, *Sports Historian*, 19(1), 97–124.

Jefferys, K. (2012) *Sport and Politics in Modern Britain*. Basingstoke: Palgrave.

Jennings, A. (2006) *FOUL! The Secret World of FIFA: Bribes, Vote Rigging and Ticket Scandals*. London: HarperCollins.

Jordana, J. (1999) Collective Action Theory and the Analysis of Social Capital, in van Deth, J. W., Maraffi, M., Newton, K. and Whiteley, P. F. (eds) *Social Capital and European Democracy*. Abingdon: Routledge.

Kay, T. and Jeanes, R. (2009) Women, Sport and Gender Inequality, in Houlihan, B. (ed) *Sport and Society: A Student Introduction* (2nd edition). London: Sage.

Keech, M. (2012) Youth Sport and London's 2012 Olympic Legacy, in Sugden, J. and Tomlinson, A. (eds) *Watching the Olympics: Politics, Power and Representation*. London and New York: Routledge.

Kellett, P., Hede, A. M. and Chalip, L. (2008) Social policy for sports events: leveraging (relationships with) teams from other nations for community benefit, *European Sport Management Quarterly*, 8(2), 101–21.

Kew, F. (2003) *Sport: Social Problems and Issues*. Oxford: Butterworth-Heinemann.

Keysers, C. (2013) *Unser Emphathisches Gehirn*. Munich: Bertelsmann Press.

Kidd, B. (2008) A new social movement: sport for development and peace, *Sport in Society*, 11(4), 370–80.

King, N. (2009) *Sport, Policy and Governance: Local Perspectives*. Oxford: Butterworth-Heinemann.

Kirk, D. (1992) *Defining Physical Education: The Social Construction of a School Subject in Postwar Britain*. London: Falmer Press.

Knott, B., Allen, D. and Swart, K. (2012) Stakeholder reflections of the tourism and nation-branding legacy of the 2010 FIFA World Cup for South Africa, *African Journal for Physical Health Education, Recreation and Dance: Supplement*, 2(18), 112–22.

Kuper, S. (2011) *Sport: Developing Nations Go on Offensive for Games* [online]. Available at: http://www.ft.com/cms/s/0/aa7cef8c-273f-11e0-80d700144feab49a.html#axzz1mMDENFR9 [Accessed 14.02.15].

Kurlantzick, J. (2007) *Charm Offensive: How China's Soft Power is Transforming the World*. New Haven, CT: Yale University Press.

Lasswell, H. D. (1936). Politics: Who Gets What, When, How. New York, Whittlesey House.

Lee, P. C., Bairner, A. and Tan, T. C. (2010) Taiwanese Identities and the 2008 Beijing Olympic Games, in Bairner, A. and Molnar, G. (eds) *The Politics of the Olympics*. London: Routledge, pp. 129–44.

Lee, D., Taylor, I. and Williams, P. D. (2006) *The New Multilateralism in South African Diplomacy*. Basingstoke: Palgrave.

Lenskyj, H. J. (2000) *Inside the Olympic Industry: Power, Politics and Activism*. New York: State University of New York Press.

Lenskyj, H. J. (2010) Olympic Power, Olympic Politics: Behind the Scenes, in Bairner, A. and Molnar, G. (eds) *The Politics of the Olympics: A Survey*. London and New York: Routledge.

Lepp, A. and Gibson, H. (2011) Reimaging a nation: South Africa and the 2010 FIFA World Cup, *Journal of Sport & Tourism*, 16(3), 211–30.

Levermore, R. and Budd, A. (eds) (2004) *Sport and International Relations*. London: Routledge.

Lueschen, G. (2000) Doping in Sport as Deviant Behaviour and its Social Control, in Coakley, J. and Dunning, E. (eds) *Handbook of Sports Studies*. London: Sage.

Lukes, S. (2007) Power and the Battle for Hearts and Minds: On the Bluntness of Soft Power, in Berenskoetter, F. and Williams, M. J. (eds) *Power in World Politics*. London: Routledge.

Mackay, D. (2013) *Munich Citizens Vote Against Bid for 2022 Winter Olympics and Paralympics* [online [10th November]]. *Inside the Games*. Available at: http://www.insidethegames.biz/olympics/winter-olympics/2022/1016892-munich-citizens-against-bid-for-2022-winter-olympics-and-paralympics [Accessed 01.03.15].

Magdalinski, T. (2000) The reinvention of Australia for the Sydney 2000 Olympic Games, *The International Journal of the History of Sport*, 17(2–3), 305–22.

Maguire, J. (1999) *Global Sport: Identities, Societies, Civilizations*. Cambridge: Polity.

Mangan, J. A. (1981) *Athleticism in the Victorian and Edwardian Public School – The Emergence and Consolidation of an Educational Ideology*. Cambridge: Cambridge University Press.

Manzenreiter, W. (2010) The Beijing Games in the Western imagination of China: the weak power of soft power, *Journal of Sport and Social Issues*, 34(1), 29–48.

Markovits, A. S. and Rensmann, L. (2010) *Gaming the World: How Sports are Reshaping Global Politics and Culture*. Princeton, NJ and Oxford: Princeton University Press.

Marsh, D. (2008a) Understanding British government: analysing competing models, *The British Journal of Politics & International Relations*, 10(2), 251–68.

Marsh, D. (2008b) What is at stake? A response to Bevir and Rhodes, *The British Journal of Politics & International Relations*, 10(4), 735–9.

Marsh, D. and Stoker, G. (eds) (2002) *Theory and Methods in Political Science* (2nd edition). Basingstoke: Macmillan.

Matheson, V. (2009) Economic multipliers and mega-event analysis, *International Journal of Sport Finance*, 4, 63–70.

Mattern, J. B. (2005) Why soft power isn't so soft: representational force and the sociolinguistic construction of attraction in world politics, *Millennium-Journal of International Studies*, 33(3), 583–612.

McFee, G. (2012) The Promise of Olympism, in Sugden, J. and Tomlinson, A. (eds) *Watching the Olympics: Politics, Power and Representation*. London and New York: Routledge.

Medical Dictionary. (2014) *Exercise* [online]. Available at: http://medical-dictionary.thefreedictionary.com/physical+exercise [Accessed on 04.03.14].

Melissen, J. (ed) (2005) *The New Public Diplomacy: Soft Power in International Relations*. Basingstoke: Palgrave.

Merkel, U. (2008) The politics of sport diplomacy and reunification in divided Korea: One nation, two countries and three flags, *International Review for the Sociology of Sport*, 43(3), 289–311.

Miah, A. and Garcia, B. (2012) *The Olympics: The Basics.* London and New York: Routledge.

Milne, S. (2012) *This is a Corporate Lockdown, Why Not an Olympics for All?* [online [10th July]]. Available at: http://www.theguard ian.com/commentisfree/2012/jul/10/london-olympics-lockdown-2012-games [Accessed 11.07.12].

Morgan, L. (2015) *Nevada Investigates Lifting Ban on Olympic Betting* [online [11th February]]. Available at: http://www.insidethegames. biz/olympics/1025513-nevada-investigates-lifting-ban-on-olympic-betting [Accessed 20.02.14].

Morris, J. (2011) How great is Britain, *British Journal of Politics and International Relations*, 13(3), 326–47.

National Audit Office. (2005) *UK Sport: Supporting Elite Athletes.* London: Stationery Office.

National Health Performance Authority. (2013) *Overweight and Obesity Rates Across Australia*, 2011–12. Available at: http://www. nhpa.gov.au/internet/nhpa/publishing.nsf/Content/Our-reports [Accessed 30.03.15].

Nauright, J. and Schimmel, K. S. (2005) *The Political Economy of Sport.* Basingstoke: Palgrave.

Ndlovu-Gatsheni, S. J. (2011) Pan-Africanism and the 2010 FIFA World Cup in South Africa, *Development Southern Africa*, 28(3), 401–13.

Newman, J. (2005) *Remaking Governance: Peoples, Politics and Public Space.* Bristol: Policy Press.

Newton, K. (1999) Social Capital and European Democracy, in van Deth, J. W., Maraffi, M., Newton, K. and Whiteley, P. F. (eds) *Social Capital and European Democracy*. Abingdon: Routledge.

New York Times. (2010) *Russia and Qatar Win World Cup Bids* [online [2nd December]]. Available at: http://www .nytimes.com/2010/12/03/sports/soccer/03worldcup.html? pagewanted=all&_r=0_[Accessed 08.02.13].

New Zealand Herald. (2014) *All Blacks: Haka Arousing Second Thought* [online [29th June]]. Available at: http://www.nzher ald.co.nz/sport/news/article.cfm?c_id=4&objectid=11283849 [Accessed 11.11.14].

NHS. (2011) *Statistics on Obesity, Physical Activity and Diet: England, 2011* [online]. Available at: http://www.ic.nhs.uk/statis tics-and-data-collections/health-and-lifestyles/obesity/statistics-on-obesity-physical-activity-and-diet-england-2011 [Accessed 20.09.12].

Nicholson, M. and Hoye, R. (eds) (2008) *Sport and Social Capital.* Oxford: Butterworth-Heinemann.

Nicholson, M., Hoye, R. and Houlihan, B. (2011) *Participation in Sport: International Policy Perspectives.* Abingdon: Routledge.

Niemann, A., Garcia, B. and Grant, W. (eds) (2011) *The Transformation of European Football: Towards the Europeanisation of the National Game*. Manchester: Manchester University Press.

Nye, J. S. (Jnr) (1990) 'Soft power', *Foreign Policy*, 80(Autumn), 153–71.

Nye, J. S. (Jnr) (2004) *Soft Power: The Means to Success in World Politics*. New York: Public Affairs.

Nye, J. S. (Jnr) (2008) Public diplomacy and soft power, *The Annals of the American Academy of Political and Social Science*, 616(1), 94–109.

O'Brien, D. (2007) Points of leverage: maximizing host community benefit from a regional surfing festival, *European Sport Management Quarterly*, 7(2), 141–65.

O'Brien, D. and Chalip, L. (2007) Executive training exercise in sport event leverage, *International Journal of Culture, Tourism and Hospitality Research*, 1(4), 296–304.

O'Brien, D. and Gardiner, S. (2006) Creating sustainable mega-event impacts: networking and relationship development through pre-event training, *Sport Management Review*, 9, 25–47.

Offe, C. (1999) How Can We Trust Our Fellow Citizens?, in Warren, M. E. (ed) *Democracy and Trust*. Cambridge: Cambridge University Press.

Olaveson, T. (2001) Collective effervescence and communitas: processual models of ritual and society in Emile Durkheim and Victor Turner, *Dialectical Anthropology*, 26(2), 89–124.

Online Etymology Dictionary. (2014) *Entry for 'Sport'* [online]. Available at: http://www.etymonline.com/index.php [Accessed 06.03.14].

Orwell, G. (1945) *The Sporting Spirit*. Chicago Tribune, December 14.

Osborne, P. (2014) *Independent Audit Recommends "Urgent" Improvements to UCI Anti-doping Practices* [online]. Available at: http://www.insidethegames.biz/sports/summer/cycling/1018745-independent-audit-recommends-urgent-improvements-to-uci-anti-doping-practices [Accessed 06.03.14].

Oughton, C. and Tacon, R. (2006) *The Economic and Social Impact of Sport*. Report for the Economic and Social Research Council. Swindon: ESRC.

Owen, D. (2014) *Does Sport Need a Plan to Counter Diplo-Doping?* [online [26th February]]. *Inside the Games*. Available at: http://www.insidethegames.biz/blogs/1018575-david-owen-does-sport-need-a-plan-to-counter-diplo-doping [Accessed 12.12.14].

Parker, O. (2012) *London 2012: Olympic Ceremonies Through the Ages* [online [27th July]]. Available at: http://www.telegraph.co.uk/sport/olympics/9429085/London-2012-Olympic-ceremonies-through-the-ages.html [Accessed 16.03.14].

Penney, D. and Evans, J. (1999) *Politics, Policy and Practice in Physical Education*. London: E & FN Spon.

Perryman, M. (2012) *Why the Olympics Aren't Good for Us and How They Might Be*. New York.

Perryman, M. (ed) (2013) *London 2012: How Was it for Us?* London: Lawrence and Wishart.

Phillpots, L., Grix, J. and Quarmby, T. (2011) Centralized grassroots sport policy and 'new governance': a case study of County Sports Partnerships in the UK – unpacking the paradox, *International Review for the Sociology of Sport*, 46(3), 265–81.

Piggin, J., Jackson, S. and Lewis, M. (2009) Knowledge, power and politics – contesting 'evidence-based' national sport policy, *International Review for the Sociology of Sport*, 44(1), 87–101.

Poggi, G. (1983) Clientelism, *Political Studies*, 31(4), 662–67.

Polley, M. (1998) *Moving the Goalposts: A History of Sport and Society Since 1945*. London: Psychology Press.

Polley, M. (2012) Book review of the politics of the Olympics, *International Journal of Sport Policy and Politics* (i-First), DOI: 10.1080/19406940.2012.719029.

Potter, E. H. (2009) *Branding Canada: Projecting Canada's Soft Power through Public Diplomacy*. Montreal & Kingston: McGill-Queen's University Press.

Portes, A. and Landolt, P. (1996) Unsolved mysteries: the Tocqueville Files II – the downside of social capital, *The American Prospect*, 26, 18–21.

Preuss, H. (2007) The conceptualisation of measurement of mega sport event legacies, *Journal of Sport and Tourism*, 12(3–4), 207–27.

Preuss, H. (2014) Legacy Revisited, in Grix, J. (ed) *Leveraging Legacies from Sports Mega-Events: Concepts and Cases*. Basingstoke: Palgrave.

Preuss, H. and Alfs, C. (2011) Signalling through the 2008 Beijing Olympics – using mega sport events to change the perception and image of the host, *European Sport Management Quarterly*, 11(1), 55–71.

Pricewaterhouse Coopers. (2012) *Beyond the Bid. The Legacy of Mega-Events in Intellectual Capital* [online]. Available at: http://www.pwc.com/us/en/point-of-view/assets/pwc-benefits-bidding-mega-events.pdf [Accessed 06.03.14].

Putnam, R. (1993) *Making Democracy Work: Civic Traditions in Modern Italy*, Princeton, NJ: Princeton University Press.

Putnam, R. (1995) Bowling alone: America's declining social capital, *Journal of Democracy*, 6(1), 65–78.

Putnam, R. (2000) *Bowling Alone: The Collapse and Revival of American Community*. New York: Simon & Schuster.

Raco, M. and Imrie, R. (2000) Governmentality and rights and responsibilities in urban policy, *Environment and Planning A*, 32(12), 2187–204.

Reuters. (2014) *IOC Mulls Revamp of Games Bid Process, Sports and Risk* [online [5th February]]. Available at: http://www.reuters.com/article/2014/02/05/us-olympics-future-idUSBREA140EJ20140205 [Accessed 06.03.14].

Reuters. (2015) *Olympics-Snowboarding-White's Flop May Give a Lift to Boarding* [online [12th February]]. Available at: http://www.reuters.com/article/2014/02/12/olympics-snowboarding-white-idUSL3N0LH4AZ20140212 [Accessed 04.03.15].

Riefenstahl, L. (1938/2006) *Olympia*, Arthaus DVD.

Riordan, J. (1991) *Sport, Politics and Communism*. Manchester: Manchester University Press.

Riordan, J. (1999) The Impact of Communism on Sport, in Riordan, J. and Krüger, A. (eds) *The International Politics of Sport in the Twentieth Century*. London: Spon Press.

Ritchie, B. W. and Adair, D. (eds) (2004) *Sport Tourism: Interrelationships, Impacts and Issues*. Clevedon: Channel View.

Roche, M. (1993) Sport and Community: Rhetoric and Reality in the Development of British Sport Policy, in Binfield, J. and Stevenson, J. (eds) *Sport, Culture and Politics*. Sheffield: Sheffield Academic Press.

Roche, M. (1994) Mega-events and urban policy, *Annals of Tourism Research*, 21(1), 1–19.

Rofe, S. (2014) 'It is a squad game: Manchester United as a diplomatic non-state actor in international affairs', *Sport in Society: Cultures, Commerce, Media and Politics*, 17(9), 1136–54.

Rohter, L. (2012) *Brazil on the Rise: The Story of a Country Transformed*. New York: Palgrave.

Rose, R., Mishler, W. and Haerfer, C. (1996) *'Getting Real': Social Capital in Post-Communist Societies*. Paper presented to the Society for Comparative Research Conference on 'The Erosion of Confidence in Advanced Democracies.' Brussels, December 7–9.

Rowbottom, M. (2013) *FOUL PLAY: The Dark Arts of Cheating in Sport*. London: Bloomsbury.

Sage, G. H. (2010) *Globalizing Sport: How Organizations, Corporations, Media, and Politics are Changing Sports*. Boulder, CO: Paradigm Publishers.

Sala, B. R., Scott, J. T. and Spriggs, J. F. (2007) The Cold War on ice: constructivism and the politics of Olympic figure skating judging, *Perspectives on Politics*, 5(1), 17–29.

Sam, M. P. (2009) The public management of sport: wicked problems, challenges and dilemmas, *Public Management Review*, 11(4), 499–514.

Schiller, K. and Young, C. (2010) *The 1972 Olympics and the Making of Germany*. Berkeley: University of California Press.

Seiler, S. (2013) Evaluating the (your country here) Olympic medal count, *International Journal of Sports Physiology and Performance*, 8(2), 203–10.

Senn, A. E. (1999) *Power, Politics and the Olympic Games*. Illinois, Champaign: Human Kinetics.

Shepard, A. C. (1999) *An Olympian Scandal* [online]. Available at: http://ajrarchive.org/article.asp?id=505 [Accessed 06.03.14].

Signitzer, B. and Coombs, T. (1992) Public relations and public diplomacy: conceptual divergence, *Public Relations Review*, 18(2), 137–47.

Silk, M. (2014) Neoliberalism and Sports Mega-Events, in Grix, J. (ed) *Leveraging Legacies from Sports Mega-Events: Concepts and Cases*. Basingstoke: Palgrave.

Singler, A. and Treutlein, G. (2008) 'Doping in der Bundesrepublik Deutschland: Historische und soziologische Aspekte abweichenden Verhaltens im Spitzensport', in Hormone und Hochleistung, Doping in Ost und West. ed. K. and L. Latzel (Köln, Weimar and Wien: Boehlau), 41–65.

Skelcher, C. (2000) Changing images of the state: overloaded, hollowed-out, congested, *Public Policy and Administration*, 15(3), 3–19.

Skelcher, C. (2008) Does Governance Perform? Concepts, Evidence, Causalities, and Research Strategies, in Hartley, J., Donaldson, C., Skelcher, C. and Wallace, M. (eds) *Managing to Improve Public Services*. Cambridge: Cambridge University Press.

Slack, T. (ed) (2004) *The Commercialisation of Sport*. Abingdon: Routledge.

Smith, E. (2009) *What Sport Tells Us about Life*. London: Penguin.

South Africa Information. (2011) *More Tourists Flock to South Africa* [online]. Available at: http://www.southafrica.info/travel/tour ism-020311.htm#.VRmfCfnF-So [Accessed 30.03.15].

Sparvero, E., Chalip, L. and Green, C. (2008) United States, in Houlihan, B. and Green, M. (eds) *Comparative Elite Sport Development*. London: Elsevier.

Spitzer, G. (1998) Remarks to the Hidden System of Stately Organized Doping in the German Democratic Republic (GDR), in *Sport und sozialer Wandel: Proceedings of the ISHPES Congress*, pp. 161–170.

Sports Council. (1982) *Sport in the Community: The Next Ten Years*. London: Sports Council.

Sport England. (2015) *Active People Survey 9*, June 2015. Available at: https://www.sportengland.org/research/who-plays-sport/national-picture/ [Accessed 10.06.2015].

Sport England. (2015) *The National Picture* [online]. Available at: http://www.sportengland.org/research/who-plays-sport/national-picture/ [Accessed 30.03.15].

Sports Marketing (IMR). (2013) *Australia/New Zealand Sponsorship Worth $880 Million* [online]. Available at: http://www.imrpublica tions.com/newsdetails.aspx?nid=44 [Accessed 20.02.15].

Sport and Recreation Alliance. (2015) *Sport and Recreation in the UK – Facts and Figures* [online]. Available at: http://www.sportandrec reation.org.uk/lobbying-and-campaigning/sport-research/UK-fact-figures [Accessed 20.02.15].

Sports Business Daily, 2013. *TV Rights Push IOC Revenue to Record*. Available at: http://www.sportsbusinessdaily.com/Journal/Issues/2013/08/26/Olympics/IOC-revenue.aspx [Accessed 25.05.15].

Standard. (2011) *Lessons of Barcelona: 1992 Games Provided Model for London...and a Few Warnings* [21st March]. Available at: http://www.standard.co.uk/news/lessons-of-barcelona-1992-games-provided-model-for-london-and-few-warnings-6382929.html [Accessed 23.03.15].

Statistic Brain. (2015) *Facebook Statistics* [23rd March]. Available at: http://www.statisticbrain.com/facebook-statistics/ [Accessed 23.03.15].

Stawell Gift. (2015) *Home* [online]. Available at: http://www.stawell gift.com/ [Accessed 20.02.14].

Steele, J. (2009) *Why We Must Keep Investing in Elite Sport* [Online]. Available at: http://www.uksport.gov.uk/news/steele_why_we_must_keep_investing_in_elite_sport/ [Accessed 02.02.15].

Stewart, B., Nicholson, M., Smith, A. and Westerbeek, H. (2005) *Australian Sport: Better by Design? The Evolution of Australian Sport Policy*. London: Routledge.

Stoker, G. and Marsh, D. (2002) Introduction, in Marsh, D. and Stoker, G. (eds) *Theory and Methods in Political Science* (2nd edition). Basingstoke: Palgrave Macmillan.

Stolle, D. and Rochon, T. R. (1999) The Myth of American Exceptionalism: A Three-Nation Comparison of Associational Membership and Social Capital, in van Deth, J. W., Maraffi, M., Newton, K. and Whiteley, P. F. (eds) *Social Capital and European Democracy*. Abingdon: Routledge.

Stotlar, D. K. and Wonders, A. (2006) Developing elite athletes: a content analysis of US national governing body systems, *International Journal of Applied Sports Sciences*, 18(2), 121–44.

Strenk, A. (1978) Diplomats in Track Suits, in Lowe, B., Kanin, D. and Strenk, A. (eds) *Sport and International Relations*. Champaign, IL: Stipes Publishing.

Sugden, J. (2010) Critical left-realism and sport interventions in divided societies, *International Review for the Sociology of Sport*, 45(3), 258–72.

Sugden, J. and Bairner, A. (1986) Northern Ireland: Sport in a Divided Society, in Allison, L. (ed) *The Politics of Sport*. Manchester: Manchester University Press.

Sugden, J. and Bairner, A. (1993) *Sport, Sectarianism and Society in a Divided Ireland*. Leicester: Leicester University Press.

Sugden, J. and Bairner, A. (eds) (1999) *Sports in Divided Societies*. Aachen: Meyer & Meyer Sport.

Sugden, J. and Tomlinson, A. (eds) (2012) *Watching the Olympics: Politics, Power and Representation*. London and New York: Routledge.

Sunday Times. (2014) *Inspiring a Nation Gets a Big Fat Zero* [online]. Available at: http://www.thesundaytimes.co.uk/sto/sport/olympics/article1376539.ece [Accessed 23.03.15].

Szymanski, S. (2009) *The Comparative Economics of Sport*. Basingstoke: Palgrave Macmillan.

Talbot, M. (1995) Physical education and the national curriculum: some political issues, *Leisure Studies Association Newsletter*, 41, 20–30.

Taylor, A. (2000) Hollowing out or filling in? Taskforces and the management of cross-cutting issues in British government, *British Journal of Politics and International Relations*, 2(1), 46–71.

Taylor, P. and Gratton, C. (2002) *The Economics of Sport and Recreation: An Economic Analysis*. London: Routledge.

Taylor, T. (1986) Sport and International Relations: A Case of Mutual Neglect, in Allison, L. (ed) *The Politics of Sport*. Manchester: Manchester University Press.

Telegraph. (2012a) *NBC Criticised Paralympics After Opening Ceremony Blackout* [30th August]. Available at: http://www.telegraph.co.uk/sport/olympics/paralympic-sport/9509190/NBC-criticised-Paralympics-after-opening-ceremony-blackout.html [Accessed 23.03.15].

Telegraph. (2012b) *London Olympics 2012: Four-in-10 Team GB Medallists 'Educated Privately'* [online [14th August]]. Available at: http://www.telegraph.co.uk/sport/olympics/news/9473344/London-Olympics-2012-four-in-10-Team-GB-medallists-educated-privately.html [Accessed 13.01.15].

Telegraph. (2012c) *lensk* [online [27th July]]. Available at: http://www.telegraph.co.uk/sport/olympics/9429085/London-2012-Olympic-ceremonies-through-the-ages.html [Accessed 04.02.15].

The Economist. (2015) *The End Zone* [online [31st January]]. Available at: http://www.economist.com/news/united-states/21641250-nations-favourite-entertainment-faces-many-charges-one-them-will-finish-it-end [Accessed 06.02.15].

The Guardian. (2002) *Bet You Won't be Shouting for this Lot on Sunday* [online [28th June]]. Available at: http://www.guardian.co.uk/uk/2002/jun/28/race.germany [Accessed 08.02.13].

The Guardian. (2003) *What Zola did Next* [online]. Available at: http://www.theguardian.com/sport/2003/feb/24/athletics.rorycar roll [Accessed 30.03.15].

The Guardian. (2004) *Kenyan Sport in Crisis as Athletes Go on the Run* [online [31st January]]. Available at: http://www.theguard ian.com/world/2004/jan/31/sport.jeevanvasagar [Accessed 25.02.13].

The Guardian. (2012a) *Cultural invasion of Britain Celebrates Germany's Big Shift* [online [1st March]]. Available at: http://www.guardian.co.uk/world/2012/mar/04/german-cultural-invasion-london [Accessed 08.02.13].

The Guardian. (2012b) *Olympics 2012 Security: Welcome to Lockdown London* [online [12th March]]. Available at: http://www.guardian.co.uk/sport/2012/mar/12/london-olympics-secu rity-lockdown-london [Accessed 06.02.13].

The Guardian. (2012c) *Fifa Corruption Intrigue Deepens as Brazil's Ricardo Teixeira Resigns* [online [12th March]]. Available at: http://www.theguardian.com/football/2012/mar/12/fifa-ricardo-teixeira-resigns [Accessed 23.03.15].

The Guardian. (2013a) *Do Man Utd Really have 659m Supporters?* [online [18th February]]. Available at: http://www.bbc.co.uk/news/magazine-21478857 [Accessed 22.02.15].

The Guardian. (2013b) *Brian Moore: This much I Know* [online [8th June]]. Available at: http://www.theguardian.com/life andstyle/2013/jun/08/rugby-player-brian-moore-much-know [Accessed 11.12.14].

The Guardian. (2013c) *Fewer Adults Playing Sport Since London Olympics* [online [14th June]]. Available at: http://www.theguard ian.com/uk/2013/jun/13/fewer-playing-sport-since-london-olym pics [Accessed 12.12.14].

The Guardian. (2013d) *Chris Froome Says Cycling's Code of Omerta has been Broken* [online [22nd June]]. Available at: http://www.theguardian.com/sport/2013/jun/22/chris-froome-cycling-code-omerta-broken [Accessed 12.02.15].

The Guardian. (2014) *Volgograd Train Station Rocked by Suicide Bombing* [online [30th December]]. Available at: http://www.theguardian.com/world/2013/dec/29/volgograd-train-station-suicide-bombing [Accessed 14.03.14].

The Guardian. (2015) *Football is Just One Example of the Inequalities that Bedevil Us* [online [15th February]]. Available at: http://www.theguardian.com/commentisfree/2015/feb/15/football-one-of-the-inequalities-that-bedevil-us-premier-league [Accessed 03.03.15].

The Independent. (2015) *Millions Face Becoming 'Mortgage Prisoners' as Rise in Interest Rates Could Trap to 2.3m Homeowners* [online [20th May]]. Available at: http://www.independent.co.uk/money/

mortgages/millions-face-becoming-mortgage-prisoners-as-risc-in-interest-rates-could-trap-to-23m-homeowners-9399137.html [Accessed 20.02.14].

Time (Magazine). (2011) *Sports as Diplomacy: How Small Gulf Countries Use Big Sports to Gain Global Influence.* Available at: http://content.time.com/time/world/article/0,8599,2080062,00. html [Accessed 25.05.15].

Time. (2015) *5 Ways This Year's Super Bowl Ads Will Be Like No Other* [online [26th January]]. Available at: http://time.com/ money/3681227/super-bowl-ads-2015 [Accessed 24.02.15].

Toledo, R. M., Grix, J. and Bega, M. T. S. (2015) Megaeventos Esportivos e seus Legados: uma análise dos efeitos institucionais da dupla condição do Brasil de país-sede, *Revista de Sociologia e Política* (in press).

Tomlinson, A. (2005) The commercialization of the Olympics: cities, corporations and the Olympic commodity, *Global Olympics: Historical and sociological studies of the modern Games*, 3, 179.

Tomlinson, A. and Young, C. (eds) (2006) *National Identity and Global Sports Events: Culture, Politics, and Spectacle in the Olympics and the Football World Cup*. Albany: SUNY Press.

Tomlinson, R. (2010) Whose accolades? An alternative perspective on motivation for hosting the Olympics, *Urban Forum*, 21(2), 139–52.

Tonts, M. (2005) Competitive sport and social capital in rural Australia, *Journal of Rural Studies*, 21(2), 137–49.

Transparency International. (2013) *Corruption Perception Index 2013*. Available at: http://www.transparency.org/cpi2013/results [Accessed 13.02.14].

Turner, V. (1968) *The Ritual Process*. Chicago, IL: Aldine Publishing.

Turner, V. (1979) Frame, flow and reflection: ritual and drama as public liminality, *Japanese Journal of Religious Studies*, 6(4), 465–99.

Twitter. (2015) *About Twitter.* [23rd March] Available at: https:// about.twitter.com/company [Accessed 23.03.15].

UK Sport. (2006) *Sports Policy Factors Leading to International Sporting Success. An International Comparative Study*. London: UK Sport.

UK Sport. (2008) *World Class Governance* [online]. Available at: http:// www.uksport.gov.uk/pages/world_class_governance/ [Accessed 03.06.11].

UK Sport. (2014) *Historical Funding Figures* [online]. Available at: http://www.uksport.gov.uk/our-work/investing-in-sport/historical-funding-figures [Accessed 30.03.15].

Ulbricht, W. (2011) *Jeder Mann, an jedem Ort, einmal in der Woche Sport* [online]. Available at: http://www.ddr-wissen.de/wiki/ddr. pl?Sport [Accessed 12.04.11].

UN. (2015) *Member States of the United Nations* [online]. Available at: http://www.un.org/en/members/ [Accessed 30.03.15].

United States Olympic Committee. (2015) *About USOC* [online]. Available at: http://www.teamusa.org/About-the-USOC [Accessed 30.03.15].

Van Bottenburg, M. (2002) Sport for All and Elite Sport Policy: Do They Benefit One Another?, in *Proceedings, World Sport for All Congress*, Vol. 20. Available at: www.vanbottenburg.nl/down loads/147.% 20Van% 20Bottenburg [Accessed 20.01.15].

Van Ham, P. (2001) The rise of the brand state: the postmodern politics of image and reputation, *Foreign Affairs*, 80(5), 2–6.

Verroken, M. (1996) Drug Use and Abuse in Sport, in Mottram, D. (ed) *Drugs in Sport*. London: E & FN Spon.

Verroken, M. and Mottram, D. R. (1996) Doping Control in Sport, in Mottram, D. R. (ed) *Drugs in Sport* (2nd edition). London and New York: Spon Press.

Vieira (2012) Rising states and distributive justice: reforming international order in the 21st century, *Global Society*, 26(3), 311–29.

Vuori, I. and Fentem, P. (1995) *Health: Position Paper*. Strasbourg: Council of Europe.

Vuori, I., Fentem, P., Svoboda, B., Patriksson, G., Andreff, W. and Weber, W. (1995) *The Significance of Sport for Society: Health, Socialisation, Economy*. Strasbourg: Council of Europe.

Waddington, I. (2000) *Sport, Health and Drugs: A Critical Sociological Perspective*. London: E & FN Spon.

Waddington, I. and Smith, A. (2009) *An Introduction to Drugs in Sport: Addicted to Winning?*. London: Routledge.

Walters, G. (2008) *Bidding for Major Sporting Events: Key Issues and Challenges Faced by Sports Governing Bodies in the UK*. London: CCPR.

Weed, M. (2008) Sports tourism experiences, *Journal of Sport & Tourism*, 13(1), 1–4.

Weed, M. (2009) Progress in sports tourism research? A meta-review and exploration of futures, *Tourism Management*, 30(5), 615–28.

Weed, M. (ed) (2014) *Sport and Leisure Management*. London: Sage.

Weed, M., Coren, E. and Fiore, J. (2009) *A Systematic Review of the Evidence Base for Developing a Physical Activity and Health Legacy from the London 2012 Olympic and Paralympic Games*. London: Department of Health.

Wetzel, D. (2014) Why no one wants to host the 2022 Olympics. Available at: http://sports.yahoo.com/news/why-no-one-wants-to-host-the-2022-olympics-225450509.html [Accessed 20.03.15].

Whiteley, P. F. (ed) (1999) *Social Capital and European Democracy*. Abingdon: Routledge.

Wilkinson, R. and Pickett, K. (2010) *The Spirit Level: Why Equality is Better for Everyone*. London: Penguin.

Williams, K. (2003) *Understanding Media Theory*. London: Hodder and Stoughton.

Woolcock, M. (2001) Microenterprise and social capital: a framework for theory, research, and policy, *The Journal of Socio-Economics*, 30(2), 193–98.

World Bank. (2014) *Gross Domestic Product 2013* [online]. Available at: http://databank.worldbank.org/data/download/GDP.pdf [Accessed 20.02.14].

World Health Organisation. (2015) *Noncommunicable Diseases*. Available at: http://www.who.int/mediacentre/factsheets/fs355/en/ [Accessed 25.05.15].

Xu, X. (2006) Modernizing China in the Olympic Spotlight: China's National Identity and the 2008 Beijing Olympiad, in Horne, J. and Manzenreiter, W. (eds) *Sports Mega-Events*.

Young, C. (2010) Berlin 1936, in Bairner, A. and Molnar, G. (eds) *The Politics of the Olympics: A Survey*. London and New York: Routledge.

Young, K. (1993) Violence, risk, and liability in male sports culture, *Sociology of Sport Journal*, 10(4), 373–96.

Young, K. (2000) Sport and Violence, in Coakley, J. and Dunning, E. (eds) *Handbook of Sports Studies*. London: Sage.

Zirin, D. (2014) *The Relationship Between Money and Sport* [online [2nd June]]. *BBC Radio 4*. Available at: http://www.bbc.co.uk/programmes/p01p5y3d [Accessed 03.01.15].

Index